C-4730   CAREER EXAMINATION SERIES

This is your
PASSBOOK for...

Emergency Medical Technician

Test Preparation Study Guide
Questions & Answers

COPYRIGHT NOTICE

This book is SOLELY intended for, is sold ONLY to, and its use is RESTRICTED to individual, bona fide applicants or candidates who qualify by virtue of having seriously filed applications for appropriate license, certificate, professional and/or promotional advancement, higher school matriculation, scholarship, or other legitimate requirements of education and/or governmental authorities.

This book is NOT intended for use, class instruction, tutoring, training, duplication, copying, reprinting, excerption, or adaptation, etc., by:

1) Other publishers
2) Proprietors and/or Instructors of "Coaching" and/or Preparatory Courses
3) Personnel and/or Training Divisions of commercial, industrial, and governmental organizations
4) Schools, colleges, or universities and/or their departments and staffs, including teachers and other personnel
5) Testing Agencies or Bureaus
6) Study groups which seek by the purchase of a single volume to copy and/or duplicate and/or adapt this material for use by the group as a whole without having purchased individual volumes for each of the members of the group
7) Et al.

Such persons would be in violation of appropriate Federal and State statutes.

PROVISION OF LICENSING AGREEMENTS – Recognized educational, commercial, industrial, and governmental institutions and organizations, and others legitimately engaged in educational pursuits, including training, testing, and measurement activities, may address request for a licensing agreement to the copyright owners, who will determine whether, and under what conditions, including fees and charges, the materials in this book may be used them. In other words, a licensing facility exists for the legitimate use of the material in this book on other than an individual basis. However, it is asseverated and affirmed here that the material in this book CANNOT be used without the receipt of the express permission of such a licensing agreement from the Publishers. Inquiries re licensing should be addressed to the company, attention rights and permissions department.

All rights reserved, including the right of reproduction in whole or in part, in any form or by any means, electronic or mechanical, including photocopying, recording, or by any information storage and retrieval system, without permission in writing from the Publisher.

Copyright © 2024 by
National Learning Corporation

212 Michael Drive, Syosset, NY 11791
(516) 921-8888 • www.passbooks.com
E-mail: info@passbooks.com

PUBLISHED IN THE UNITED STATES OF AMERICA

PASSBOOK® SERIES

THE *PASSBOOK® SERIES* has been created to prepare applicants and candidates for the ultimate academic battlefield – the examination room.

At some time in our lives, each and every one of us may be required to take an examination – for validation, matriculation, admission, qualification, registration, certification, or licensure.

Based on the assumption that every applicant or candidate has met the basic formal educational standards, has taken the required number of courses, and read the necessary texts, the *PASSBOOK® SERIES* furnishes the one special preparation which may assure passing with confidence, instead of failing with insecurity. Examination questions – together with answers – are furnished as the basic vehicle for study so that the mysteries of the examination and its compounding difficulties may be eliminated or diminished by a sure method.

This book is meant to help you pass your examination provided that you qualify and are serious in your objective.

The entire field is reviewed through the huge store of content information which is succinctly presented through a provocative and challenging approach – the question-and-answer method.

A climate of success is established by furnishing the correct answers at the end of each test.

You soon learn to recognize types of questions, forms of questions, and patterns of questioning. You may even begin to anticipate expected outcomes.

You perceive that many questions are repeated or adapted so that you can gain acute insights, which may enable you to score many sure points.

You learn how to confront new questions, or types of questions, and to attack them confidently and work out the correct answers.

You note objectives and emphases, and recognize pitfalls and dangers, so that you may make positive educational adjustments.

Moreover, you are kept fully informed in relation to new concepts, methods, practices, and directions in the field.

You discover that you are actually taking the examination all the time: you are preparing for the examination by "taking" an examination, not by reading extraneous and/or supererogatory textbooks.

In short, this PASSBOOK®, used directedly, should be an important factor in helping you to pass your test.

EMERGENCY MEDICAL TECHNICIAN

DUTIES:
This work involves responsibility for administering initial first-aid treatment or emergency medical care to individuals who have suffered physical trauma such as stroke, car accident, poisoning, heart attack, etc. at the scene and/or during transport in an ambulance to a hospital for more intensive treatment. The work is performed under general supervision of higher level personnel with leeway allowed for the exercise of independent judgment. The incumbent does related work as required.

TYPICAL WORK ACTIVITIES:
- Respond to calls when dispatched, gain access to the patient and assess the extent of their injuries or illness. Act as crew chief for Advanced Life Support (ALS) calls. Basic Life Support (BLS) calls may be passed off to a qualified BLS provider after sufficient evaluation to confirm the BLS nature;
- Provide life support services to stabilize persons in life threatening situations resulting from trauma and other-medical conditions;
- Use prescribed techniques and equipment to provide patient care and provide additional emergency care following established protocols;
- Assess and monitor vital signs and general appearance of patient for change;
- Determine appropriate medical facility to which patient will be transported and transport patient; provide ongoing medical care on route, if required;
- Communicate with dispatcher requesting additional assistance or services, as necessary. Receive and transmit communications from the public and agencies requesting emergency services Report verbally and in writing, the nature of patient's injury/illness and observations of patient's emergency care provided, to departmental staff of medical facility;
- Report verbally and in writing, the nature of patient's injury/illness and observations of patient's emergency care provided, to departmental staff of medical facility;
- Provide response for ALS link up's and/or Mutual Aid as set forth in current mutual aid agreements. Provide response for hospital transfers as directed by the Rescue Chief;
- Complete Patient Care Report call sheets in a timely fashion including all required information in accordance with established PCR policy. Enter PCR data into computer on a weekly basis;
- Maintain a daily log of calls and duties completed. Provide assistance with billing responsibilities as directed;
- Properly dispose of medical waste, decontaminate interior of ambulance and related equipment according to established guidelines;
- Maintain the cleanliness of the ambulance and facility as needed, including performing housekeeping duties such as vacuuming, cleaning garage, kitchen and bathrooms, sweeping sidewalks, snow removal, and maintaining the property in general. Notify Rescue chief and drivers of necessary repairs to rig or other equipment;
- Inventory the duty ambulance daily, inventory second run truck weekly, inventory all 3 ALS drug boxes weekly, and restock all as needed and notify Rescue Chief or other designated person of items to order on a weekly basis;
- Provide Preceptor responsibilities to student and intern providers of all levels;
- May assist in driving emergency services vehicles, as needed.

FULL PERFORMANCE, KNOWLEDGE, SKILLS, ABILITIES, AND PERSONAL CHARACTERISTICS:
Good knowledge of the principles, practices and techniques of emergency treatment procedures; good knowledge of equipment and supplies used in administrating emergency medical treatment; good knowledge of recent developments in the field of emergency medical treatment; ability to act calmly and effectively in emergency situations; ability to evaluate the extent of illness or injury; ability to prepare and maintain accurate records; physical condition commensurate with the demands of the position.

SCOPE OF THE EXAMINATION
The written test will cover knowledge, skills, and/or abilities in such areas as:
1. Patient assessment;
2. Patient transport;
3. First aid and emergency procedures;
4. Medication administration; and
5. Ekg monitoring.

HOW TO TAKE A TEST

I. YOU MUST PASS AN EXAMINATION

A. *WHAT EVERY CANDIDATE SHOULD KNOW*

Examination applicants often ask us for help in preparing for the written test. What can I study in advance? What kinds of questions will be asked? How will the test be given? How will the papers be graded?

As an applicant for a civil service examination, you may be wondering about some of these things. Our purpose here is to suggest effective methods of advance study and to describe civil service examinations.

Your chances for success on this examination can be increased if you know how to prepare. Those "pre-examination jitters" can be reduced if you know what to expect. You can even experience an adventure in good citizenship if you know why civil service exams are given.

B. *WHY ARE CIVIL SERVICE EXAMINATIONS GIVEN?*

Civil service examinations are important to you in two ways. As a citizen, you want public jobs filled by employees who know how to do their work. As a job seeker, you want a fair chance to compete for that job on an equal footing with other candidates. The best-known means of accomplishing this two-fold goal is the competitive examination.

Exams are widely publicized throughout the nation. They may be administered for jobs in federal, state, city, municipal, town or village governments or agencies.

Any citizen may apply, with some limitations, such as the age or residence of applicants. Your experience and education may be reviewed to see whether you meet the requirements for the particular examination. When these requirements exist, they are reasonable and applied consistently to all applicants. Thus, a competitive examination may cause you some uneasiness now, but it is your privilege and safeguard.

C. *HOW ARE CIVIL SERVICE EXAMS DEVELOPED?*

Examinations are carefully written by trained technicians who are specialists in the field known as "psychological measurement," in consultation with recognized authorities in the field of work that the test will cover. These experts recommend the subject matter areas or skills to be tested; only those knowledges or skills important to your success on the job are included. The most reliable books and source materials available are used as references. Together, the experts and technicians judge the difficulty level of the questions.

Test technicians know how to phrase questions so that the problem is clearly stated. Their ethics do not permit "trick" or "catch" questions. Questions may have been tried out on sample groups, or subjected to statistical analysis, to determine their usefulness.

Written tests are often used in combination with performance tests, ratings of training and experience, and oral interviews. All of these measures combine to form the best-known means of finding the right person for the right job.

II. HOW TO PASS THE WRITTEN TEST

A. NATURE OF THE EXAMINATION

To prepare intelligently for civil service examinations, you should know how they differ from school examinations you have taken. In school you were assigned certain definite pages to read or subjects to cover. The examination questions were quite detailed and usually emphasized memory. Civil service exams, on the other hand, try to discover your present ability to perform the duties of a position, plus your potentiality to learn these duties. In other words, a civil service exam attempts to predict how successful you will be. Questions cover such a broad area that they cannot be as minute and detailed as school exam questions.

In the public service similar kinds of work, or positions, are grouped together in one "class." This process is known as *position-classification*. All the positions in a class are paid according to the salary range for that class. One class title covers all of these positions, and they are all tested by the same examination.

B. FOUR BASIC STEPS

1) Study the announcement

How, then, can you know what subjects to study? Our best answer is: "Learn as much as possible about the class of positions for which you've applied." The exam will test the knowledge, skills and abilities needed to do the work.

Your most valuable source of information about the position you want is the official exam announcement. This announcement lists the training and experience qualifications. Check these standards and apply only if you come reasonably close to meeting them.

The brief description of the position in the examination announcement offers some clues to the subjects which will be tested. Think about the job itself. Review the duties in your mind. Can you perform them, or are there some in which you are rusty? Fill in the blank spots in your preparation.

Many jurisdictions preview the written test in the exam announcement by including a section called "Knowledge and Abilities Required," "Scope of the Examination," or some similar heading. Here you will find out specifically what fields will be tested.

2) Review your own background

Once you learn in general what the position is all about, and what you need to know to do the work, ask yourself which subjects you already know fairly well and which need improvement. You may wonder whether to concentrate on improving your strong areas or on building some background in your fields of weakness. When the announcement has specified "some knowledge" or "considerable knowledge," or has used adjectives like "beginning principles of…" or "advanced … methods," you can get a clue as to the number and difficulty of questions to be asked in any given field. More questions, and hence broader coverage, would be included for those subjects which are more important in the work. Now weigh your strengths and weaknesses against the job requirements and prepare accordingly.

3) Determine the level of the position

Another way to tell how intensively you should prepare is to understand the level of the job for which you are applying. Is it the entering level? In other words, is this the position in which beginners in a field of work are hired? Or is it an intermediate or advanced level? Sometimes this is indicated by such words as "Junior" or "Senior" in the class title. Other jurisdictions use Roman numerals to designate the level – Clerk I, Clerk II, for example. The word "Supervisor" sometimes appears in the title. If the level is not indicated by the title, check the description of duties. Will you be working under very close supervision, or will you have responsibility for independent decisions in this work?

4) Choose appropriate study materials

Now that you know the subjects to be examined and the relative amount of each subject to be covered, you can choose suitable study materials. For beginning level jobs, or even advanced ones, if you have a pronounced weakness in some aspect of your training, read a modern, standard textbook in that field. Be sure it is up to date and has general coverage. Such books are normally available at your library, and the librarian will be glad to help you locate one. For entry-level positions, questions of appropriate difficulty are chosen – neither highly advanced questions, nor those too simple. Such questions require careful thought but not advanced training.

If the position for which you are applying is technical or advanced, you will read more advanced, specialized material. If you are already familiar with the basic principles of your field, elementary textbooks would waste your time. Concentrate on advanced textbooks and technical periodicals. Think through the concepts and review difficult problems in your field.

These are all general sources. You can get more ideas on your own initiative, following these leads. For example, training manuals and publications of the government agency which employs workers in your field can be useful, particularly for technical and professional positions. A letter or visit to the government department involved may result in more specific study suggestions, and certainly will provide you with a more definite idea of the exact nature of the position you are seeking.

III. KINDS OF TESTS

Tests are used for purposes other than measuring knowledge and ability to perform specified duties. For some positions, it is equally important to test ability to make adjustments to new situations or to profit from training. In others, basic mental abilities not dependent on information are essential. Questions which test these things may not appear as pertinent to the duties of the position as those which test for knowledge and information. Yet they are often highly important parts of a fair examination. For very general questions, it is almost impossible to help you direct your study efforts. What we can do is to point out some of the more common of these general abilities needed in public service positions and describe some typical questions.

1) General information

Broad, general information has been found useful for predicting job success in some kinds of work. This is tested in a variety of ways, from vocabulary lists to questions about current events. Basic background in some field of work, such as sociology or economics, may be sampled in a group of questions. Often these are principles which have become familiar to most persons through exposure rather than through formal training. It is difficult to advise you how to study for these questions; being alert to the world around you is our best suggestion.

2) Verbal ability

An example of an ability needed in many positions is verbal or language ability. Verbal ability is, in brief, the ability to use and understand words. Vocabulary and grammar tests are typical measures of this ability. Reading comprehension or paragraph interpretation questions are common in many kinds of civil service tests. You are given a paragraph of written material and asked to find its central meaning.

3) Numerical ability

Number skills can be tested by the familiar arithmetic problem, by checking paired lists of numbers to see which are alike and which are different, or by interpreting charts and graphs. In the latter test, a graph may be printed in the test booklet which you are asked to use as the basis for answering questions.

4) Observation

A popular test for law-enforcement positions is the observation test. A picture is shown to you for several minutes, then taken away. Questions about the picture test your ability to observe both details and larger elements.

5) Following directions

In many positions in the public service, the employee must be able to carry out written instructions dependably and accurately. You may be given a chart with several columns, each column listing a variety of information. The questions require you to carry out directions involving the information given in the chart.

6) Skills and aptitudes

Performance tests effectively measure some manual skills and aptitudes. When the skill is one in which you are trained, such as typing or shorthand, you can practice. These tests are often very much like those given in business school or high school courses. For many of the other skills and aptitudes, however, no short-time preparation can be made. Skills and abilities natural to you or that you have developed throughout your lifetime are being tested.

Many of the general questions just described provide all the data needed to answer the questions and ask you to use your reasoning ability to find the answers. Your best preparation for these tests, as well as for tests of facts and ideas, is to be at your physical and mental best. You, no doubt, have your own methods of getting into an exam-taking mood and keeping "in shape." The next section lists some ideas on this subject.

IV. KINDS OF QUESTIONS

Only rarely is the "essay" question, which you answer in narrative form, used in civil service tests. Civil service tests are usually of the short-answer type. Full instructions for answering these questions will be given to you at the examination. But in case this is your first experience with short-answer questions and separate answer sheets, here is what you need to know:

1) Multiple-choice Questions

Most popular of the short-answer questions is the "multiple choice" or "best answer" question. It can be used, for example, to test for factual knowledge, ability to solve problems or judgment in meeting situations found at work.

A multiple-choice question is normally one of three types—
- It can begin with an incomplete statement followed by several possible endings. You are to find the one ending which *best* completes the statement, although some of the others may not be entirely wrong.
- It can also be a complete statement in the form of a question which is answered by choosing one of the statements listed.

- It can be in the form of a problem – again you select the best answer.

Here is an example of a multiple-choice question with a discussion which should give you some clues as to the method for choosing the right answer:

When an employee has a complaint about his assignment, the action which will *best* help him overcome his difficulty is to
- A. discuss his difficulty with his coworkers
- B. take the problem to the head of the organization
- C. take the problem to the person who gave him the assignment
- D. say nothing to anyone about his complaint

In answering this question, you should study each of the choices to find which is best. Consider choice "A" – Certainly an employee may discuss his complaint with fellow employees, but no change or improvement can result, and the complaint remains unresolved. Choice "B" is a poor choice since the head of the organization probably does not know what assignment you have been given, and taking your problem to him is known as "going over the head" of the supervisor. The supervisor, or person who made the assignment, is the person who can clarify it or correct any injustice. Choice "C" is, therefore, correct. To say nothing, as in choice "D," is unwise. Supervisors have and interest in knowing the problems employees are facing, and the employee is seeking a solution to his problem.

2) True/False Questions

The "true/false" or "right/wrong" form of question is sometimes used. Here a complete statement is given. Your job is to decide whether the statement is right or wrong.

SAMPLE: A roaming cell-phone call to a nearby city costs less than a non-roaming call to a distant city.

This statement is wrong, or false, since roaming calls are more expensive.

This is not a complete list of all possible question forms, although most of the others are variations of these common types. You will always get complete directions for answering questions. Be sure you understand *how* to mark your answers – ask questions until you do.

V. RECORDING YOUR ANSWERS

Computer terminals are used more and more today for many different kinds of exams.

For an examination with very few applicants, you may be told to record your answers in the test booklet itself. Separate answer sheets are much more common. If this separate answer sheet is to be scored by machine – and this is often the case – it is highly important that you mark your answers correctly in order to get credit.

An electronic scoring machine is often used in civil service offices because of the speed with which papers can be scored. Machine-scored answer sheets must be marked with a pencil, which will be given to you. This pencil has a high graphite content which responds to the electronic scoring machine. As a matter of fact, stray dots may register as answers, so do not let your pencil rest on the answer sheet while you are pondering the correct answer. Also, if your pencil lead breaks or is otherwise defective, ask for another.

Since the answer sheet will be dropped in a slot in the scoring machine, be careful not to bend the corners or get the paper crumpled.

The answer sheet normally has five vertical columns of numbers, with 30 numbers to a column. These numbers correspond to the question numbers in your test booklet. After each number, going across the page are four or five pairs of dotted lines. These short dotted lines have small letters or numbers above them. The first two pairs may also have a "T" or "F" above the letters. This indicates that the first two pairs only are to be used if the questions are of the true-false type. If the questions are multiple choice, disregard the "T" and "F" and pay attention only to the small letters or numbers.

Answer your questions in the manner of the sample that follows:

32. The largest city in the United States is
    A. Washington, D.C.
    B. New York City
    C. Chicago
    D. Detroit
    E. San Francisco

1) Choose the answer you think is best. (New York City is the largest, so "B" is correct.)
2) Find the row of dotted lines numbered the same as the question you are answering. (Find row number 32)
3) Find the pair of dotted lines corresponding to the answer. (Find the pair of lines under the mark "B.")
4) Make a solid black mark between the dotted lines.

VI. BEFORE THE TEST

Common sense will help you find procedures to follow to get ready for an examination. Too many of us, however, overlook these sensible measures. Indeed, nervousness and fatigue have been found to be the most serious reasons why applicants fail to do their best on civil service tests. Here is a list of reminders:

- Begin your preparation early – Don't wait until the last minute to go scurrying around for books and materials or to find out what the position is all about.
- Prepare continuously – An hour a night for a week is better than an all-night cram session. This has been definitely established. What is more, a night a week for a month will return better dividends than crowding your study into a shorter period of time.
- Locate the place of the exam – You have been sent a notice telling you when and where to report for the examination. If the location is in a different town or otherwise unfamiliar to you, it would be well to inquire the best route and learn something about the building.
- Relax the night before the test – Allow your mind to rest. Do not study at all that night. Plan some mild recreation or diversion; then go to bed early and get a good night's sleep.
- Get up early enough to make a leisurely trip to the place for the test – This way unforeseen events, traffic snarls, unfamiliar buildings, etc. will not upset you.
- Dress comfortably – A written test is not a fashion show. You will be known by number and not by name, so wear something comfortable.

- Leave excess paraphernalia at home – Shopping bags and odd bundles will get in your way. You need bring only the items mentioned in the official notice you received; usually everything you need is provided. Do not bring reference books to the exam. They will only confuse those last minutes and be taken away from you when in the test room.
- Arrive somewhat ahead of time – If because of transportation schedules you must get there very early, bring a newspaper or magazine to take your mind off yourself while waiting.
- Locate the examination room – When you have found the proper room, you will be directed to the seat or part of the room where you will sit. Sometimes you are given a sheet of instructions to read while you are waiting. Do not fill out any forms until you are told to do so; just read them and be prepared.
- Relax and prepare to listen to the instructions
- If you have any physical problem that may keep you from doing your best, be sure to tell the test administrator. If you are sick or in poor health, you really cannot do your best on the exam. You can come back and take the test some other time.

VII. AT THE TEST

The day of the test is here and you have the test booklet in your hand. The temptation to get going is very strong. Caution! There is more to success than knowing the right answers. You must know how to identify your papers and understand variations in the type of short-answer question used in this particular examination. Follow these suggestions for maximum results from your efforts:

1) Cooperate with the monitor

The test administrator has a duty to create a situation in which you can be as much at ease as possible. He will give instructions, tell you when to begin, check to see that you are marking your answer sheet correctly, and so on. He is not there to guard you, although he will see that your competitors do not take unfair advantage. He wants to help you do your best.

2) Listen to all instructions

Don't jump the gun! Wait until you understand all directions. In most civil service tests you get more time than you need to answer the questions. So don't be in a hurry. Read each word of instructions until you clearly understand the meaning. Study the examples, listen to all announcements and follow directions. Ask questions if you do not understand what to do.

3) Identify your papers

Civil service exams are usually identified by number only. You will be assigned a number; you must not put your name on your test papers. Be sure to copy your number correctly. Since more than one exam may be given, copy your exact examination title.

4) Plan your time

Unless you are told that a test is a "speed" or "rate of work" test, speed itself is usually not important. Time enough to answer all the questions will be provided, but this does not mean that you have all day. An overall time limit has been set. Divide the total time (in minutes) by the number of questions to determine the approximate time you have for each question.

5) Do not linger over difficult questions

If you come across a difficult question, mark it with a paper clip (useful to have along) and come back to it when you have been through the booklet. One caution if you do this – be sure to skip a number on your answer sheet as well. Check often to be sure that you have not lost your place and that you are marking in the row numbered the same as the question you are answering.

6) Read the questions

Be sure you know what the question asks! Many capable people are unsuccessful because they failed to *read* the questions correctly.

7) Answer all questions

Unless you have been instructed that a penalty will be deducted for incorrect answers, it is better to guess than to omit a question.

8) Speed tests

It is often better NOT to guess on speed tests. It has been found that on timed tests people are tempted to spend the last few seconds before time is called in marking answers at random – without even reading them – in the hope of picking up a few extra points. To discourage this practice, the instructions may warn you that your score will be "corrected" for guessing. That is, a penalty will be applied. The incorrect answers will be deducted from the correct ones, or some other penalty formula will be used.

9) Review your answers

If you finish before time is called, go back to the questions you guessed or omitted to give them further thought. Review other answers if you have time.

10) Return your test materials

If you are ready to leave before others have finished or time is called, take ALL your materials to the monitor and leave quietly. Never take any test material with you. The monitor can discover whose papers are not complete, and taking a test booklet may be grounds for disqualification.

VIII. EXAMINATION TECHNIQUES

1) Read the general instructions carefully. These are usually printed on the first page of the exam booklet. As a rule, these instructions refer to the timing of the examination; the fact that you should not start work until the signal and must stop work at a signal, etc. If there are any *special* instructions, such as a choice of questions to be answered, make sure that you note this instruction carefully.

2) When you are ready to start work on the examination, that is as soon as the signal has been given, read the instructions to each question booklet, underline any key words or phrases, such as *least, best, outline, describe* and the like. In this way you will tend to answer as requested rather than discover on reviewing your paper that you *listed without describing*, that you selected the *worst* choice rather than the *best* choice, etc.

3) If the examination is of the objective or multiple-choice type – that is, each question will also give a series of possible answers: A, B, C or D, and you are called upon to select the best answer and write the letter next to that answer on your answer paper – it is advisable to start answering each question in turn. There may be anywhere from 50 to 100 such questions in the three or four hours allotted and you can see how much time would be taken if you read through all the questions before beginning to answer any. Furthermore, if you come across a question or group of questions which you know would be difficult to answer, it would undoubtedly affect your handling of all the other questions.

4) If the examination is of the essay type and contains but a few questions, it is a moot point as to whether you should read all the questions before starting to answer any one. Of course, if you are given a choice – say five out of seven and the like – then it is essential to read all the questions so you can eliminate the two that are most difficult. If, however, you are asked to answer all the questions, there may be danger in trying to answer the easiest one first because you may find that you will spend too much time on it. The best technique is to answer the first question, then proceed to the second, etc.

5) Time your answers. Before the exam begins, write down the time it started, then add the time allowed for the examination and write down the time it must be completed, then divide the time available somewhat as follows:
    - If 3-1/2 hours are allowed, that would be 210 minutes. If you have 80 objective-type questions, that would be an average of 2-1/2 minutes per question. Allow yourself no more than 2 minutes per question, or a total of 160 minutes, which will permit about 50 minutes to review.
    - If for the time allotment of 210 minutes there are 7 essay questions to answer, that would average about 30 minutes a question. Give yourself only 25 minutes per question so that you have about 35 minutes to review.

6) The most important instruction is to *read each question* and make sure you know what is wanted. The second most important instruction is to *time yourself properly* so that you answer every question. The third most important instruction is to *answer every question*. Guess if you have to but include something for each question. Remember that you will receive no credit for a blank and will probably receive some credit if you write something in answer to an essay question. If you guess a letter – say "B" for a multiple-choice question – you may have guessed right. If you leave a blank as an answer to a multiple-choice question, the examiners may respect your feelings but it will not add a point to your score. Some exams may penalize you for wrong answers, so in such cases *only*, you may not want to guess unless you have some basis for your answer.

7) Suggestions
    a. Objective-type questions
        1. Examine the question booklet for proper sequence of pages and questions
        2. Read all instructions carefully
        3. Skip any question which seems too difficult; return to it after all other questions have been answered
        4. Apportion your time properly; do not spend too much time on any single question or group of questions

5. Note and underline key words – *all, most, fewest, least, best, worst, same, opposite*, etc.
6. Pay particular attention to negatives
7. Note unusual option, e.g., unduly long, short, complex, different or similar in content to the body of the question
8. Observe the use of "hedging" words – *probably, may, most likely*, etc.
9. Make sure that your answer is put next to the same number as the question
10. Do not second-guess unless you have good reason to believe the second answer is definitely more correct
11. Cross out original answer if you decide another answer is more accurate; do not erase until you are ready to hand your paper in
12. Answer all questions; guess unless instructed otherwise
13. Leave time for review

b. Essay questions
1. Read each question carefully
2. Determine exactly what is wanted. Underline key words or phrases.
3. Decide on outline or paragraph answer
4. Include many different points and elements unless asked to develop any one or two points or elements
5. Show impartiality by giving pros and cons unless directed to select one side only
6. Make and write down any assumptions you find necessary to answer the questions
7. Watch your English, grammar, punctuation and choice of words
8. Time your answers; don't crowd material

8) Answering the essay question

Most essay questions can be answered by framing the specific response around several key words or ideas. Here are a few such key words or ideas:

M's: manpower, materials, methods, money, management
P's: purpose, program, policy, plan, procedure, practice, problems, pitfalls, personnel, public relations

a. Six basic steps in handling problems:
1. Preliminary plan and background development
2. Collect information, data and facts
3. Analyze and interpret information, data and facts
4. Analyze and develop solutions as well as make recommendations
5. Prepare report and sell recommendations
6. Install recommendations and follow up effectiveness

b. Pitfalls to avoid
1. *Taking things for granted* – A statement of the situation does not necessarily imply that each of the elements is necessarily true; for example, a complaint may be invalid and biased so that all that can be taken for granted is that a complaint has been registered

2. *Considering only one side of a situation* – Wherever possible, indicate several alternatives and then point out the reasons you selected the best one
3. *Failing to indicate follow up* – Whenever your answer indicates action on your part, make certain that you will take proper follow-up action to see how successful your recommendations, procedures or actions turn out to be
4. *Taking too long in answering any single question* – Remember to time your answers properly

IX. AFTER THE TEST

Scoring procedures differ in detail among civil service jurisdictions although the general principles are the same. Whether the papers are hand-scored or graded by machine we have described, they are nearly always graded by number. That is, the person who marks the paper knows only the number – never the name – of the applicant. Not until all the papers have been graded will they be matched with names. If other tests, such as training and experience or oral interview ratings have been given, scores will be combined. Different parts of the examination usually have different weights. For example, the written test might count 60 percent of the final grade, and a rating of training and experience 40 percent. In many jurisdictions, veterans will have a certain number of points added to their grades.

After the final grade has been determined, the names are placed in grade order and an eligible list is established. There are various methods for resolving ties between those who get the same final grade – probably the most common is to place first the name of the person whose application was received first. Job offers are made from the eligible list in the order the names appear on it. You will be notified of your grade and your rank as soon as all these computations have been made. This will be done as rapidly as possible.

People who are found to meet the requirements in the announcement are called "eligibles." Their names are put on a list of eligible candidates. An eligible's chances of getting a job depend on how high he stands on this list and how fast agencies are filling jobs from the list.

When a job is to be filled from a list of eligibles, the agency asks for the names of people on the list of eligibles for that job. When the civil service commission receives this request, it sends to the agency the names of the three people highest on this list. Or, if the job to be filled has specialized requirements, the office sends the agency the names of the top three persons who meet these requirements from the general list.

The appointing officer makes a choice from among the three people whose names were sent to him. If the selected person accepts the appointment, the names of the others are put back on the list to be considered for future openings.

That is the rule in hiring from all kinds of eligible lists, whether they are for typist, carpenter, chemist, or something else. For every vacancy, the appointing officer has his choice of any one of the top three eligibles on the list. This explains why the person whose name is on top of the list sometimes does not get an appointment when some of the persons lower on the list do. If the appointing officer chooses the second or third eligible, the No. 1 eligible does not get a job at once, but stays on the list until he is appointed or the list is terminated.

X. HOW TO PASS THE INTERVIEW TEST

The examination for which you applied requires an oral interview test. You have already taken the written test and you are now being called for the interview test – the final part of the formal examination.

You may think that it is not possible to prepare for an interview test and that there are no procedures to follow during an interview. Our purpose is to point out some things you can do in advance that will help you and some good rules to follow and pitfalls to avoid while you are being interviewed.

What is an interview supposed to test?

The written examination is designed to test the technical knowledge and competence of the candidate; the oral is designed to evaluate intangible qualities, not readily measured otherwise, and to establish a list showing the relative fitness of each candidate – as measured against his competitors – for the position sought. Scoring is not on the basis of "right" and "wrong," but on a sliding scale of values ranging from "not passable" to "outstanding." As a matter of fact, it is possible to achieve a relatively low score without a single "incorrect" answer because of evident weakness in the qualities being measured.

Occasionally, an examination may consist entirely of an oral test – either an individual or a group oral. In such cases, information is sought concerning the technical knowledges and abilities of the candidate, since there has been no written examination for this purpose. More commonly, however, an oral test is used to supplement a written examination.

Who conducts interviews?

The composition of oral boards varies among different jurisdictions. In nearly all, a representative of the personnel department serves as chairman. One of the members of the board may be a representative of the department in which the candidate would work. In some cases, "outside experts" are used, and, frequently, a businessman or some other representative of the general public is asked to serve. Labor and management or other special groups may be represented. The aim is to secure the services of experts in the appropriate field.

However the board is composed, it is a good idea (and not at all improper or unethical) to ascertain in advance of the interview who the members are and what groups they represent. When you are introduced to them, you will have some idea of their backgrounds and interests, and at least you will not stutter and stammer over their names.

What should be done before the interview?

While knowledge about the board members is useful and takes some of the surprise element out of the interview, there is other preparation which is more substantive. It *is* possible to prepare for an oral interview – in several ways:

1) Keep a copy of your application and review it carefully before the interview

This may be the only document before the oral board, and the starting point of the interview. Know what education and experience you have listed there, and the sequence and dates of all of it. Sometimes the board will ask you to review the highlights of your experience for them; you should not have to hem and haw doing it.

2) Study the class specification and the examination announcement

Usually, the oral board has one or both of these to guide them. The qualities, characteristics or knowledges required by the position sought are stated in these documents. They offer valuable clues as to the nature of the oral interview. For example, if the job involves supervisory responsibilities, the announcement will usually indicate that knowledge of modern supervisory methods and the qualifications of the candidate as a supervisor will be tested. If so, you can expect such questions, frequently in the form of a hypothetical situation which you are expected to solve. NEVER go into an oral without knowledge of the duties and responsibilities of the job you seek.

3) Think through each qualification required

Try to visualize the kind of questions you would ask if you were a board member. How well could you answer them? Try especially to appraise your own knowledge and background in each area, *measured against the job sought*, and identify any areas in which you are weak. Be critical and realistic – do not flatter yourself.

4) Do some general reading in areas in which you feel you may be weak

For example, if the job involves supervision and your past experience has NOT, some general reading in supervisory methods and practices, particularly in the field of human relations, might be useful. Do NOT study agency procedures or detailed manuals. The oral board will be testing your understanding and capacity, not your memory.

5) Get a good night's sleep and watch your general health and mental attitude

You will want a clear head at the interview. Take care of a cold or any other minor ailment, and of course, no hangovers.

What should be done on the day of the interview?

Now comes the day of the interview itself. Give yourself plenty of time to get there. Plan to arrive somewhat ahead of the scheduled time, particularly if your appointment is in the fore part of the day. If a previous candidate fails to appear, the board might be ready for you a bit early. By early afternoon an oral board is almost invariably behind schedule if there are many candidates, and you may have to wait. Take along a book or magazine to read, or your application to review, but leave any extraneous material in the waiting room when you go in for your interview. In any event, relax and compose yourself.

The matter of dress is important. The board is forming impressions about you – from your experience, your manners, your attitude, and your appearance. Give your personal appearance careful attention. Dress your best, but not your flashiest. Choose conservative, appropriate clothing, and be sure it is immaculate. This is a business interview, and your appearance should indicate that you regard it as such. Besides, being well groomed and properly dressed will help boost your confidence.

Sooner or later, someone will call your name and escort you into the interview room. *This is it.* From here on you are on your own. It is too late for any more preparation. But remember, you asked for this opportunity to prove your fitness, and you are here because your request was granted.

What happens when you go in?

The usual sequence of events will be as follows: The clerk (who is often the board stenographer) will introduce you to the chairman of the oral board, who will introduce you to the other members of the board. Acknowledge the introductions before you sit down. Do not be surprised if you find a microphone facing you or a stenotypist sitting by. Oral interviews are usually recorded in the event of an appeal or other review.

Usually the chairman of the board will open the interview by reviewing the highlights of your education and work experience from your application – primarily for the benefit of the other members of the board, as well as to get the material into the record. Do not interrupt or comment unless there is an error or significant misinterpretation; if that is the case, do not hesitate. But do not quibble about insignificant matters. Also, he will usually ask you some question about your education, experience or your present job – partly to get you to start talking and to establish the interviewing "rapport." He may start the actual questioning, or turn it over to one of the other members. Frequently, each member undertakes the questioning on a particular area, one in which he is perhaps most competent, so you can expect each member to participate in the examination. Because time is limited, you may also expect some rather abrupt switches in the direction the questioning takes, so do not be upset by it. Normally, a board member will not pursue a single line of questioning unless he discovers a particular strength or weakness.

After each member has participated, the chairman will usually ask whether any member has any further questions, then will ask you if you have anything you wish to add. Unless you are expecting this question, it may floor you. Worse, it may start you off on an extended, extemporaneous speech. The board is not usually seeking more information. The question is principally to offer you a last opportunity to present further qualifications or to indicate that you have nothing to add. So, if you feel that a significant qualification or characteristic has been overlooked, it is proper to point it out in a sentence or so. Do not compliment the board on the thoroughness of their examination – they have been sketchy, and you know it. If you wish, merely say, "No thank you, I have nothing further to add." This is a point where you can "talk yourself out" of a good impression or fail to present an important bit of information. Remember, *you close the interview yourself.*

The chairman will then say, "That is all, Mr. _____, thank you." Do not be startled; the interview is over, and quicker than you think. Thank him, gather your belongings and take your leave. Save your sigh of relief for the other side of the door.

How to put your best foot forward

Throughout this entire process, you may feel that the board individually and collectively is trying to pierce your defenses, seek out your hidden weaknesses and embarrass and confuse you. Actually, this is not true. They are obliged to make an appraisal of your qualifications for the job you are seeking, and they want to see you in your best light. Remember, they must interview all candidates and a non-cooperative candidate may become a failure in spite of their best efforts to bring out his qualifications. Here are 15 suggestions that will help you:

1) Be natural – Keep your attitude confident, not cocky

If you are not confident that you can do the job, do not expect the board to be. Do not apologize for your weaknesses, try to bring out your strong points. The board is interested in a positive, not negative, presentation. Cockiness will antagonize any board member and make him wonder if you are covering up a weakness by a false show of strength.

2) Get comfortable, but don't lounge or sprawl

Sit erectly but not stiffly. A careless posture may lead the board to conclude that you are careless in other things, or at least that you are not impressed by the importance of the occasion. Either conclusion is natural, even if incorrect. Do not fuss with your clothing, a pencil or an ashtray. Your hands may occasionally be useful to emphasize a point; do not let them become a point of distraction.

3) Do not wisecrack or make small talk

This is a serious situation, and your attitude should show that you consider it as such. Further, the time of the board is limited – they do not want to waste it, and neither should you.

4) Do not exaggerate your experience or abilities

In the first place, from information in the application or other interviews and sources, the board may know more about you than you think. Secondly, you probably will not get away with it. An experienced board is rather adept at spotting such a situation, so do not take the chance.

5) If you know a board member, do not make a point of it, yet do not hide it

Certainly you are not fooling him, and probably not the other members of the board. Do not try to take advantage of your acquaintanceship – it will probably do you little good.

6) Do not dominate the interview

Let the board do that. They will give you the clues – do not assume that you have to do all the talking. Realize that the board has a number of questions to ask you, and do not try to take up all the interview time by showing off your extensive knowledge of the answer to the first one.

7) Be attentive

You only have 20 minutes or so, and you should keep your attention at its sharpest throughout. When a member is addressing a problem or question to you, give him your undivided attention. Address your reply principally to him, but do not exclude the other board members.

8) Do not interrupt

A board member may be stating a problem for you to analyze. He will ask you a question when the time comes. Let him state the problem, and wait for the question.

9) Make sure you understand the question

Do not try to answer until you are sure what the question is. If it is not clear, restate it in your own words or ask the board member to clarify it for you. However, do not haggle about minor elements.

10) Reply promptly but not hastily

A common entry on oral board rating sheets is "candidate responded readily," or "candidate hesitated in replies." Respond as promptly and quickly as you can, but do not jump to a hasty, ill-considered answer.

11) Do not be peremptory in your answers

A brief answer is proper – but do not fire your answer back. That is a losing game from your point of view. The board member can probably ask questions much faster than you can answer them.

12) Do not try to create the answer you think the board member wants

He is interested in what kind of mind you have and how it works – not in playing games. Furthermore, he can usually spot this practice and will actually grade you down on it.

13) Do not switch sides in your reply merely to agree with a board member

Frequently, a member will take a contrary position merely to draw you out and to see if you are willing and able to defend your point of view. Do not start a debate, yet do not surrender a good position. If a position is worth taking, it is worth defending.

14) Do not be afraid to admit an error in judgment if you are shown to be wrong

The board knows that you are forced to reply without any opportunity for careful consideration. Your answer may be demonstrably wrong. If so, admit it and get on with the interview.

15) Do not dwell at length on your present job

The opening question may relate to your present assignment. Answer the question but do not go into an extended discussion. You are being examined for a *new* job, not your present one. As a matter of fact, try to phrase ALL your answers in terms of the job for which you are being examined.

Basis of Rating

Probably you will forget most of these "do's" and "don'ts" when you walk into the oral interview room. Even remembering them all will not ensure you a passing grade. Perhaps you did not have the qualifications in the first place. But remembering them will help you to put your best foot forward, without treading on the toes of the board members.

Rumor and popular opinion to the contrary notwithstanding, an oral board wants you to make the best appearance possible. They know you are under pressure – but they also want to see how you respond to it as a guide to what your reaction would be under the pressures of the job you seek. They will be influenced by the degree of poise you display, the personal traits you show and the manner in which you respond.

ABOUT THIS BOOK

This book contains tests divided into Examination Sections. Go through each test, answering every question in the margin. We have also attached a sample answer sheet at the back of the book that can be removed and used. At the end of each test look at the answer key and check your answers. On the ones you got wrong, look at the right answer choice and learn. Do not fill in the answers first. Do not memorize the questions and answers, but understand the answer and principles involved. On your test, the questions will likely be different from the samples. Questions are changed and new ones added. If you understand these past questions you should have success with any changes that arise. Tests may consist of several types of questions. We have additional books on each subject should more study be advisable or necessary for you. Finally, the more you study, the better prepared you will be. This book is intended to be the last thing you study before you walk into the examination room. Prior study of relevant texts is also recommended. NLC publishes some of these in our Fundamental Series. Knowledge and good sense are important factors in passing your exam. Good luck also helps. So now study this Passbook, absorb the material contained within and take that knowledge into the examination. Then do your best to pass that exam.

EXAMINATION SECTION

EXAMINATION SECTION
TEST 1

DIRECTIONS: Each question or incomplete statement is followed by several suggested answers or completions. Select the one that BEST answers the question or completes the statement. *PRINT THE LETTER OF THE CORRECT ANSWER IN THE SPACE AT THE RIGHT.*

1. The *Father of the Paramedics* is Dr.   1._____
   A. James Warren
   B. William Grace
   C. Eugene Nagel
   D. Williams

2. A paramedic is a professional who   2._____
   A. treats the patient
   B. provides pre-hospital emergency care
   C. provides in-house care of patients
   D. all of the above

3. The paramedic carries out a variety of invasive procedures, which he can perform   3._____
   A. whenever he thinks they are necessary
   B. after discussion with other paramedics
   C. only after ordered by a licensed physician through medical control
   D. none of the above

4. The paramedic must master a variety of complex skills, including   4._____
   A. endotracheal intubation
   B. pneumothorax decompression
   C. traction and splinting
   D. all of the above

Questions 5-8.

DIRECTIONS: In Questions 5 through 8, match the numbered descriptions with the appropriate lettered title or term listed in Column I. Place the letter of the correct answer in the space at the right.

COLUMN I
A. EMT - A
B. EMT - I
C. EMT - P
D. Medical Control

5. An individual who has passed a nationally standardized course that includes all the required material plus instruction regarding invasive techniques, ACLS, and administration of medication.   5._____

6. An individual who has passed a nationally standardized course that includes CPR, airway management, artificial ventilation, basic trauma life support, emergency childbirth rescue, and extrication and other non-invasive skills.   6._____

7. The supervision of paramedics by physicians, which provides the legal framework within which paramedics can function.

8. An individual who has passed a nationally standardized course that includes all the required material plus instruction regarding esophageal obturator airway IV infusion, endotracheal intubation, and defibrillation.

9. ANY act of touching another person without that person's consent is called
   A. battery
   B. assault
   C. negligence
   D. none of the above

10. _____ is the creation of a fear of immediate bodily harm or invasion of bodily security in another person.
    A. Battery
    B. Assault
    C. Negligence
    D. All of the above

11. A wrongful act which gives rise to a civil suit is called
    A. tort
    B. civil suit
    C. negligence
    D. none of the above

12. When one intentionally and unjustifiably detains another person against that person's will, he commits
    A. assault
    B. false imprisonment
    C. emergency doctrine
    D. good samaritan act

13. An action instituted by a private individual against another private individual is
    A. consent
    B. criminal suit
    C. civil suit
    D. tort

14. When the government institutes an action against a private individual for a violation of criminal law, it is known as a
    A. criminal suit
    B. civil suit
    C. battery
    D. none of the above

15. The process by which a professional association grants recognition to an individual who has met predetermined qualifications specified by that association is referred to as
    A. licensure
    B. certification
    C. reciprocity
    D. all of the above

16. _____ is the process by which a governmental agency, upon verifying that an applicant has attained the minimal degree of necessary competency, grants permission to that individual to engage in a given occupation.
    A. Licensure
    B. Certification
    C. Reciprocity
    D. None of the above

17. Abrupt termination of contact with a patient without giving that patient sufficient opportunity to find another suitable health professional to take over his medical treatment is called
    A. negligence
    B. emergency doctoring
    C. abandonment
    D. all of the above

18. Paramedics function within a legal framework provided by _____, or the supervision of paramedics by licensed physicians.   18.____

    A. medical control
    B. messenger service
    C. teaching service
    D. none of the above

19. The criteria for determining mental competence should be spelled out in detail in the protocols of every ambulance service.   19.____
    As a rule, such criteria will include reminders to check if the patient

    A. is oriented to person, place, and time
    B. has no significant mental impairment from alcohol, drugs, head injury or other organic illnesses
    C. understands the nature of his condition and the risk of not going to the hospital for immediate care
    D. all of the above

20. Criteria for determining hospital categorization includes   20.____

    A. the number of physicians on the staff and their availability
    B. the medical specialties of the staff physicians
    C. the medical specialties of the nurses
    D. all of the above

Questions 21-25.

   DIRECTIONS: In Questions 21 through 25, match the numbered definition with the appropriate lettered term listed in Column I. Place the letter of the correct answer in the space at the right.

   COLUMN I
   A. Good Samaritan Act
   B. Duty to act
   C. Liability
   D. Negligence
   E. Emergency doctrine

21. The legal obligation of public and certain other ambulance services to respond to a call for help within their jurisdiction.   21.____

22. A statute providing limited immunity from liability for the person responding voluntarily and in good faith to the aid of an injured person outside the hospital.   22.____

23. A form of implied consent to medical treatment when a person's life or limb is in imminent danger and the person is unable to consent to treatment for him/herself. The law implies consent to emergency treatment that the person would consent to if otherwise able.   23.____

24. A finding in civil cases that the preponderance of the evidence shows the defendant to be responsible for the plaintiff's injury.   24.____

25. A professional action or inaction on the part of the health worker that does not meet the standard of ordinary care expected of similarly trained and prudent health practitioners and that results in injury to the patient.   25.____

KEY (CORRECT ANSWERS)

1.	C	11.	A
2.	B	12.	B
3.	C	13.	C
4.	D	14.	A
5.	C	15.	B
6.	A	16.	A
7.	D	17.	C
8.	B	18.	A
9.	A	19.	D
10.	B	20.	D

21. B
22. A
23. E
24. C
25. D

HUMAN SYSTEMS & PATIENT ASSESSMENT
EXAMINATION SECTION
TEST 1

DIRECTIONS: Each question or incomplete statement is followed by several suggested answers or completions. Select the one that BEST answers the question or completes the statement. *PRINT THE LETTER OF THE CORRECT ANSWER IN THE SPACE AT THE RIGHT.*

1. When the patient is facing the examiner, the front is called the   1._____
   A. posterior   B. anterior   C. inferior   D. superior

2. The part of an extremity that is NEARER to the point of attachment to the body is the   2._____
   _____ part.
   A. proximal   B. distal   C. medial   D. superior

3. Someone who is in a lying down position is   3._____
   A. supine   B. prone   C. recumbent   D. erect

4. If a patient is lying face-down, he is   4._____
   A. prone   B. lateral recumbent
   C. recumbent   D. supine

5. _____ is the act of bending a part of the body, or the state of being bent.   5._____
   A. Extension   B. Flexion   C. Abduction   D. Adduction

6. Any movement AWAY from the midline of the body is called   6._____
   A. abduction   B. adduction   C. extension   D. flexion

7. The external rotation of the arm, causing the palm to face forward, is referred to as   7._____
   A. pronation   B. adduction   C. supination   D. abduction

8. When the arm is INTERNALLY rotated so that the back (dorsum) of the hand faces forward, the arm is said to be in   8._____
   A. pronation   B. supination
   C. flexion   D. extension

9. In humans, homeostasis is the maintenance of a stable internal environment. This environment includes   9._____
   A. oxygen supply   B. carbon dioxide level
   C. temperature   D. all of the above

10. What is the PRINCIPLE function of human cells?   10._____
    A. Exchanging materials with the immediate environment
    B. Obtaining energy from nutrients
    C. Synthesizing proteins and reproducing
    D. All of the above

11. The term *cauded* means towards the

    A. tail end B. midline
    C. head D. cranium

12. A vertical line dividing left from right is called

    A. transverse B. sagittal
    C. cephaled D. cranial

13. A vertical cut dividing the body into anterior and posterior portions is a _____ line.

    A. sagittal B. mesial
    C. coronal D. transverse

14. Which of the following statements describes how food is converted into energy?

    A. Protein is transformed into simple amino acids in the digestive system, and carbohydrates and fats are similarly broken down.
    B. Broken-down food is absorbed into the bloodstream and penetrates the cell membranes.
    C. Metabolism is the chemical reaction responsible for changing nutrients into energy.
    D. All of the above.

15. Each of the following terms regarding bone structure is correctly matched with its definition EXCEPT

    A. diaphysis - the shaft of a long bone
    B. endosteum - connective tissue inside the bone
    C. epiphysis - the end of a long bone
    D. periosteum - connective tissue around the bone

16. _____ bones are in the normal human skeleton.

    A. 100 B. 280 C. 206 D. 300

17. The respiratory system performs all of the following functions EXCEPT:

    A. Air is inspired to the lung
    B. Oxygen attaches to hemoglobin
    C. Blood carries hemoglobin to the cells
    D. Red blood cells are reproduced

18. It is NOT true that

    A. blood passes from the right atrium to the right ventricle
    B. the right ventricle pumps blood to the lungs through the pulmonary arteries
    C. from the left atrium, the blood passes to the right atrium
    D. oxygenated blood goes from the lungs through the pulmonary vein to the left atrium

19. The functions of the digestive system include all of the following EXCEPT:

    A. Proteins, carbohydrates, and fats are broken down to simple compounds
    B. Compounds are absorbed by villi into the bloodstream and lymphatic system
    C. Waste products are excreted
    D. Waste products are reabsorbed

20. Which of the following statements is NOT true about the lymphatic system?

    A. Tissue fluid (lymph) is filtered out of the blood capillaries and is returned to the bloodstream by the lymphatic system.
    B. Lymph is excreted directly through the kidneys.
    C. Special function tissue adds lymphocytes and antibodies to the system.
    D. Flow is maintained by pressure differences in the system, formation of lymph, muscle activity, etc.

21. The peripheral nervous system

    A. transmits messages from the various parts of the body
    B. is composed of afferent fibers which transmit impulses to the brain
    C. is composed of efferent fibers which transmit impulses from the brain
    D. all of the above

22. The very FIRST step upon reaching the scene of an emergency (for example, MVA) is to look around and determine whether

    A. the vehicles are positioned on the road in such a way that other vehicles are likely to pile into them
    B. either of the vehicles is on fire, or there is spilled gasoline on the road
    C. there are downed electrical wires at the scene
    D. all of the above

23. When you reach the scene of any emergency, the survey of the scene should include all of the following EXCEPT

    A. a check for hazards to the rescuers or patients and an elimination of any hazards detected
    B. an initial determination of whether back-up is needed
    C. a determination of whether special equipment is needed to gain access to the patient
    D. securing parking for transport

24. What is the purpose of a primary survey or assessment of an emergency situation?

    A. To rapidly identify existing life-threatening situations
    B. To exclude the need of a physical examination
    C. All of the above
    D. None of the above

25. The FIRST step in the primary survey of every patient is to determine if the patient

    A. has an open airway
    B. is breathing
    C. has adequate circulation
    D. all of the above

KEY (CORRECT ANSWERS)

1. B
2. A
3. C
4. A
5. B

6. A
7. C
8. A
9. D
10. D

11. A
12. B
13. C
14. D
15. B

16. C
17. D
18. C
19. D
20. B

21. D
22. D
23. D
24. A
25. D

TEST 2

DIRECTIONS: Each question or incomplete statement is followed by several suggested answers or completions. Select the one that BEST answers the question or completes the statement. *PRINT THE LETTER OF THE CORRECT ANSWER IN THE SPACE AT THE RIGHT.*

1. With regard to secondary survey or assessment, it is TRUE that it should   1.____

    A. be performed after all life-threatening situations are treated
    B. evaluate the entire patient to determine if underlying problems are present
    C. gather information to communicate to the hospital
    D. all of the above

2. Which of the following parts of history is of IMMEDIATE importance in the field of patient assessment?   2.____

    A. History of immediate situation
    B. The patient's past medical history
    C. Family medical history
    D. A and B *only*

3. You are called in to examine a patient with MVA.   3.____
   The inspection of the head should check specifically for all of the following problems EXCEPT

    A. any obvious hemorrhage
    B. ecchymosis, erythema, contusion
    C. pain on compression of skull
    D. scalp lesions

4. Palpation of the head will reveal any   4.____

    A. lumps
    B. depression
    C. pain of compression of the scalp
    D. all of the above

5. Battle's sign is   5.____

    A. ecchymosis over the mastoid
    B. ecchymosis over the eyes
    C. presence of rhinorrhea
    D. bleeding from the nose

6. The one of the following which is NOT a first-priority injury is   6.____

    A. airway and breathing difficulties
    B. major multiple fractures
    C. cardiac arrest
    D. uncontrolled bleeding

7. When examining a patient's skin, you should observe the _____ of the skin.

   A. color
   B. temperature
   C. moisture
   D. all of the above

8. An examination of the thorax should include an inspection of

   A. respiratory rate and depth
   B. retraction of intercostal space between the ribs
   C. chest elevation symmetry, laceration, punctures, or ecchymosis
   D. all of the above

9. On palpation of a patient with thoraxic injury, you want to find out all of the following EXCEPT

   A. any compression of the clavicle
   B. heart rate
   C. any anterior to posterior compress of the thorax
   D. compression on the costovertebral angles

10. Percussion on a patient with respiratory difficulty does NOT intend to find the presence of

    A. fluid in the thorax
    B. pneumothorax
    C. rhonchi
    D. a collapsed lung

11. True statements regarding the sequence of taking signs include all of the following EXCEPT:
    If the patient is _____, take the signs _____.

    A. communicative with a traumatic injury; after assessing the site(s) of the injury
    B. non-communicative; after secondary survey
    C. communicative with a medical problem; after primary assessment and in conjunction with taking the medical history, if possible
    D. non-communicative; immediately after the primary assessment

12. If a patient complains of abdominal pain, a palpation must be done to find

    A. local tenderness and/or abdominal distension
    B. garding
    C. rebound pain
    D. all of the above

13. A patient with respiratory difficulty requires the performance of an auscultation in order to find the

    A. absence of or unequal quality of breath sound
    B. characteristics of breath sound (rales, rhonchi, wheezing)
    C. heart sound
    D. all of the above

14. Important functions of the renal system include all of the following EXCEPT

    A. maintenance of salt and water balance
    B. maintenance of acid and base balance
    C. control of production and elimination of urine
    D. production of lymphocytes

15. Bones are composed of

   A. water
   B. inorganic minerals
   C. organic compounds
   D. all of the above

16. Assessing the pulse provides an initial, rapid check of the patient's cardiovascular status. The pulse is BEST palpated over the _____ artery.

   A. radial or carotid
   B. subclavical
   C. axillary
   D. none of the above

17. Severe vasoconstriction causes the pulse to feel

   A. strong or bounding
   B. weak or thready
   C. normal
   D. all of the above

18. A patient with periods of rapid, irregular breathing which start shallow, become deeper, then shallow again, alternating with periods of non-breathing, MOST likely suffers from

   A. cheyne stokes respiration
   B. kussmaul's respiration
   C. none of the above
   D. all of the above

19. The bilateral symmetric periorbital ecchymoses that is seen with some skull fractures is called a

   A. Battle's sign
   B. raccoon sign
   C. consensual reaction
   D. all of the above

20. The female reproductive system consists of all of the following EXCEPT the

   A. ovaries   B. uterus   C. ureter   D. vagina

Questions 21-25.

DIRECTIONS: In Questions 21 through 25, match the numbered gland or organ with the lettered substance MOST closely associated with it listed in Column I. Place the letter of the CORRECT answer in the appropriate space at the right.

COLUMN I
A. Insulin
B. Calcium
C. Cortisol
D. Growth hormone
E. Estrogen

21. Parathyroid gland

22. Pancreas

23. Pituitary gland

24. Ovaries

25. Adrenal gland

Questions 26-30.

DIRECTIONS: In Questions 26 through 30, match the numbered system or internal body part with its lettered function listed in Column I. Place the letter of the CORRECT answer in the appropriate space at the right.

COLUMN I
A. In action when the body is at rest
B. In action when the body is in action
C. A conducting pathway
D. A regulatory center
E. Pumping blood to the lungs

26. Sympathetic nervous system   26.___

27. Parasympathetic nervous system   27.___

28. Spinal cord   28.___

29. Brain   29.___

30. Heart   30.___

KEY (CORRECT ANSWERS)

1.	D	11.	B	21.	B
2.	D	12.	D	22.	A
3.	C	13.	D	23.	D
4.	D	14.	D	24.	E
5.	A	15.	D	25.	C
6.	B	16.	A	26.	B
7.	D	17.	B	27.	A
8.	D	18.	A	28.	C
9.	B	19.	B	29.	D
10.	C	20.	C	30.	E

SHOCK AND FLUID THERAPY
EXAMINATION SECTION
TEST 1

DIRECTIONS: Each question or incomplete statement is followed by several suggested answers or completions. Select the one that BEST answers the question or completes the statement. *PRINT THE LETTER OF THE CORRECT ANSWER IN THE SPACE AT THE RIGHT.*

1. Water constitutes 60% of the total weight of an adult man and is distributed among numerous compartments. The compartment below which contains MOST of the water is the _____ compartment.

    A. intracellular fluid (ICF)
    B. extracellular fluid (ECF)
    C. interstitial fluid
    D. intravascular fluid

    1._____

2. In a man weighing 70 kg, there are about 42 liters of water. How much water is in the extracellular fluid compartment? _____ liters.

    A. 31.5   B. 20   C. 10.5   D. 15.8

    2._____

3. Ions with a positive charge are called cations.
   The one of the following which is NOT among the most important cations in the body is

    A. sodium   B. bicarbonate
    C. potassium   D. calcium

    3._____

4. The MOST common anions in the body include

    A. magnesium   B. potassium
    C. chloride   D. all of the above

    4._____

5. If two solutions are separated by a semipermeable membrane, water will flow across the membrane from the solution of lower concentration to the solution of higher concentration.
   This process is called

    A. diffusion   B. osmosis
    C. absorption   D. all of the above

    5._____

6. The normal concentration of glucose in the blood is APPROXIMATELY _____ to _____ mg per 100 ml.

    A. 70; 110   B. 200; 250   C. 300; 350   D. 400; 500

    6._____

7. The one of the following solutions which does NOT contain protein or other large molecules is

    A. dextran   B. albumin
    C. normal saline   D. none of the above

    7._____

8. The MOST important extracellular cation which has primary role in regulating the distribution of water throughout the body is

   A. sodium B. potassium C. magnesium D. calcium

9. What chief cation of the intracellular fluid has a critical role in mediating electric impulses in the nerves and muscles, including the heart muscle?

   A. Sodium B. Potassium C. Calcium D. Magnesium

10. The presence of a tall, peaked T wave on an electrocardiogram suggests

    A. hyponatremia
    C. hyperkalemia
    B. hypercalcemia
    D. hypokalemia

11. _____ serves as the chief buffer in the human body.

    A. Phosphate
    C. Lactic acid
    B. Bicarbonate
    D. Proteins

12. The deficit of the electrolyte _____ may cause tetany and convulsions.

    A. magnesium B. chloride C. calcium D. phosphate

13. Among the most important functions of the blood is(are) the

    A. transport of oxygen and nutrients to the cells
    B. transport of white blood cells to combat infection
    C. maintenance of vascular volume
    D. all of the above

14. Of the following, the presence of _____ does NOT symptomize dehydration.

    A. sunken eyes
    C. postural syncope
    B. strong bounding pulse
    D. poor skin turger

15. If the pH of the body fluids is below 7.35 and the concentration of the hydrogen ion is increased, the resulting condition will MOST likely be

    A. normal
    C. acidosis
    B. alkalosis
    D. none of the above

16. A patient has hypoventilation, increased CO_2, decreased pH, and normal-to-increased H_2CO_3.
    The MOST likely diagnosis is

    A. respiratory acidosis
    C. metabolic acidosis
    B. respiratory alkalosis
    D. all of the above

17. A classic finding of respiratory alkaiosis is _____ CO_2 and _____ pH.

    A. increased; increased
    C. decreased; decreased
    B. decreased; increased
    D. normal; normal

18. The definitive treatment for metabolic acidosis is to

    A. administer sodium bicarbonate intravenously
    B. blow off CO_2
    C. eliminate the cause
    D. none of the above

19. All of the following statements are true regarding blood EXCEPT:

    A. Blood develops in bone marrow and lymph nodes
    B. The normal blood volume in a 70 kg man is 12 to 15 liters
    C. Blood carries hormones and other chemical substances that regulate organs
    D. Blood carries waste products from the cells to the organs of excretion

20. Which of the following is NOT a function of the leukocyte?

    A. To engulf bacteria and foreign bodies
    B. To isolate infection
    C. To assist in the clotting process
    D. Antibody reaction

21. The blood type known as the *universal donor* is Type

    A. A   B. B   C. O   D. AB

22. The blood type known as the *universal recipient* is Type

    A. A   B. B   C. O   D. AB

23. The MOST common adverse reaction to a blood transfusion is

    A. fever   B. bradycardia
    C. hypotension   D. diaphoresis

24. Common causes of hypovolumic shock include the loss of all of the following EXCEPT

    A. blood   B. plasma
    C. gastrointestinal fluid   D. all of the above

25. Of the following patients, those at a HIGH risk of developing shock include

    A. one suffering from trauma or bleeding from any cause
    B. a patient with massive myocardial infarction
    C. an elderly man with a urinary tract infection
    D. all of the above

KEY (CORRECT ANSWERS)

1.	A	11.	B
2.	C	12.	C
3.	B	13.	D
4.	C	14.	B
5.	B	15.	C
6.	A	16.	A
7.	C	17.	B
8.	A	18.	C
9.	B	19.	B
10.	C	20.	C

21. C
22. D
23. A
24. D
25. D

TEST 2

DIRECTIONS: Each question or incomplete statement is followed by several suggested answers or completions. Select the one that BEST answers the question or completes the statement. *PRINT THE LETTER OF THE CORRECT ANSWER IN THE SPACE AT THE RIGHT.*

1. In treating shock, it is NOT necessary to

    A. maintain an airway and give oxygen
    B. control bleeding and apply mast
    C. monitor cardiac rhythm and cardiovert
    D. give IV fluids and keep the patient in a recumbent position

    1._____

2. The BEST solution to give to a patient with hypovolumic shock due to vomiting and diarrhea is a solution of

    A. whole blood
    B. normal saline or lactated ringer's
    C. packed red blood cells
    D. none of the above

    2._____

3. All of the following indicate mast use EXCEPT

    A. hypovolumic shock with systolic blood pressure less than 80-90 mmhg
    B. neurogenic shock with systolic blood pressure less than 80-90 mmhg
    C. subdural hematoma
    D. pelvic fractures which need to be stabilized

    3._____

4. _____ does NOT contraindicate mast use.

    A. Diffuse bleeding of the lower extremities
    B. Chest injury
    C. Head injury
    D. Heart failure with pulmonary edema

    4._____

5. IVs are needed for fluid replacement by all of the following EXCEPT a patient who

    A. is in hypovolumic shock
    B. is in neurogenic and septic shock
    C. needs the mast
    D. is young and has epiglottitis

    5._____

6. Potential complications of intravenous therapy include

    A. thrombophlebitis   B. air embolism
    C. pyrogenic reaction   D. all of the above

    6._____

7. The _____ is the site of choice for a peripheral IV.

    A. antecubital fossa   B. dorsum of the hand
    C. femoral vein   D. back of the forearm

    7._____

17

8. All of the following are disadvantages of central venous lines in prehospital care EXCEPT the fact that they

   A. take less time to establish
   B. require strict sterile techniques
   C. have a high complication rate
   D. should be accompanied by a chest x-ray immediately after placement to ensure correct positioning

9. Possible hazards and complications of central venous cannulation include

   A. hematoma
   B. pneumothorax
   C. hemothorax
   D. all of the above

10. *Homeostasis* refers to

    A. the disruption of red blood cells that results from some adverse factor
    B. a tendency to constancy or stability in the body's internal environment
    C. the oxygen-carrying pigment in the red blood cells
    D. none of the above

11. The use of military anti-shock trousers presents the risk of

    A. restricted lung extensibility
    B. severe acidosis and permanent impairment of the lower extremities
    C. abdominal pressure triggering urination, defecation, or emesis
    D. all of the above

12. A(n) _____ is NOT among the possible complications associated with subclavian IV insertion.

    A. puncture of the heart chamber
    B. intracranial hemorrhage
    C. cardiac tamponade
    D. arrhythmia from a catheter initiation

13. The common causes of cardiogenic shock include all of the following EXCEPT

    A. myocardial infarction
    B. pulmonary embolism
    C. peritonitis
    D. arrhythmias

14. Regarding neurogenic shock, it is NOT true that

    A. the loss of sympathetic control of vessels leads to marked vasodilation
    B. true volume deficit always occurs
    C. a decrease in peripheral resistance occurs
    D. the effective circulatory volume is lost into dilated vessels

15. A 25-year-old male sustained burns on 30% of his body surface area. He is MOST prone to developing _____ shock.

    A. cardiogenic
    B. neurogenic
    C. hypovolumic
    D. obstructive

16. A 35-year-old male sustained a stab wound on the left 5th intercostal space and then developed distended neck veins and a paradoxal pulse.
    He is MOST likely in _____ shock.

    A. hypovolumic
    C. neurogenic
    B. cardiogenic
    D. septic

17. A 60-year-old male who has a temperature of 104° F, dysurea, and frequency and suddenly develops hypotension and tachycardia is PROBABLY in _____ shock.

    A. cardiogenic
    C. septic
    B. hypovolumic
    D. neurogenic

18. Excessive retention of body fluids, specifically water and salt, frequently occurs in a patient with

    A. siadh
    B. diabetes insipidis
    C. congestive heart failure
    D. all of the above

19. The physician orders an infusion of 1 liter of normal saline to be run over 2 hours. Using a macrodrop administration set, the number of drops per minute that would be required would equal _____ gtt/min.

    A. 42
    B. 84
    C. 124
    D. 240

20. Metabolic alkalosis can be caused by all of the following EXCEPT the

    A. ingestion of large amounts of sodium bicarbonate as an antacid
    B. excessive administration of sodium bicarbonate IV by a physician or paramedic
    C. intravenous use of morphine sulphate
    D. chronic use of diuretics

KEY (CORRECT ANSWERS)

1.	C	11.	D
2.	B	12.	B
3.	C	13.	C
4.	A	14.	B
5.	D	15.	C
6.	D	16.	B
7.	A	17.	C
8.	A	18.	C
9.	D	19.	B
10.	B	20.	C

GENERAL PHARMACOLOGY
EXAMINATION SECTION
TEST 1

DIRECTIONS: Each question or incomplete statement is followed by several suggested answers or completions. Select the one that BEST answers the question or completes the statement. *PRINT THE LETTER OF THE CORRECT ANSWER IN THE SPACE AT THE RIGHT.*

1. _____ are important sources of drugs.

    A. Animals
    B. Vegetables and plants
    C. Minerals and synthetics
    D. All of the above

1.____

2. Drugs NOT made from animal sources include

    A. insulin
    B. thyroid
    C. epinephrine
    D. all of the above

2.____

3. The dried leaves of the wild flower *foxglove* are an important source of

    A. digitalis
    B. opium
    C. insulin
    D. all of the above

3.____

4. The different names which a drug may have are

    A. official, chemical
    B. generic, trade
    C. all of the above
    D. none of the above

4.____

5. The Federal Food, Drug and Cosmetic Act (1938; amended in 1952 and 1962) added several important provisions that are not contained in earlier laws.
These provisions do all of the following EXCEPT

    A. require that labels list any possible habit–forming drugs contained within a product and give warning regarding possible side effects
    B. not authorize the FDA to determine the safety and efficacy of a drug before it is marketed
    C. authorize the FDA to determine the safety and efficacy of a drug before it is marketed
    D. require that dangerous drugs be issued only upon the prescription of a physician, dentist, or veterinarian

5.____

6. The type of drug having the HIGHEST abuse potential and no legal medical use is Schedule

    A. I   B. II   C. III   D. IV

6.____

7. The drug NOT belonging to Schedule I is

    A. heroin
    B. cocaine
    C. marijuana
    D. lysergic acid diethylamide (LSD)

7.____

8. Cocaine is classified into Schedule

   A. I B. II C. III D. IV

9. All of the following are Schedule II drugs EXCEPT

   A. meperidine hydrochloride
   B. opiates
   C. diazepam
   D. short–acting barbiturates

10. Drugs that may lead to limited dependence (Schedule III) do NOT include

    A. paregoric
    B. codeine combinations
    C. amphetamine combinations
    D. chloral hydrate

11. Drugs that may lead to limited dependence (Schedule IV) include all of the following EXCEPT

    A. meprobomate
    B. phenobarbital
    C. demerol
    D. valium

12. The regulation of drugs in the United States falls under the jurisdiction of several agencies
    It does NOT, however, fall under the jurisdiction of the

    A. FDA, which is charged with enforcement of the Federal Food, Drug, and Cosmetic Act
    B. Agriculture Department, which is responsible for controlled substances and the registration of physicians
    C. Public Health Service (PHS), which regulates biologic products such as vaccines and antitoxins
    D. Federal Trade Commission (FTC), which is empowered to suppress misleading drug advertising

13. A liquid containing one or more chemical substances ENTIRELY dissolved, usually in water, is called a

    A. syrup
    B. solution
    C. suspension
    D. all of the above

14. _____ is the preparation of a finely divided drug intended to be incorporated into a suitable liquid.

    A. Suspension
    B. Ointment
    C. Syrup
    D. Solution

15. A drug suspended in sugar and water in order to improve its taste is called a(n)

    A. emulsion
    B. elixir
    C. syrup
    D. none of the above

16. The _____ of a patient does NOT affect the action of administered drugs.

    A. age B. weight C. race D. condition

17. The route of drug administration RARELY indicated is the _____ route.

    A. oral B. rectal
    C. intravenous D. intramuscular

18. The medication FREQUENTLY administered via the oral route is

    A. activated charcoal B. syrup of ipecac
    C. cough syrup D. A and B *only*

19. The MOST rapidly effective, as well as most dangerous, route of administration is the _____ route.

    A. intravenous B. inhalation
    C. subcutaneous D. rectal

20. All of the following drugs can be administered by way of the endotracheal route EXCEPT

    A. narcan, atropine
    B. valium, lidocaine
    C. digitalis, nitroglycerine
    D. all epinephrine

21. The SLOWEST absorption occurs along the _____ route.

    A. oral B. rectal
    C. topical D. sublingual

22. When the combined effect of two drugs is greater than the sum of their individual effects, it is known as

    A. addition B. synergism
    C. potentiation D. all of the above

23. The enhancement of the action of one drug by another substance which does not perform that action itself is called

    A. potentiation B. addition
    C. antagonism D. stimulant

24. _____ refers to a decrease in the action of a drug *A* caused by the administration of drug *B*.

    A. Antagonism B. Cumulative action
    C. Depressant D. Untoward reaction

25. *An abnormal susceptibility to a drug peculiar to an individual* defines

    A. therapeutic action B. idiosyncrasy
    C. physiologic action D. hypersensitivity

KEY (CORRECT ANSWERS)

1. D
2. D
3. A
4. C
5. B

6. A
7. B
8. B
9. C
10. D

11. C
12. B
13. B
14. A
15. C

16. C
17. B
18. D
19. A
20. C

21. C
22. B
23. A
24. A
25. B

TEST 2

DIRECTIONS: Each question or incomplete statement is followed by several suggested answers or completions. Select the one that BEST answers the question or completes the statement. *PRINT THE LETTER OF THE CORRECT ANSWER IN THE SPACE AT THE RIGHT.*

1. The body's SECOND most important mechanism for terminating the action of a drug is to metabolize the drug to an inactive compound.
   This action USUALLY takes place in the

   A. kidneys   B. lungs   C. liver   D. brain

   1.____

2. Important locations of drug sources in vegetables and plants include

   A. dried roots and seeds   B. leaves and flowers
   C. bark and sap   D. all of the above

   2.____

3. Resulting from the repeated consumption of a drug, a desire to continue the drug's use, but little or no tendency to increase the dosage.
   The condition described above is

   A. additive   B. habituation
   C. tolerance   D. none of the above

   3.____

4. Whenever you administer a drug, you should be aware of

   A. its indications and contraindications
   B. its side effects and incompatibilities
   C. how it is supplied and administered, and its proper dosage
   D. all of the above

   4.____

5. The one of the following which is NOT a unit of solid measure in the apothecaries system is the

   A. pound   B. minim   C. ounce   D. grain

   5.____

6. The one of the following which is NOT a unit of liquid measure in the apothecaries system is the

   A. gallon   B. pint   C. dram   D. fluidram

   6.____

7. What is (are) the advantage(s) of the metric system?

   A. It is the most frequently used system in the official listing of drugs
   B. It is very logical and organized
   C. All of the above
   D. None of the above

   7.____

8. In the metric system, all of the following are units of solid measure EXCEPT the

   A. milliliter   B. gram
   C. milligram   D. kilogram

   8.____

9. To convert pounds to kilograms, divide the number of pounds by

   A. 1.5   B. 2.2   C. 3.5   D. 4

   9.____

10. A patient who weighs 220 lbs. weighs _____ kilograms according to the metric system.

   A. 50   B. 75   C. 100   D. 150

11. Volatile substances dissolved in alcohol form

   A. spirits
   C. elixirs
   B. tintures
   D. none of the above

12. Ointments are described by the statement(s) that they

   A. are a mixture of drugs in a fatty base
   B. are soft enough to spread at room temperature
   C. may have soothing, astringent, and bacteriostatic effects
   D. all of the above

13. The official name of a drug provides

   A. the name registered by the company and restricted to its use
   B. the name under which the drug is listed in official publications
   C. a detailed denotation of the chemical constitution of the drug
   D. all of the above

14. Which of the following statements is (are) TRUE regarding the generic name of a drug? It is

   A. given to the drug before becoming the official name
   B. usually derived from the chemical name, but given in a simpler form
   C. not capitalized
   D. all of the above

15. The mineral present in animal bones and teeth is

   A. calcium   B. insulin   C. opium   D. epinephrine

16. Whether administering medication according to voice orders or to protocols,

   A. always administer the medication immediately
   B. do not waste time to check the dosage
   C. always recheck the correct dosage before administering a drug
   D. none of the above

17. A physician has ordered you to administer medication to a patient, but you do not clearly understand the dosage and route of administration.
You should

   A. administer the drug on the basis of your knowledge
   B. check the route and dosage in your notebook and administer the drug
   C. ask the physician to repeat the order
   D. all of the above

18. A patient is known to be taking lithium.
You should, therefore, NOT administer _____ to the patient.

   A. albuterol
   C. penicillin
   B. furosemide
   D. none of the above

19. When administering a drug via intravenous lines, it is IMPORTANT to 19._____
    A. prep the drug administration port
    B. pinch off the tubing and inject the drug
    C. open the regulator clamp to flush the system
    D. all of the above

20. Proper technique for an intramuscular injection includes 20._____
    A. choosing an injection site in the deltoid muscle and prepping the skin over the site
    B. inserting the needle at a 90° angle to the muscle and aspirating for the blood
    C. returning the inject if there is no blood, and applying pressure to the injection
    D. all of the above

Questions 21–25.

DIRECTIONS: In Questions 21 through 25, match each numbered definition with the lettered term it describes listed in Column I. Place the letter of the CORRECT answer in the appropriate space at the right.

COLUMN I
A. Biotransformation
B. Physiologic action
C. Addition
D. Therapeutic action
E. Hypersensitivity

21. Increased effect that may occur when two drugs that have the same action are given together. 21._____

22. Action caused by a drug when given in the concentration normally present in the body. 22._____

23. Beneficial action of a drug to correct a bodily dysfunction. 23._____

24. Allergic reaction to a drug, occurring after previous exposure to the drug. 24._____

25. Metabolic process by which a drug is deactivated. 25._____

KEY (CORRECT ANSWERS)

1. C
2. D
3. B
4. D
5. B

6. C
7. C
8. A
9. B
10. C

11. A
12. D
13. B
14. D
15. A

16. C
17. C
18. B
19. D
20. D

21. C
22. B
23. D
24. E
25. A

GENERAL PHARMACOLOGY

EXAMINATION SECTION
TEST 1

DIRECTIONS: Each question or incomplete statement is followed by several suggested answers or completions. Select the one that BEST answers the question or completes the statement. *PRINT THE LETTER OF THE CORRECT ANSWER IN THE SPACE AT THE RIGHT.*

1. Important Beta-1 sympathetic effects of epinephrine include all of the following EXCEPT   1.____

   A. increased myocardial contractility
   B. production of vasoconstriction
   C. possible restoration of electric activity in the systole
   D. lowering of the threshold for defibrillation

2. Beta-2 sympathetic effects of epinephrine include the production of   2.____

   A. bronchodilatation   B. bronchoconstriction
   C. peripheral vasodilation   D. none of the above

3. The *trade name* of epinephrine is   3.____

   A. epinephrine hydrochloride
   B. adrenalin
   C. tyrosine
   D. none of the above

4. The one of the following which does NOT indicate epinephrine is   4.____

   A. anaphylactic shock   B. cardiac arrest
   C. hypertension   D. asthma

5. Possible side effects of epinephrine include all of the following EXCEPT   5.____

   A. angina   B. hypoglycemia
   C. tachycardia   D. ectopic beats

6. _____ is an indication to epinephrine.   6.____

   A. Glaucoma   B. Hyperthyroidism
   C. Tachyarrhythmias   D. Angina

7. The proper dosage and route of administration of epinephrine in the treatment of a patient under cardiac arrest is   7.____

   A. 0.5 to 1.0 mg of 1:10,000 solution via the endotracheal tube
   B. 0.5 to 1.0 mg of 1:10,000 solution via IV
   C. all of the above
   D. none of the above

8. Racemic epinephrine provides therapeutic action for conditions of   8.____

   A. bronchoconstriction   B. bronchodilatation
   C. hypotension   D. none of the above

9. Racemic epinephrine is indicated by

    A. anaphylaxis with progressive laryngeal edema
    B. severe croup
    C. epiglottitis
    D. A and B *only*

10. The side effects of racemic epinephrine may include all of the following EXCEPT

    A. paradoxical bronchospasm
    B. bradycardia
    C. dysrhythmias
    D. palpitations

11. The medication which MOST effectively increases urine output is

    A. vassopressor   B. vassodilator
    C. diuretics   D. none of the above

12. _____ is an indication of diuretic use.

    A. Congestive heart failure
    B. Pregnancy
    C. Dehydration
    D. Hypotension

13. Which of the following is NOT a side effect of furosemide?

    A. Hypokalemia   B. Acute urinary retention
    C. Hypernatremia   D. Nausea and vomiting

14. Corticosteroids are known by the trade name(s)

    A. Solu-cortef   B. Solu-medrol
    C. Decadron   D. all of the above

15. Corticosteroids may be used to do all of the following EXCEPT

    A. treat acute myocardial infarction
    B. decrease cerebral edema
    C. minimize the damage from a spinal cord injury
    D. treat acute mountain sickness

16. An important therapeutic effect of isoproterenol is that it

    A. produces bronchodilation
    B. increases peripheral resistance
    C. decreases peripheral resistance
    D. increases heart rate and force

17. Contraindications of isoproterenol include all of the following EXCEPT

    A. cardiogenic shock
    B. acute myocardial infarction
    C. bradycardia due to heart block
    D. none of the above

18. A common side effect of isoproterenol is 18._____

   A. tremors
   B. bradycardia
   C. flushing
   D. tachycardia

19. _____ is NOT a therapeutic effect of magnesium. 19._____

   A. Serving as a central nervous system stimulant
   B. Smooth muscle relaxation
   C. Muscle cell membranes stabilized by interaction with the sodium/potassium exchange system
   D. Serving as a central nervous system depressant

20. Magnesium sulfate is useful in the 20._____

   A. treatment of eclampsia
   B. prophylaxis of cardiac dysrhythmias in acute myocardial infarction
   C. treatment of heart block
   D. treatment of selected tachyarrhythmias

Questions 21-25.

DIRECTIONS: In Questions 21 through 25, match the numbered description with the lettered substance or item it describes listed in Column I. Place the letter of the CORRECT answer in the appropriate space at the right.

COLUMN I
A. Patch
B. Ointment
C. Extract
D. Powder
E. Palvule

21. A semi-solid preparation for external application to the body, usually containing medicinal substances. 21._____

22. A medication impregnated into a membrane or adhesive which is applied onto the surface of the skin. 22._____

23. It resembles a capsule, but it is not made of gelatin and it does not separate. 23._____

24. A drug that has been ground into pulverized form. 24._____

25. A concentrated preparation of a drug; made by putting the drug into solution and evaporating off the excess solvent to a prescribed standard. 25._____

KEY (CORRECT ANSWERS)

1. B
2. A
3. B
4. C
5. B

6. A
7. C
8. B
9. D
10. B

11. C
12. A
13. C
14. D
15. A

16. B
17. C
18. B
19. A
20. C

21. B
22. A
23. E
24. D
25. C

TEST 2

DIRECTIONS: Each question or incomplete statement is followed by several suggested answers or completions. Select the one that BEST answers the question or completes the statement. *PRINT THE LETTER OF THE CORRECT ANSWER IN THE SPACE AT THE RIGHT.*

1. All of the following are common side effects of magnesium sulfate EXCEPT

    A. respiratory depression
    B. bronchoconstriction
    C. cardiac arrest
    D. A and C *only*

    1.____

2. The one of the following which is NOT a common indication for manitol use is

    A. pregnancy
    B. cerebral edema
    C. selected drug overdose
    D. crush injury or electric injury

    2.____

3. MAJOR contraindications to manitol use include

    A. anuria
    B. intracranial hemorrhage
    C. dehydration
    D. all of the above

    3.____

4. Possible side effects of manitol include all of the following EXCEPT

    A. a fall in serum sodium concentration
    B. precipitation of congestive heart failure
    C. fluid retention
    D. extravasation causing local tissue necrosis

    4.____

5. Common therapeutic effects of morphine sulphate include the _____ effect.

    A. vasodilator
    B. potent analgesic
    C. potent bronchodilater
    D. A and B *only*

    5.____

6. Morphine sulphate provides effective treatment for

    A. pulmonary edema associated with congestive heart failure
    B. increased intracranial hypertension
    C. hypotension
    D. all of the above

    6.____

7. The common side effects of morphine sulphate may include all of the following EXCEPT

    A. respiratory depression
    B. hypertension
    C. urinary retention
    D. increased vagal tone leading to bradycardia

    7.____

8. The one of the following which indicates morphine sulphate is

    A. chronic obstructive pulmonary disease
    B. congestive heart failure
    C. head injury
    D. undiagnosed abdominal pain

    8.____

33

9. Therapeutic effects of nitroglycerin do NOT include

   A. relaxation of vascular smooth muscle
   B. increased myocardial oxygen demand
   C. promotion of pooling of blood in systemic circulation
   D. decreased myocardial oxygen demand

10. Which of the following is the BEST indication for nitroglycerin use?

    A. Angina pectoris
    B. Heart failure
    C. Asthma
    D. All of the above

11. Of the following, _____ contraindicate(s) nitroglycerine use.

    A. glaucoma
    B. hypovolemia
    C. selected cases of pulmonary edema
    D. increased intracranial pressure

12. Common side effects of nitroglycerin include all of the following EXCEPT

    A. hypotension
    B. hypertension
    C. flushing
    D. throbbing headache

13. Norepinephrine has the trade name

    A. adrenaline
    B. trandate
    C. levophed
    D. bronkosol

14. Of the following, the condition which is NOT among the common indicators of norepinephrine is

    A. myocardial infarction
    B. neurogenic shock
    C. cardiogenic shock
    D. blood pressure support after CPR

15. Among the common side effects of norepinephrine is(are)

    A. ventricular dysrhythmias
    B. severe hypertension
    C. necrosis of tissue if IV infiltrate
    D. all of the above

16. All of the following are considered therapeutic effects of propranolol EXCEPT

    A. decreasing of the sinus rate
    B. slow atrial conduction
    C. stimulation of spontaneous electric activity and muscular force
    D. delayed conduction through the atrioventricular node (AV node)

17. Propranolol is indicated by all of the following EXCEPT

    A. supraventricular tacharrhythmias
    B. atrial flutter
    C. heart failure
    D. atrial fibrillation

18. Contraindication to propranolol use does NOT include

    A. hypertension
    B. asthma
    C. third degree heart block
    D. hay fever

19. 50% dextrose (DSO) use's common indicators include

    A. hypoglycemia
    B. coma of unknown cause
    C. status epilepticus of uncertain cause
    D. all of the above

20. By which of the following is 50% dextrose (DSO) use contraindicated?

    A. Intracranial hemorrhage   B. Known stroke
    C. All of the above   D. None of the above

KEY (CORRECT ANSWERS)

1.	D	11.	C
2.	A	12.	B
3.	D	13.	C
4.	C	14.	A
5.	D	15.	D
6.	A	16.	C
7.	B	17.	C
8.	B	18.	A
9.	B	19.	D
10.	A	20.	C

RESPIRATORY SYSTEM
EXAMINATION SECTION
TEST 1

DIRECTIONS: Each question or incomplete statement is followed by several suggested answers or completions. Select the one that BEST answers the question or completes the statement. *PRINT THE LETTER OF THE CORRECT ANSWER IN THE SPACE AT THE RIGHT.*

1. In the upper respiratory tract,   1.____

   A. air is filtered in the nasopharynx
   B. air is warmed to 37° C before reaching the lungs
   C. cilia sweep foreign matter towards the oropharynx where it may be expectorated or swallowed
   D. all of the above

2. The left lung consists of _____ lobe(s).   2.____

   A. two
   B. three
   C. one
   D. none of the above

3. Alveoli are NOT   3.____

   A. hollow sacs
   B. thick-walled
   C. the agents through which oxygenation occurs
   D. the most important functional unit of the respiratory system

4. By definition, normal ventilation is that which maintains the arterial PCO_2 at APPROXIMATELY _____ to _____ torr.   4.____

   A. 10; 15   B. 20; 30   C. 35; 40   D. 50; 60

5. If the arterial PO_2 falls below 80 torr., the patient is considered   5.____

   A. hypercapnic
   B. hypocapnic
   C. hyoxemic
   D. tachypnic

6. Elevated PCO_2 is commonly associated with all of the following conditions EXCEPT   6.____

   A. myasthenia gravis
   B. stroke
   C. hyperventilation syndrome
   D. head injury

7. Which of the following conditions is(are) associated with hypoxemia?   7.____

   A. Near drowning
   B. Pulmonary edema
   C. Chest trauma
   D. All of the above

37

8. The respiratory control center is located in the part of the brain known as the

   A. medulla
   B. frontal lobe
   C. pineal gland
   D. temporal lobe

9. The one of the following conditions which is NOT a cause of lower airway obstruction is

   A. epiglottitis
   B. emphysema
   C. chronic bronchitis
   D. asthma

10. Causes of respiratory center depression include all of the following EXCEPT

    A. a stroke
    B. pulmonary edema
    C. depressant drugs
    D. head trauma

11. _____ is NOT among the conditions which frequently affect alveoli.

    A. Flail chest
    B. Pneumothorax
    C. Croup
    D. Pulmonary edema

12. Regarding chronic obstructive pulmonary disease, it is FALSE that

    A. the condition is more common among men than women
    B. 82 percent of mortality is attributed to alcohol use
    C. the condition is more common among city dwellers than in rural populations
    D. it is seen primarily in individuals between the ages of 45 and 65

13. All of the following are considered classic features of pink puffers (emphysema) EXCEPT

    A. pain and wasted appearance
    B. barrel-shaped chest which is hyperresonant to percussion owing to air trapping within the lungs
    C. obvious shortness of breath and frequent pursing of the lips during exhalation
    D. none of the above

14. Symptoms and signs of decompensation in COPD include

    A. increasing dyspnea and sleep disturbance
    B. confusion, agitation, and combativeness resulting from hypoxemia
    C. lethargy and drowsiness resulting from hypercarbia
    D. all of the above

15. Of the following, _____ is(are) NOT helpful in the management of COPD.

    A. oxygen by nasal canvia or mask
    B. aminophylline
    C. sedatives and tranquilizers
    D. establishment of an IV lifeline with D5W

16. Among the common clinical features of the acute asthmatic attack is(are)

    A. wheezing that is audible without a stethoscope
    B. spasmodic coughing
    C. prominent use of accessor muscles of respiration
    D. all of the above

17. It is NOT a sign of a severe asthmatic attack when 17.____
    A. pulse rate is greater than 130 per minute
    B. respiratory rate is less than 20 per minute
    C. pulus paradoxus is greater than 15 mmhg
    D. chest is silent

18. Pre-hospital management of an acute asthmatic attack may employ all of the following EXCEPT 18.____
    A. albuterol   B. aminophylline
    C. cromolyn sodium   D. epinephrine

19. Of the following statements, which is(are) TRUE regarding bacterial pneumonia? 19.____
    A. Elderly patients with chronic illnesses and smokers are at greater risk to contract the illness.
    B. The most common form of bacterial pnemonia is pneumococcal pneumonia.
    C. The peak incidence occurs in winter and early spring.
    D. All of the above

20. The MOST effective treatment of pneumonia would be the use of 20.____
    A. antibiotics
    B. oxygen
    C. multiple doses of epinephrine
    D. all of the above

21. Specialized respiratory functions include 21.____
    A. coughing or sneezing   B. hiccupping
    C. sighing   D. all of the above

Questions 22-25.

DIRECTIONS: In Questions 22 through 25, match the numbered description with the lettered symptomatic sound it describes listed in Column I. Place the letter of the CORRECT answer in the appropriate space at the right.

COLUMN I

A. Rales
B. Rhonchi
C. Wheezing
D. Stridor

22. Harsh, high-pitched sound upon inspiration indicating an upper airway obstruction. 22.____

23. Harsher sound indicating the presence of fluid in a larger airway. 23.____

24. High-pitched whistling sound of air moving through narrowed airways. 24.____

25. Fine, crackling sound indicating the presence of fluid in a small airway. 25.____

KEY (CORRECT ANSWERS)

1.	D	11.	C
2.	A	12.	B
3.	B	13.	D
4.	C	14.	D
5.	C	15.	C
6.	C	16.	D
7.	D	17.	B
8.	A	18.	C
9.	A	19.	D
10.	B	20.	B

21. D
22. D
23. B
24. C
25. A

TEST 2

DIRECTIONS: Each question or incomplete statement is followed by several suggested answers or completions. Select the one that BEST answers the question or completes the statement. *PRINT THE LETTER OF THE CORRECT ANSWER IN THE SPACE AT THE RIGHT.*

1. Physical factors influencing the respiratory center include all of the following EXCEPT _____ respiratory rate. 1.____

   A. high temperature increasing
   B. low temperature increasing
   C. low blood pressure increasing
   D. high blood pressure decreasing

2. Regarding the effect of carbon dioxide and oxygen on inspiratory activity, it is NOT true that 2.____

   A. high CO_2 concentration decreases respiratory activity
   B. high CO_2 concentration increases respiratory activity
   C. low CO_2 concentration decreases respiratory activity
   D. hypoxemia is the most profound stimulus to respiration in the normal individual

3. The single MOST common cause of airway obstruction in the unconscious victim is due to 3.____

   A. dentures   B. the tongue
   C. a foreign body   D. glottic edema

4. In order to eliminate airway obstruction due to the presence of a foreign body, you should NOT 4.____

   A. discourage the victim from coughing
   B. deliver four blows to the back of the victim
   C. apply abdominal thrust (Heimlich maneuver)
   D. do more than one but not all of the above

5. Among adults, the MOST common factor associated with drowning is 5.____

   A. alcohol intoxication   B. cocaine abuse
   C. heroin intoxication   D. none of the above

6. *A severe prolonged asthmatic attack that cannot be broken with epinephrine* is the definition of 6.____

   A. bronchitis   B. status asthmaticus
   C. asthmatic bronchitis   D. COPD

7. All of the following are true statements regarding near-drowning EXCEPT: 7.____

   A. 10 percent of drowning victims do not aspirate any water at all
   B. The mortality rate from drowning is less than 5 percent
   C. In freshwater drowning, the hypotonic solution has been absorbed through the lungs
   D. In saltwater drowning, pulmonary edema occurs as a result of aspiration

8. Management techniques for cases of near-drowning include

   A. early performance of endotracheal intubation to prevent aspiration
   B. determination of whether the victim has a pulse; if not, starting of external chest compression
   C. insertion of a nasogastric tube to decompress the stomach (only after an endotracheal tube is in place)
   D. all of the above

9. The treatment of choice for severe metabolic acidosis in drowning victims is

   A. hyperventilation by ambu bag
   B. sodium bicarbonate
   C. calcium carbonate
   D. 100% oxygen

10. The one of the following conditions that CANNOT produce pulmonary edema is

    A. heroin overdose
    B. left heart failure
    C. ingestion of furosemide
    D. inhalation of toxic fumes

11. The signs and symptoms of pulmonary edema include all of the following EXCEPT

    A. presence of hypoxia, dyspnea, and cyanosis
    B. patient laboring to breathe, often sitting bolt upright
    C. low arterial CO_2 concentration and high oxygen concentration
    D. rales heard when listening to the posterior bases of both lungs

12. In the management of pulmonary edema, it is NOT necessary to

    A. manage and transport the patient in a sitting position
    B. administer morphine if ordered by a physician
    C. apply rotating tourniquets, if indicated
    D. strictly avoid administering oxygen in high concentration

13. Among the common symptoms of acute mountain sickness is (are) included

    A. throbbing bilateral frontal headache which is worse in the morning and in the supine position
    B. sleep disturbance
    C. dyspnea on exertion
    D. all of the above

14. The MOST useful sign of progression from mild to moderate mountain sickness is

    A. ataxia
    B. lassitude
    C. anorexia
    D. dyspnea on exertion

15. If you anticipate a long delay in arranging rescue for a patient with acute mountain sickness, you should administer

    A. epinephrine
    B. dexamethasone
    C. bronchodilator
    D. none of the above

16. Common signs and symptoms of high altitude pulmonary edema include   16._____

    A. tachpnea, severe dysmnea, and chyne-stokes respirations
    B. cough, cyanosis, and tachycardia
    C. confusion and coma
    D. all of the above

17. The MOST important element in treating high altitude pulmonary edema is   17._____

    A. descent to lower altitude
    B. intravenous morphine
    C. intravenous diuretics
    D. all of the above

18. _____ are the MOST common scenarios of exposure to toxic gases.   18._____

    A. Municipal swimming pools
    B. Fires
    C. Transport accidents
    D. Industrial settings

19. The *dunglung* syndrome of pulmonary edema, metabolic acidosis, and cardiovascular collapse is produced by   19._____

    A. hydrogen sulfide   B. acrylics
    C. cotton   D. nitrogen dioxide

20. An IMPORTANT part of the treatment of suspected pulmonary embolism is to   20._____

    A. ensure an open airway and administer 100% oxygen
    B. monitor cardiac rhythm
    C. establish an IV lifeline with normal saline
    D. all of the above

Questions 21-25.

DIRECTIONS: In Questions 21 through 25, match the numbered characteristic with the lettered disorder listed in Column I with which it is MOST closely associated. Place the letter of the CORRECT answer in the appropriate space at the right.

21. Birth control pill.   COLUMN I   21._____

22. Patient is often young, thin, and tall.   22._____
    A. Pickwickian syndrome
    B. Hyperventilation syndrome
23. Carpopedal spasms and low CO_2.   C. Chronic obstructive pulmonary disease   23._____
    D. Pulmonary embolism
24. Extreme obesity, periods of apnea, and dysrhythmias during sleep.   E. Spontaneous pneumothorax   24._____

25. Oxygen is the mainstay of treatment.   25._____

KEY (CORRECT ANSWERS)

1. B
2. A
3. B
4. A
5. A

6. B
7. B
8. D
9. B
10. C

11. C
12. D
13. D
14. A
15. B

16. D
17. A
18. B
19. A
20. D

21. D
22. E
23. B
24. A
25. C

RESPIRATORY SYSTEM

EXAMINATION SECTION
TEST 1

DIRECTIONS: Each question or incomplete statement is followed by several suggested answers or completions. Select the one that BEST answers the question or completes the statement. *PRINT THE LETTER OF THE CORRECT ANSWER IN THE SPACE AT THE RIGHT.*

1. All of the following are important actions to take in the management of a patient exposed to toxic fumes EXCEPT: 1._____

    A. Remove the patient from the environment of exposure
    B. Establish and maintain an open airway
    C. Cease constant supervision since it is not necessary for all victims of intense exposure to smoke or toxic fumes
    D. Assist breathing as required, with the demand value or bag value mask plus peep

2. The MOST common source of pulmonary embolism is   2._____

    A. fat particles   B. blood clot
    C. amniotic fluid   D. air

3. The typical pulmonary embolism patient is prone to sudden onsets of severe, unexplained   3._____

    A. dyspnea
    B. sharp chest pain made worse by coughing
    C. tachycardia and achpnea
    D. all of the above

4. All of the following are immediate life-threatening chest injuries that must be detected and managed during the primary survey EXCEPT   4._____

    A. tension pneumothorax   B. pulmonary contusion
    C. cardiac tamponade   D. airway obstruction

5. Regarding chest trauma, it is TRUE that   5._____

    A. 75 percent of those who die as a result of automobile accidents have suffered chest injuries
    B. simple rib fractures usually involve the fourth, fifth, sixth, and seventh ribs
    C. rib fractures are usually very painful, and they restrict respiratory activity
    D. all of the above

6. Regarding simple pneumothorax, it is NOT true that   6._____

    A. it never requires any treatment
    B. it is often caused by blunt trauma
    C. small pneumothorax may absorb slowly
    D. subcutaneous emphysema may be present

7. Which of the following statements is FALSE about tension pneumothorax?

   A. The lung collapses and the mediastinum shifts to the opposite side.
   B. Venous return is compromised due to increased intra-thoracic pressure and distortion of the venae cavae.
   C. Tension should not be relieved.
   D. Mediastinal shift is augmented with every respiration.

8. The preferred site for chest decompression in tension pneumothorax is the _____ intercostal space, _____ line.

   A. second; midclavicular
   B. fifth; midclavicular
   C. third; mid axillary
   D. fourth; mid axillary

9. A 25-year-old male has a puncture of the chest wall by a knife. The result is a sucking chest wound.
   The management of choice is

   A. immediate insertion of a chest tube
   B. application of a sterile occlusive dressing
   C. immediate endotracheal intubation
   D. all of the above

10. A 30-year-old male sustained a puncture wound on the fifth intercostal space. The wound was caused by a knife during a fight. Thirty minutes later, he developed a distended neck vein and muffled heart sound.
    The MOST likely diagnosis is

    A. tension pneumothorax
    B. flail chest
    C. cardiac tamponade
    D. none of the above

11. In pre-hospital treatment of flail chest, it is VITAL to

    A. assist ventilation with a bag valve mask if the patient is unable to take deep breaths on his own
    B. stabilize the flail segment by applying constant, firm, manual pressure, or buttressing the segment with sandbags or pillows
    C. start an IV en route, but restrict intravenous fluids unless there is a sign of shock
    D. all of the above

12. It is important to remember to do all of the following when suctioning through an endotracheal tube EXCEPT

    A. carry out frequent endotracheal suction in the pre-hospital setting
    B. always pre-oxygenate the patient for 3 minutes
    C. observe strict sterile techniques
    D. re-oxygenate the patient the moment you finish suctioning

13. All of the following indicate endotracheal intubation EXCEPT

    A. cardiac arrest
    B. deep coma with absent gag reflex
    C. simple pneumothorax
    D. airway obstruction due to burns

14. Advantages of endotracheal intubation do NOT include

    A. the cuffed endotracheal tube's protection of the airway from aspiration
    B. ventilation through the endotracheal tube causing severe gastric distention
    C. the allowance of intermittent positive pressure ventilation (IPPV) with 100% oxygen
    D. an endotracheal tubes enabling the delivery of aerosolized medication

15. The one of the following which is NOT an indication for blind nasotracheal intubation is

    A. suspected trauma to the cervical spine
    B. trauma to the mouth or mandible
    C. basilar skull fracture
    D. severe congestive heart failure

16. Contraindications to blind nasotracheal intubation include all of the following EXCEPT

    A. apnea
    B. respiratory depression from alcohol
    C. defect in blood clotting
    D. severe nasal polyps

17. The one of the following which is NOT a contraindication to esophageal obturator airway is

    A. a patient under 16 years of age
    B. cirrhosis of the liver
    C. a deeply unconscious patient
    D. the ingestion of caustic substances

18. The advantages of the esophageal obturator airway is(are) that it

    A. requires no visualization of the patient's airway
    B. may be inadvertently inserted in the trachea
    C. prevents gastric distension and aspiration
    D. A and C *only*

19. Common complications of cricothyrotomy include all of the following EXCEPT

    A. bleeding
    B. subcutaneous emphysema
    C. cardiac tamponade
    D. mediastinal emphysema

20. The MOST likely side effect of morphine sulphate on the respiratory system is

    A. bronchodilation
    B. respiratory acidosis
    C. respiratory alkalosis
    D. none of the above

Questions 21-25.

DIRECTIONS: In Questions 21 through 25, match the numbered function with the lettered piece of equipment it describes as listed in Column I. Place the letter of the CORRECT answer in the appropriate space at the right.

COLUMN I

A. Nasal cannula
B. Plastic face mask
C. Partial rebreathing mask
D. Nonrebreathing mask
E. Venturi mask

21. Delivers 90% oxygen. 21.___

22. Delivers 50 to 60% oxygen. 22.___

23. Is useful in long-term treatment of a patient with COPD. 23.___

24. Delivers 25 to 40% oxygen. 24.___

25. Delivers 35 to 60% oxygen. 25.___

KEY (CORRECT ANSWERS)

1. C
2. B
3. D
4. B
5. D

6. A
7. C
8. A
9. B
10. C

11. D
12. A
13. C
14. B
15. C

16. B
17. C
18. D
19. C
20. B

21. D
22. B
23. E
24. A
25. D

TEST 2

DIRECTIONS: Each question or incomplete statement is followed by several suggested answers or completions. Select the one that BEST answers the question or completes the statement. *PRINT THE LETTER OF THE CORRECT ANSWER IN THE SPACE AT THE RIGHT.*

1. In a majority of pre-hospital settings, the airway can BEST be improved INITIALLY by　　1.____

    A. proper positioning of the airway
    B. endotracheal intubation
    C. use of an esophageal obturator airway
    D. none of the above

2. Endotracheal intubation is a technique used to manage　　2.____

    A. cardiac circulation
    B. renal blood flow
    C. the unprotected airway
    D. all of the above

3. A(n) _____ is to be expected when removing an esophageal obturator airway (EOA).　　3.____

    A. esophageal rupture
    B. regurgitation of stomach contents
    C. spasm of the trachea
    D. all of the above

4. The MOST severe hazard of intubation using the esophageal obturator airway in an unconscious victim is　　4.____

    A. severe abdominal distension
    B. failure to inflate the cuff
    C. undetected intubation of the trachea
    D. uncontrollable bleeding of the trachea

5. When a patient is suffering from poor ventilation, there is an obvious reduction in oxygen flow to all parts of the body.　　5.____
   Poor ventilation quickly affects all of the following EXCEPT the

    A. anxiety level
    B. pulse rate
    C. intravascular volume
    D. acid/base balance

6. Oxygen-powered mechanical breathing devices for use during CPR are　　6.____

    A. satisfactory only if manually triggered
    B. satisfactory only if pressure cycled
    C. not capable of delivering high concentrations of oxygen to the patient
    D. all of the above

7. Tension pneumothorax　　7.____

    A. can make CPR ineffective
    B. may be detectable by tracheal shift
    C. can be caused by a broken rib
    D. all of the above

8. Multiple attempts at tracheal intubation may cause

   A. esophageal intubation
   B. laryngeal trauma
   C. anoxia
   D. all of the above

9. Bag-valve-mask devices should be

   A. designed to deliver 100% oxygen for effective CPR
   B. used only by trained persons
   C. all of the above
   D. none of the above

10. Endotracheal suction

    A. should be limited to 5 seconds
    B. can produce hypoxemia
    C. can produce bradyarrythmia
    D. all of the above

11. To manage acute laryngeal edema due to an allergic reaction, one should

    A. establish an airway
    B. administer oxygen
    C. perform a cricothyrotomy (if the patient does not respond to medication)
    D. all of the above

12. The drug of choice for treating acute laryngeal edema due to allergic reaction is

    A. epinephrine
    B. diphenhydramine
    C. oral prednisone
    D. none of the above

13. Signs of choking include

    A. inability of the victim to speak or make any sound
    B. dusky or cyanotic skin
    C. exaggerated but ineffective breathing movements
    D. all of the above

14. Treatments of decompression sickness include all of the following EXCEPT

    A. steroids
    B. nitronox for analgesia
    C. 100% oxygen
    D. hyperbaric facility

Questions 15-18.

DIRECTIONS: Questions 15 through 18 refer to a diving injury. Match the numbered mechanisms and pathophysiologies with the lettered condition with which they are MOST closely related, as listed in Column I. Place the letter of the CORRECT answer in the appropriate space at the right.

COLUMN I

A. Barotitis externa and barotitis media
B. Bargdontalgia, aerogastralgia, and blindness
C. Bend, staggers, paraplegia, and the *chokes*
D. Symptoms similar to those of alcoholic intoxication

15. Barotrauma during ascent 15.____

16. Barotrauma during descent 16.____

17. Nitrogen narcosis 17.____

18. Decompression sickness 18.____

Questions 19-25.

DIRECTIONS: In Questions 19 through 25, match the numbered descriptions with the lettered parts of the respiratory system, as listed in Column I, which they describe MOST accurately. Place the letter of the CORRECT answer in the appropriate space at the right.

COLUMN I

A. Alveoli
B. Bronchus
C. Glottis
D. Pharynx
E. Trachea
F. Vocal cords
G. Turbinates

19. One of the main branches of the trachea which carries air into various parts of the lung. 19.____

20. The saccular unit at the end of the terminal bronchiol where gas exchange takes place in the lung. 20.____

21. The portion of the airway between the nasal cavity and the larynx. 21.____

22. The opening to the trachea. 22.____

23. The cartilaginous tube extending from the larynx superiorly down to the carina. 23.____

24. It mixes up the air entering the nasopharynx. 24.____

25. The paired structures in the larynx whose vibrations produce sound. 25.____

4 (#2)

KEY (CORRECT ANSWERS)

1. A
2. C
3. B
4. C
5. B

6. A
7. D
8. D
9. C
10. D

11. D
12. A
13. D
14. B
15. B

16. A
17. D
18. C
19. B
20. A

21. D
22. C
23. E
24. G
25. F

CARDIOVASCULAR SYSTEMS
EXAMINATION SECTION
TEST 1

DIRECTIONS: Each question or incomplete statement is followed by several suggested answers or completions. Select the one that BEST answers the question or completes the statement. *PRINT THE LETTER OF THE CORRECT ANSWER IN THE SPACE AT THE RIGHT.*

1. The wall of the heart is made up of all of the following EXCEPT the 1.____

   A. pericardium B. epicardium
   C. myocardium D. endocardium

2. Among the following statements, the one which is TRUE regarding the pericardium is: 2.____

   A. It contains about 30 ml of serous fluid
   B. It is tough and fibrous and does not readily stretch
   C. If more than 100 ml of fluid accumulates within the pericardium, it may compromise heart contractility
   D. All of the above

3. The MAIN function of the heart is to 3.____

   A. transport the waste products of metabolism to the cells
   B. deliver oxygenated blood and nutrients to every cell in the body
   C. deliver non-oxygenated blood to the cells in the body
   D. deliver chemical messages to the cells

4. Of the following, the structure which collects non-oxygenated blood returning from the body is the 4.____

   A. left atrium B. right ventricle
   C. right atrium D. left ventricle

5. The vessels that carry blood to the heart are 5.____

   A. arteries B. arterioles
   C. capillaries D. veins

6. It is NOT true that the heart 6.____

   A. weighs about 300 grams in males and 250 grams in females
   B. is usually 10-12 cm long
   C. is usually located in the right mediastinum
   D. is usually 9 cm wide and 6 cm thick

7. The MOST common location of atria is in the _____ portion of the heart. 7.____

   A. superior B. inferior
   C. middle D. all of the above

53

8. The MOST common location and function of the superior vena cava are that it is located _____ and drains _____.

   A. at the right side of the heart; unoxygenated blood from the upper body
   B. at the left side of the heart; oxygenated blood from the lower body
   C. on the right side; unoxygenated blood from the lower part of the body
   D. in the right atrium; blood from the heart itself

9. The high-pressure pump that drives blood OUT of the heart against the relatively high resistance of the systemic arteries is called the

   A. right atrium
   B. left atrium
   C. left ventricle
   D. right ventricle

10. Oxygenated blood is usually supplied to the heart via the _____ artery (arteries).

    A. carotid
    B. coronary
    C. pulmonary
    D. subclavian

11. The MOST accurate definition of cardiac output is:

    A. The amount of blood pumped out by either ventricle, measured in liters per minute
    B. The amount of blood pumped out by either ventricle in a single contraction
    C. The number of cardiac contractions per minute
    D. None of the above

12. The MOST frequent location of the sino atrial node is the _____ near the _____.

    A. right atrium; inlet of the inferior vena cava
    B. right atrium; inlet of the superior vena cava
    C. left atrium; inlet of the pulmonary vein
    D. left ventricle; aortic valve

13. The sinoatrial (SA) node is the fastest pacemaker in the heart, normally firing at the rate of _____ to _____ times per minute.

    A. 20; 40
    B. 40; 60
    C. 60; 100
    D. 100; 300

14. _____ is the process by which muscle fibers are stimulated to contract.

    A. Depolarization
    B. Repolarization
    C. Dyastole
    D. Refractory period

15. The electrolyte that flows into the cell to initiate depolarization is

    A. magnesium
    B. potassium
    C. sodium
    D. phosphate

16. Of the following electrolytes, the one which flows out of the cell to initiate repolarization is

    A. sodium
    B. potassium
    C. calcium
    D. magnesium

17. Depolarization of the atria produces which of the following waves on the ECG? A(n)

    A. P wave
    B. T wave
    C. QRS complex
    D. N wave

18. Of the following waves, repolarization of the atria and ventricles produces _____ on the ECG.

    A. QRS complex   B. P waves
    C. T waves   D. none of the above

19. The coronary arteries

    A. originate from the base of the ascending aorta
    B. are above the leaflets of the aortic valve
    C. provide blood supply to the cardiac muscles
    D. all of the above

20. All of the following are caused by the stimulation of beta receptors EXCEPT

    A. bronchoconstriction
    B. increased heart rate
    C. increased heart contractability
    D. vasodilation

21. Alpha receptor stimulation does NOT cause

    A. vasoconstriction   B. bronchoconstriction
    C. no effect on the heart   D. increased heart rate

22. Which of the following is pure beta agonist?

    A. Isoproterenol   B. Metaraminol
    C. Norepinephrine   D. Dopamine

23. The agent of choice to treat increased blood pressure when hypotension has been caused by neurogenic shock (vasodilation) is

    A. isoproterenol   B. atropin
    C. norepinephrine   D. propranolol

24. Of the following sympathetic agents, the one usually indicated for asystole and anaphylactic shock is

    A. dopamine   B. epinephrine
    C. metaraminol   D. isoproterenol

25. When used in low doses, this sympathetic agent increases the force of cardiac contraction and helps to maintain urine flow and good perfusion to abdominal organs. This is a description of

    A. dopamine   B. norepinephrine
    C. metaraminol   D. isoproterenol

KEY (CORRECT ANSWERS)

1.	A	11.	A
2.	D	12.	B
3.	B	13.	C
4.	C	14.	A
5.	D	15.	C
6.	C	16.	B
7.	A	17.	A
8.	A	18.	C
9.	C	19.	D
10.	B	20.	A

21. D
22. A
23. C
24. B
25. A

TEST 2

DIRECTIONS: Each question or incomplete statement is followed by several suggested answers or completions. Select the one that BEST answers the question or completes the statement. *PRINT THE LETTER OF THE CORRECT ANSWER IN THE SPACE AT THE RIGHT.*

1. Propranolol is used clinically to

   A. slow the heart rate in certain tachyarrythmias
   B. decrease the pain of chronic angina
   C. decrease irritability in the heart
   D. all of the above

   1.____

2. All of the following are functions of the parasympathetic nervous system EXCEPT

   A. increasing salivation
   B. constricting pupils
   C. slowing the gut
   D. slowing the heart

   2.____

3. Which of the following is NOT a function of the sympathetic nervous system?

   A. Dilate pupils
   B. Increase gut motility
   C. Speed the heart
   D. Constrict blood vessels

   3.____

4. Chest pain is often the presenting sign of acute myocardial infarction. When treating a patient with chest pain, the MOST important question for you to ask him is:

   A. What provoked the pain?
   B. What is the quality and severity of the pain?
   C. Does the pain radiate?
   D. All of the above

   4.____

5. Paroxymal nocturnal dyspnea is one of the classic signs of

   A. pericarditis
   B. right heart failure
   C. left heart failure
   D. asthmatic bronchitis

   5.____

6. The MOST prevalent preventable cause of death in the United States is

   A. diabetes
   B. hypertension
   C. cigarette smoking
   D. high serum cholesterol

   6.____

7. Common sources of risk to the coronary artery include

   A. birth control pills
   B. lack of exercise
   C. male sex
   D. all of the above

   7.____

8. Among the MOST common symptoms of angina pectoris are included

   A. sensations of tightness or pressure
   B. pain induced by anything that increases oxygen requirements
   C. pain radiating to the lower jaw, upper neck, and left shoulder
   D. all of the above

   8.____

9. The difference(s) between the pain of angina pectoris and the pain from acute myocardial infarction is (are) that the pain of acute myocardial infarction

   A. may occur at rest
   B. may last for hours
   C. is not relieved by rest
   D. all of the above

10. All of the following are characteristic of angina pectoris EXCEPT that the pain usually

    A. occurs after exercise, stress and/or cold weather
    B. is relieved by rest
    C. is unresponsive to nitroglycerine
    D. lasts 3 to 5 minutes

11. Among the following, the classic symptoms of acute myocardial infarction include

    A. squeezing or crushing chest pain which is not relieved by rest
    B. a feeling of impending death
    C. diaphoresis, dyspnea, and dizziness
    D. all of the above

12. An elderly patient suffers a sudden onset of dyspnea, hypotension, and confusion. The MOST likely diagnosis is

    A. acute myocardial infarction
    B. angina pectoris
    C. pericarditis
    D. congestive heart failure

13. What is the treatment of choice for angina pectoris?

    A. Propranolol   B. Nitroglycerin
    C. Epinephrine   D. Metaraminol

14. The MAIN goal of treatment for acute myocardial infarction is to

    A. alleviate the patient's fear and pain
    B. prevent the development of serious cardiac dysrhythmias
    C. limit the size of the infarct
    D. all of the above

15. Cardiac work is minimal in the _____ position.

    A. standing   B. sitting
    C. semi-recumbent   D. none of the above

16. _____ therapy is the mainstay of emergency cardiac care.

    A. Epinephrine   B. Oxygen
    C. Propranolol   D. Norepinephrine

17. The proper treatment of uncomplicated acute myocardial infarction en route to the hospital should include all of the following EXCEPT

    A. administering oxygen by mask or nasal cannula
    B. D5W using a 250 ml bag and the infusion rate should be just enough to keep the vein open
    C. giving normal saline bolus
    D. taking blood pressure and repeating at least every 5 minutes

18. In which of the following conditions should the patient be transported before he is stabilized?
    Cardiac

    A. arrest due to uncontrollable hemorrhaging
    B. arrest secondary to cold exposure
    C. rhythms that require immediate pacemaker insertion
    D. all of the above

19. The preferred pain medication for treating a hypotensive patient with acute myocardial infarction is

    A. morphine sulphate
    B. nitrous oxide
    C. codeine
    D. acetominophen

20. Of the following medications, the one you should draw BEFORE administering morphine to a patient with an acute myocardial infarction is

    A. atropine sulphate
    B. nitroglycerine
    C. propranolol
    D. digoxin

21. It would be acceptable to administer morphine to a patient suffering from

    A. low blood pressure
    B. bronchial asthma
    C. AMI involving the inferior wall of the heart
    D. hypertension and pulmonary edema

22. Criteria for thrombolytic therapy for acute myocardial infarction includes all of the following EXCEPT

    A. recent CPR
    B. alert patient who is able to give informed consent
    C. age between 30 and 75 years
    D. chest pain lasting more than 20 minutes but less than 6 hours

23. Common signs and symptoms of left heart failure include

    A. extreme restlessness and agitation
    B. severe dyspnea and tachypnea
    C. frothy pink sputum
    D. all of the above

24. Which of the following heart chambers is MOST commonly damaged by acute myocardial infarction?

    A. Right ventricle
    B. Left ventricle
    C. Left atrium
    D. Right atrium

25. Of the following medications, the one(s) which should be drawn up ready, pending the physician's order for administration, for the treatment of left heart failure is (are)

    A. morphine sulphate
    B. furosemide
    C. digoxin
    D. all of the above

Questions 26-30.

DIRECTIONS: In Questions 26 through 30, match the numbered description with the lettered part of the circulatory system, as listed in Column I, to which it is most closely related. Place the letter of the CORRECT answer in the appropriate space at the right.

COLUMN I
A. Epicardium
B. Endocardium
C. Myocardium
D. Pericardium
E. Coronary sinus

26. The tough fibrous sac which surrounds the heart.

27. The outermost layer of the heart wall.

28. The innermost layer of the heart wall.

29. The middle layer of the heart wall.

30. A large vessel in the posterior part of the coronary sulcus into which venous blood empties.

KEY (CORRECT ANSWERS)

1.	D		16.	B
2.	C		17.	C
3.	B		18.	D
4.	D		19.	B
5.	C		20.	A
6.	C		21.	D
7.	D		22.	A
8.	D		23.	D
9.	D		24.	B
10.	C		25.	D
11.	D		26.	D
12.	A		27.	A
13.	B		28.	B
14.	D		29.	C
15.	C		30.	E

TEST 3

DIRECTIONS: Each question or incomplete statement is followed by several suggested answers or completions. Select the one that BEST answers the question or completes the statement. *PRINT THE LETTER OF THE CORRECT ANSWER IN THE SPACE AT THE RIGHT.*

1. Pre-hospital treatment of left heart failure would NOT include

    A. administration of beta blocker
    B. administration of 100% oxygen
    C. seating the patient with his feet dangling
    D. starting an intravenous line with D5W

    1.___

2. The MOST common cause of right heart failure is

    A. cor pulmonale
    B. tricuspid stenosis
    C. left heart failure
    D. cardiac tamponade

    2.___

3. All of the following can occur as a result of ventricle failure EXCEPT

    A. blood backs up into the vein
    B. back-up increases the venous pressure
    C. back-up decreases the venous pressure
    D. blood serum escapes into the tissue and produces edema

    3.___

4. Signs and symptoms of right heart failure do NOT include

    A. collapsed jugular vein
    B. hepatosplenomegaly
    C. peripheral edema
    D. tachycardia

    4.___

5. Common signs and symptoms of cardiogenic shock include all of the following EXCEPT

    A. pulse racing and thready
    B. severe hypertension
    C. respiration rapid and shallow
    D. confused or comatose state

    5.___

6. The differentiating factor(s) between the pain of a dissecting aneurysm and an acute myocardial infarction is (are) that the pain of a dissecting aneurysm

    A. is maximal from the outset
    B. is often included in the back between the shoulder blades
    C. does not abate once it has started
    D. all of the above

    6.___

7. A 60-year-old male has sudden back pain and a pulsatile abdominal mass. Ten minutes later, his blood pressure starts dropping.
   Pre-hospital management for this patient would include all of the following EXCEPT

    A. administering oxygen
    B. stabilizing the patient before transport
    C. applying (but not inflating) the mast
    D. starting an IV en route with normal saline or lactated ringer's

    7.___

8. A 35-year-old comatose male has cold and clammy skin, shallow breathing, and thready pulse.
   The FIRST thing you should do to treat this patient is

   A. start an IV D5W
   B. apply monitoring electrodes
   C. secure an open airway
   D. administer epinephrine

9. The MOST common complications of hypertension include

   A. renal damage
   B. stroke
   C. heart failure
   D. all of the above

10. Acute hypertensive crisis is usually signaled by a sudden marked rise in blood pressure to a level greater than _____ mmHg.

    A. 120/80
    B. 140/80
    C. 200/130
    D. none of the above

11. Which of the following is the drug of choice for treatment of hypertensive encephalopathy?

    A. Propranolol
    B. Diazoxide
    C. Furosemide
    D. Reserpin

12. The P wave represents depolarization of the atria. When examining the ECG, you should look for the presence of

    A. P waves in general
    B. a P wave before every QRS complex
    C. a QRS complex before every P wave
    D. all of the above

13. A P-R interval exceeding 0.2 second is called _____ degree AV block.

    A. first
    B. second
    C. third
    D. none of the above

14. Potential causes of sinus tachycardia include

    A. pain and fever
    B. shock and hypoxia
    C. hypotension and congestive heart failure
    D. all of the above

15. The treatment of choice for sinus tachycardia is

    A. atropin sulphate
    B. treatment of the underlying cause
    C. propranolol
    D. all of the above

16. You should NOT treat patients with sinus bradycardia if they have

    A. unconsciousness
    B. a good or strong pulse

C. cold and clammy skin
D. systolic blood pressure of 80 mmHg or less

17. Which of the following drugs can be used to treat sinus bradycardia?

    A. Atropin sulphate
    B. Propranolol
    C. Isoproterenol
    D. A and C *only*

18. For premature atrial contraction,

    A. epinephrine is the best treatment
    B. dopamine is the best treatment
    C. no satisfactory treatment exists
    D. all of the above

19. A 40-year-old male has paroxymal supraventricular tachycardia and stable vital signs. The physician tells you to apply vagal maneuvers but, at the same time, the patient develops hypotension.
    The treatment of choice is

    A. to continue valsalva maneuver
    B. cardioversion
    C. verapamil
    D. digoxin

20. Some maneuvers that stimulate the vagus nerve will slow the heart rate and may convert some PSVT's back to normal sinus rhythm.
    These maneuvers include all of the following EXCEPT

    A. valsalva maneuver
    B. ice water
    C. carotid sinus massage
    D. hot water

21. You are taking a patient with PSVT to the hospital, which is 30 minutes away. The physician may tell you to administer

    A. verapamil
    B. digoxin
    C. dopamine
    D. all of the above

22. You are looking at the ECG of a patient who has regular rhythm, a rate of 50 per minute, absent P wave, and normal QRS complexes.
    The MOST likely diagnosis is

    A. sinus bradycardia
    B. junctional bradycardia
    C. third degree heart block
    D. none of the above

23. If the patient in the above question develops signs of poor perfusion, you should administer

    A. atropin sulphate
    B. digoxin
    C. procainamide
    D. all of the above

24. Propranolol is known by the trade name(s)

    A. pronestyle
    B. inderal
    C. procardia
    D. all of the above

Questions 25-30.

DIRECTIONS: In Questions 25 through 30, match the numbered description or function with the appropriate lettered part of the cardiovascular system, as listed in Column I. Place the letter of the CORRECT answer in the space at the right.

COLUMN I
A. Tricuspid valve
B. Mitral valve
C. Coronary sulcus
D. Systole
E. Diastole
F. SA node

25. The groove which separates the atria and the ventricle, in which the arteries and the main coronary vein cross the heart. 25.____

26. Separates the right atrium from the right ventricle. 26.____

27. Separates the left atrium from the left ventricle. 27.____

28. Atrial and ventricular relaxation. 28.____

29. Atrial and ventricular contraction. 29.____

30. Located in the right atrium near the inlet of the superior vena cava. 30.____

KEY (CORRECT ANSWERS)

1.	A	16.	B
2.	C	17.	D
3.	C	18.	C
4.	A	19.	B
5.	B	20.	D
6.	D	21.	A
7.	B	22.	B
8.	C	23.	A
9.	D	24.	B
10.	C	25.	C
11.	B	26.	A
12.	D	27.	B
13.	A	28.	E
14.	D	29.	D
15.	B	30.	F

CARDIOVASCULAR SYSTEM
EXAMINATION SECTION
TEST 1

DIRECTIONS: Each question or incomplete statement is followed by several suggested answers or completions. Select the one that BEST answers the question or completes the statement. *PRINT THE LETTER OF THE CORRECT ANSWER IN THE SPACE AT THE RIGHT.*

Questions 1-2.

DIRECTIONS: Questions 1 and 2 are to be answered on the basis of the following EKG reading.

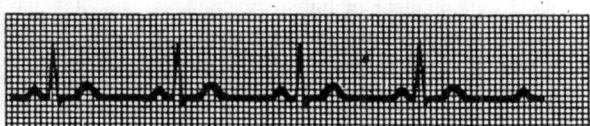

1. The MOST likely diagnosis of the above EKG is 1.____

   A. regular sinus rhythm
   B. sinus bradycardia
   C. atrial tachycardia
   D. first degree heart block

2. The MOST appropriate treatment for the patient with this EKG would be 2.____

   A. propranolol   B. isoproterenol
   C. atropin   D. none of the above

Questions 3-5.

DIRECTIONS: Questions 3 through 5 are to be answered on the basis of the following EKG reading.

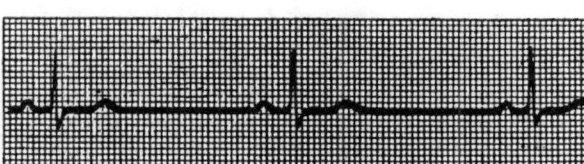

3. The MOST likely diagnosis for this patient is 3.____

   A. regular sinus rhythm
   B. sinus bradycardia
   C. first degree heart block
   D. second degree heart block

4. The cause of the above rhythm is (are) PROBABLY 4.____

   A. damage to the conduction system
   B. increased vagal tone
   C. possible toxic levels of certain cardiac drugs (digitalis quinidine)
   D. all of the above

5. If the victim with the above EKG develops a weak pulse and confusion, the treatment of choice would be

   A. atropin sulfate
   B. lidocaine
   C. isoproterenol
   D. all of the above

Questions 6-8.

DIRECTIONS: Questions 6 through 8 are to be answered on the basis of the following EKG reading.

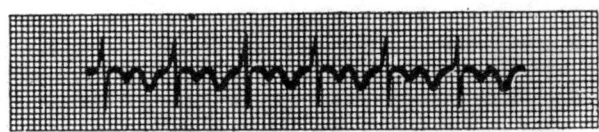

6. The MOST likely diagnosis for this patient is

   A. regular sinus rhythm
   B. sinus tachycardia
   C. atrial tachycardia
   D. atrial flutter

7. Common causes of the above rhythm include

   A. fever
   B. hypoxia
   C. shock
   D. all of the above

8. The BEST treatment for the above victim would be

   A. epinephrine
   B. atropine
   C. lidocaine
   D. treatment of the underlying cause

Questions 9-11.

DIRECTIONS: Questions 9 through 11 are to be answered on the basis of the following EKG reading.

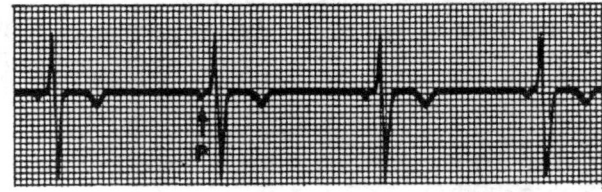

9. What is the MOST likely diagnosis of the above EKG?

   A. Sinus rhythm
   B. Junctional rhythm
   C. Coronary sinus rhythm
   D. None of the above

10. The MOST likely abnormality of the above EKG rhythm is a(n)

    A. inverted P wave
    B. U wave
    C. absent F wave
    D. small T wave

11. If the above victim does not respond to atropine and the transport time is prolonged, the physician may order a(n) 11.____

    A. isoproterenol drip
    B. pacemaker
    C. repeat dose of sodium bicarbonate
    D. none of the above

12. The one of the following which is NOT a common cause of junctional rhythm is 12.____

    A. anoxia and vagotonic drugs
    B. fever
    C. congestive heart failure
    D. acidosis and hyperkalemia

Questions 13-15.

DIRECTIONS: Questions 13 through 15 are to be answered on the basis of the following EKG reading.

13. The MOST likely diagnosis of a patient with the above EKG is 13.____

    A. the syndrome of short P-R interval and normal QRS
    B. first degree heart block
    C. second degree heart block
    D. all of the above

14. Among the following, the drug whose toxicity could NOT cause the above EKG problem is 14.____

    A. digitalis   B. quinidine
    C. atropine sulphate   D. procainamide

15. The treatment of choice for the victim with the above EKG is 15.____

    A. cardioversion   B. defibrillation
    C. pacemaker   D. none of the above

Questions 16-17.

DIRECTIONS: Questions 16 and 17 are to be answered on the basis of the following EKG reading.

16. The MOST likely diagnosis of a patient with the above EKG is _____ degree heart block.

   A. first
   B. second
   C. third
   D. none of the above

17. The PROPER treatment for a victim with the above EKG and poor cardiac output is

   A. atropin sulfate
   B. cardioversion
   C. defibrillation
   D. none of the above

Questions 18-19.

DIRECTIONS: Questions 18 and 19 are to be answered on the basis of the following EKG reading.

18. What is the MOST likely diagnosis of a patient with the above EKG? _____ heart block.

   A. First degree
   B. AV dissociation without
   C. complete
   D. all of the above

19. The definitive treatment of a victim with the above EKG, if he does not respond to atropin, is

   A. epinephrine
   B. lidocaine
   C. pacemaker
   D. bretylium tosylate

Questions 20-22.

DIRECTIONS: Questions 20 through 22 are to be answered on the basis of the following EKG reading.

20. What is the MOST likely diagnosis of a patient with the above EKG?

   A. Atrial flutter
   B. Atrial fibrillation
   C. Ventricular tachycardia
   D. None of the above

21. If a victim with the above cardiogram is unstable, the treatment of choice is

   A. digitalis
   B. atropin
   C. cardioversion
   D. defibrillation

22. It is very important to inform the physician if a patient is taking a certain medication; otherwise the above-mentioned procedure will be hazardous to the victim.
This medication is

    A. lasix
    B. digitalis
    C. hydralazine
    D. none of the above

Questions 23-24.

DIRECTIONS: Questions 23 and 24 are to be answered on the basis of the following EKG reading.

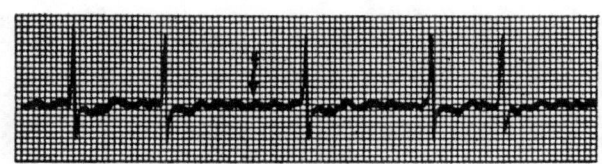

23. The MOST likely diagnosis of a patient with the above EKG is

    A. atrial flutter
    B. atrial fibrillation
    C. ventricular fibrillation
    D. all of the above

24. Which of the following would be the drug of choice if the victim developed a very rapid pulse?

    A. Digitalis
    B. Atropin sulphate
    C. Lidocaine
    D. All of the above

25. The MOST likely diagnosis of a patient with the EKG shown at the right is
    A. atrial flutter
    B. ventricular flutter
    C. ventricular fibrillation
    D. all of the above

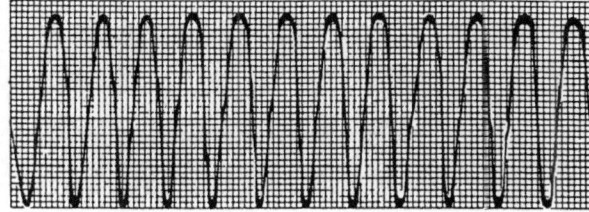

KEY (CORRECT ANSWERS)

1.	A		11.	A
2.	D		12.	B
3.	B		13.	B
4.	D		14.	C
5.	A		15.	D
6.	B		16.	B
7.	D		17.	A
8.	D		18.	C
9.	B		19.	C
10.	A		20.	A

21. C
22. B
23. B
24. A
25. B

TEST 2

DIRECTIONS: Each question or incomplete statement is followed by several suggested answers or completions. Select the one that BEST answers the question or completes the statement. *PRINT THE LETTER OF THE CORRECT ANSWER IN THE SPACE AT THE RIGHT.*

1. Of the following dysrhythmias, the one which does NOT originate in the atrium is 1._____

   A. paroxysmal supraventricular tachycardia
   B. wandering atrial pacemaker
   C. junctional rhythm
   D. atrial fibrillation

2. Dysrhythmias originating in the AV node or AV junction include all of the following EXCEPT 2._____

   A. Type I wenckeback   B. junctional extrasystoles
   C. bundle branch block   D. third degree AV block

Questions 3-4.

DIRECTIONS: Questions 3 and 4 are to be answered on the basis of the following information.

   A patient is stable, with atrial flutter.

3. The treatment of choice for this patient is 3._____

   A. verapamil   B. propranolol
   C. cardioversion   D. no treatment is indicated

4. The patient develops hypotension with tachycardia.
   The treatment of choice is NOW 4._____

   A. verapamil   B. propranolol
   C. cardioversion   D. all of the above

5. A monitored patient is observed to go into ventricular fibrillation, and a defibrillator is NOT immediately available.
   The treatment of choice is 5._____

   A. precordial thump   B. epinephrine
   C. verapamil   D. quinidine

6. If ventricular fibrillation occurs in the rescuer's presence, he should treat it with 6._____

   A. epinephrine
   B. immediate counter shock
   C. immediate cardioversion
   D. all of the above

7. A patient develops a systole on the way to the hospital. _____ should be administered. 7._____

   A. CPR   B. Epinephrine
   C. Defibrillation   D. All of the above

73

Questions 8-10.

DIRECTIONS: Questions 8 through 10 are to be answered on the basis of the following information.

A patient suffering from ventricular tachycardia is alert and shows no signs of inadequate cardiac output.

8. The INITIAL treatment of choice for this patient is

    A. epinephrine
    B. lidocaine
    C. defibrillation
    D. quinidine

9. If the initial treatment proves ineffective in converting the rhythm to sinus, the physician MAY order the use of

    A. procainamide
    B. bretylium tosylate
    C. propranolol
    D. verapamil

10. If the above patient suddenly falls into a coma and develops hypotension, the treatment of choice is

    A. defibrillation
    B. cardioversion
    C. lidocaine
    D. none of the above

Questions 11-12.

DIRECTIONS: Questions 11 and 12 are to be answered on the basis of the following EKG reading.

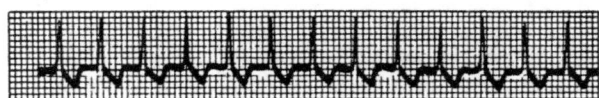

11. What is the MOST likely diagnosis of a patient with the above EKG? _____ tachycardia.

    A. Junctional
    B. Paroxysmal atrial
    C. Supraventricular
    D. Multifocal atrial

12. The BEST initial treatment for a victim with the above rhythm is

    A. vagal maneuver
    B. lidocaine
    C. atropin
    D. all of the above

Questions 13-14.

DIRECTIONS: Questions 13 and 14 are to be answered on the basis of the following EKG reading.

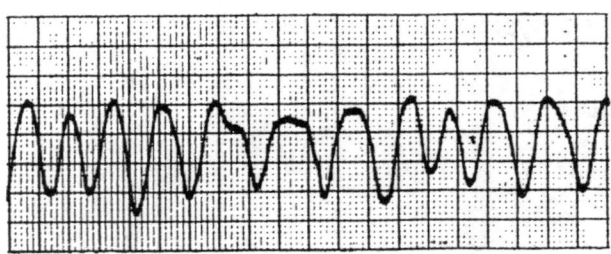

13. The MOST likely diagnosis of a patient with the above EKG is

    A. ventricular tachycardia
    B. ventricular fibrillation
    C. paroxysmal atrial tachycardia
    D. none of the above

14. What would be the treatment of choice for a victim with the above EKG?

    A. Epinephrine   B. Procainamide
    C. Countershock   D. None of the above

Questions 15-18.

DIRECTIONS: Questions 15 through 18 are to be answered on the basis of the following EKG reading.

15. _____ tachycardia is the MOST likely diagnosis of a patient with the above EKG.

    A. Sinus   B. Junctional
    C. Ventricular   D. None of the above

16. If the victim with the above EKG is alert and not in distress, the drug of choice for INITIAL management is

    A. digitalis   B. lidocaine
    C. bretylium tosylate D. procainamide

17. If a victim with the above EKG becomes unconscious,

    A. administer bretylium tosylate as an infusion of 10 mg/kg given over 10 minutes
    B. a sharp, quick precordial thump may be delivered over the midsternum
    C. defibrillate at 200 joules
    D. all of the above

18. If the victim does not respond to the above treatment, the NEXT best approach is to administer

    A. procainamide   B. epinephrine
    C. cardioversion   D. defibrillation

Questions 19-20.

DIRECTIONS: Questions 19 and 20 are to be answered on the basis of the following EKG reading.

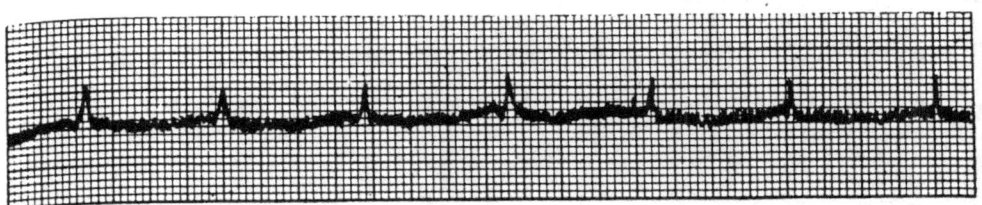

19. What is the MOST likely diagnosis of a patient with the above EKG?   19.___

    A. Ventricular fibrillation
    B. Atrial fibrillation
    C. Muscle tremor
    D. None of the above

20. The BEST treatment of a victim with the above rhythm is   20.___

    A. lidocaine
    B. cardioversion
    C. defibrillation
    D. none of the above

Questions 21-25.

DIRECTIONS: In Questions 21 through 25, match the numbered condition with the lettered pulse rate which is associated with it. Place the letter of the CORRECT answer in the appropriate space at the right.

PULSE RATES (PER MINUTE)
A. Less than 60
B. 60 to 100
C. 100 to 150
D. 250 to 350
E. Greater than 350

21. Normal sinus rhythm   21.___

22. Sinus bradycardia   22.___

23. Sinus tachycardia   23.___

24. Atrial fibrillation   24.___

25. Atrial flutter   25.___

KEY (CORRECT ANSWERS)

1. C
2. B
3. D
4. C
5. A

6. B
7. D
8. B
9. B
10. B

11. C
12. A
13. B
14. C
15. C

16. B
17. B
18. C
19. C
20. D

21. B
22. A
23. C
24. E
25. D

TEST 3

DIRECTIONS: Each question or incomplete statement is followed by several suggested answers or completions. Select the one that BEST answers the question or completes the statement. *PRINT THE LETTER OF THE CORRECT ANSWER IN THE SPACE AT THE RIGHT.*

1. Among the drugs that decrease excitability in tachyarrhythmias is(are)

    A. lidocaine
    B. procainamide
    C. quinidine
    D. all of the above

2. All of the following indicate cardioversion EXCEPT

    A. rapid ventricular tachycardia
    B. atrial flutter with hypotension; signs of perfusion
    C. ventricular fibrillation
    D. atrial fibrillation with a rapid ventricular response and hypotension

3. Advantages of mechanical CPR devices do NOT include

    A. reduction or elimination of operator fatigue
    B. decrease in the number of personnel required to perform CPR
    C. lack of effectiveness in adults
    D. usefulness in extended CPR during transport

4. The fibrous strands, shaped like umbrella stays, that attach the free edges of the AV valve leaflets to the papillary muscles are called

    A. bundle of his
    B. chordae tendinae
    C. bundle branches
    D. atrioventricular node

5. Of the following arrhythmias, _____ resemble(s) ventricular tachycardia.

    A. atrial tachycardia with second degree atrioventricular block
    B. supraventricular tachycardia (SUT) with aberration defect
    C. rapid SUT with an interventricular conduction defect
    D. all of the above

6. Which of the following statements is NOT true regarding cardiac tamponade? It

    A. usually results in excess fluid in the pericardium
    B. is usually associated with increased cardiac output
    C. usually results in inadequate filling of the heart
    D. can be caused by the use of an intracardiac needle

7. The MOST suitable vein for IV insertion during cardiac arrest while resuscitation is in progress is the _____ vein.

    A. external jugular
    B. peripheral arm (in the antecubital space)
    C. internal carotid
    D. femoral

8. A victim who has acute chest pain which radiates to the neck and left arm should be

    A. given supplemental oxygen
    B. monitored for arrhythmias
    C. made as comfortable as possible
    D. all of the above

9. A patient who is receiving cardioversion for ventricular tachycardia develops ventricular fibrillation and pulselessness.
   You should

    A. give bretylium IV
    B. repeat synchronized countershock immediately
    C. defibrillate at 200 joules
    D. none of the above

10. Among the following, the GREATEST risk of failure to recognize and properly treat complete heart block comes from

    A. myocardial infarction
    B. ventricular asystole
    C. ventricular aneurysm
    D. atrial fibrillation

11. You suspect a victim is in congestive heart failure.
    Of the following, the drug you should NOT give to this victim is

    A. morphine sulphate
    B. furosemide
    C. propranolol
    D. nitroprusside

12. An EKG MOST nearly represents

    A. total cardiac output
    B. left ventricular endodiastolic pressure
    C. total venous return to the heart
    D. electrical activity of the heart

13. An EKG of a victim which shows a straight line or asystole means there is

    A. no cardiac electric activity
    B. congestive heart failure
    C. decreased conduction through the AV node only
    D. decreased conduction through the bundle of his

14. All of the following are recommended treatments for asystole EXCEPT

    A. epinephrine
    B. atropine
    C. calcium chloride
    D. pacemaker insertion

15. _____ is NOT useful in the treatment of paroxysmal supraventricular tachycardia.

    A. Infusion of isoproterenol
    B. Carotid sinus massage
    C. Verapamil
    D. Digitalization

16. In order for an external chest compression to be effective in an adult victim of cardiac arrest, the sternum must be depressed _____ inch(es).

    A. $\frac{1}{2}$ B. 1 C. $1\frac{1}{2}$ to 2 D. $2\frac{1}{2}$ to $3\frac{1}{2}$

17. Supraventricular bradydysrhythmias with acute myocardial infarction is
    A. usually treated by epinephrine drip
    B. usually common during the first hour following the onset of symptoms
    C. always associated with anterior wall infarction
    D. none of the above

18. How many pounds of pressure should be exerted on each electrode paddle during adult defibrillation?
    A. 7 B. 15 C. 25 D. 35

19. Relatively simple techniques useful in certain arrythmias include
    A. precordial thump   B. coughing
    C. carotid sinus massage   D. all of the above

20. All of the following are potential hazards of intracardiac injection EXCEPT
    A. pneumothorax
    B. cardiac tamponade
    C. constrictive pericarditis
    D. inadvertent laceration of the coronary artery

Questions 21-25.

DIRECTIONS: In Questions 21 through 25, match the numbered description with the lettered substance or structure, listed in Column I, which it MOST NEARLY defines. Place the letter of the CORRECT answer in the appropriate space at the right.

COLUMN I
A. Tunica intima
B. Tunica adventitia
C. Tunica media
D. Arteriole
E. Plasmine

21. Nautrally occurring clot-dissolving enzyme.

22. Thin, innermost layer of a blood vessel.

23. Muscular layer of a blood vessel that gives the vessel its contractility.

24. Small blood vessel that carries oxygenated blood.

25. Protective fibrous covering that gives a blood vessel the strength to withstand pressure against its wall.

KEY (CORRECT ANSWERS)

1.	D	11.	C
2.	C	12.	D
3.	C	13.	A
4.	B	14.	C
5.	D	15.	A
6.	B	16.	C
7.	B	17.	B
8.	D	18.	C
9.	C	19.	D
10.	B	20.	C

21. E
22. A
23. C
24. D
25. B

CENTRAL NERVOUS SYSTEM
EXAMINATION SECTION
TEST 1

DIRECTIONS: Each question or incomplete statement is followed by several suggested answers or completions. Select the one that BEST answers the question or completes the statement. *PRINT THE LETTER OF THE CORRECT ANSWER IN THE SPACE AT THE RIGHT.*

1. The skull is made up of _____ bones, which can be categorized as either cranial or facial bones.

    A. 20   B. 18   C. 29   D. 35

    1.____

2. The facial bones MOST important in emergency medicine include the

    A. maxilla
    B. mandible
    C. zygomata
    D. all of the above

    2.____

3. The opening in the base of the skull where the brain stem is continuous with the beginning of the spinal cord is called the foramen

    A. magnum
    B. of monro
    C. rotundum
    D. spinosum

    3.____

4. The one of the following NOT among the three layers of fibrous covering of the brain (meninges) is the

    A. dura mater
    B. tia mater
    C. arachnoid
    D. pia mater

    4.____

5. The dura mater is firmly attached to the internal wall of the skull. In certain places, however, it splits into two surfaces and forms venous sinuses. During head injury, those sinuses can be disrupted, allowing the blood to collect beneath the dura.
This condition is known as _____ hematoma.

    A. subdural
    B. epidural
    C. subarachnoid
    D. all of the above

    5.____

6. The meningeal arteries are located between the dura and the skull.
Disruption of one of these arteries results in bleeding above the dura, forming

    A. subdural hematoma
    B. epidural hematoma
    C. subarachnoid hemorrhage
    D. none of the above

    6.____

7. The brain is

    A. a very soft and moist organ
    B. richly supplied with blood
    C. contained in the skull cavity
    D. all of the above

    7.____

8. The cerebellum is located in the _____ part of the brain.

   A. anterior
   B. superior
   C. inferoposterior
   D. anteriolateral

9. The MAIN function of the cerebellum is the control of

   A. posture and equilibrium and the coordination of skills
   B. heart rate
   C. vision
   D. speech

10. The brain stem is located at the _____ of the brain.

    A. anterior part
    B. anteriolateral part
    C. base
    D. none of the above

Questions 11-14.

DIRECTIONS: In Questions 11 through 14, match the numbered region of the brain with its lettered function, listed in Column I. Place the letter of the CORRECT answer in the appropriate space at the right.

COLUMN I

A. Speech center
B. Vision center
C. Respiratory center
D. Concerned with emotion

11. Occipital lobe

12. Temporal lobe

13. Frontal lobe

14. Brain stem

15. The functions of brain stem include

    A. the medulla's control of respiration and heart rate
    B. control of the eye, throat, and facial muscles
    C. the oculomotor nerve's causing the eye to constrict
    D. all of the above

16. All of the following are true regarding the spinal cord EXCEPT:

    A. It is 10 mm in diameter.
    B. If the vertebral body is displaced 5 mm, injury to the cord and paralysis may result.
    C. It controls movement of the eye muscles.
    D. There are segmental neurons that supply local anatomical structures.

17. The _____ mediates the position and vibratory sense.

    A. anterior column
    B. posterior column
    C. corticospinal tract
    D. all of the above

18. Of the following, the mediators of pain and temperature sense include the

    A. corticospinal tract
    B. posterior column
    C. lateral spinothalmic tract
    D. all of the above

19. Movement is usually controlled by

    A. the corticospinal tract
    B. the lateral spinal tract
    C. all of the above
    D. none of the above

20. The chemical mediator of the parasympathetic nervous system is

    A. norepinephrine
    B. epinephrine
    C. acetylcholine
    D. all of the above

21. Regarding cerebrospinal fluid, it is TRUE that

    A. it is a clear and water-like fluid
    B. it serves as a shock absorber and as a source of nourishment for some of the brain cells
    C. leakage of the fluid indicates that the skull has been fractured and the dura mater has been lacerated
    D. all of the above

22. When sympathetic nerves are damaged or interrupted, all of the following conditions may occur EXCEPT

    A. a sudden increase in blood pressure
    B. arteries no longer constricting in response to changes in posture and core body temperature
    C. dramatic pooling of blood within the suddenly dilated vessels
    D. a fall in blood pressure

Questions 23-25.

DIRECTIONS: In Questions 23 through 25, match the numbered description with the lettered structure of the central nervous system, listed in Column I, which it most accurately describes. Place the letter of the CORRECT answer in the appropriate space at the right.

COLUMN I

    A. Dura mater
    B. Arachnoid mater
    C. Pia mater

23. Middle meningeal layer; a delicate, transparent membrane.

24. A thin, highly vascular membrane firmly adherent to the surface of the brain.

25. Outermost layer; a strong, fibrous wrapping.

KEY (CORRECT ANSWERS)

1. C
2. D
3. A
4. B
5. A

6. B
7. D
8. C
9. A
10. C

11. B
12. A
13. D
14. C
15. D

16. C
17. B
18. C
19. A
20. C

21. D
22. A
23. B
24. C
25. A

TEST 2

DIRECTIONS: Each question or incomplete statement is followed by several suggested answers or completions. Select the one that BEST answers the question or completes the statement. *PRINT THE LETTER OF THE CORRECT ANSWER IN THE SPACE AT THE RIGHT.*

1. Signs and symptoms of increased intracranial pressure include

    A. rising blood pressure
    B. slow pulse
    C. rapid or irregular respiration
    D. all of the above

1._____

2. A 25-year-old male is hit with a baseball bat on the right side of his head during a fight. He loses consciousness for a few minutes; then he regains consciousness, but one hour later he starts getting sleepy with a change of mental status. On examination, his right pupil is fixed and dilated.
The MOST likely diagnosis is

    A. subdural hematoma B. epidural hematoma
    C. subarachnoid hemorrhage D. all of the above

2._____

Questions 3-5.

DIRECTIONS: Questions 3 through 5 are to be answered on the basis of the following information.

You receive a call for a 30-year-old male who fell from the stairs. When you get to the scene, you find an unconscious patient with multiple lacerations on his head and slightly elevated blood pressure.

3. The best FIRST management is

    A. nasotracheal intubation
    B. epinephrine IV
    C. to try to stop the bleeding
    D. to start an IV lifeline

3._____

4. The MOST likely initial treatment for increased intracranial pressure would be to maintain a ventilation rate of about _____ breaths per minute.

    A. 10 B. 15
    C. 20 D. none of the above

4._____

5. Which of the following drugs might the physician order if the patient's condition does NOT improve?

    A. Furosemide B. Manitol
    C. Diazepam D. A and B *only*

5._____

6. If a patient with head trauma develops seizures in a pre-hospital setting, you should notify the physician and then administer

   A. phenytoin
   B. diazepam
   C. phenobarbital
   D. none of the above

7. The single MOST important sign in the evaluation of a head-injured patient is

   A. rising blood pressure
   B. decreasing pulse rate
   C. changing state of consciousness
   D. none of the above

8. The Glasgow coma scale assigns a numerical score to the patient's responses in three categories.
   The one of the following categories which does NOT receive a score according to this scale is

   A. eye opening
   B. breathing response
   C. best motor response
   D. verbal response

9. _____ is the MOST likely cause of hypotension in a patient with head injury.

   A. Epidural hematoma
   B. Subdural hematoma
   C. Major hemorrhaging elsewhere in the body
   D. All of the above

10. You should suspect spinal cord injury as a result of

    A. vehicular trauma
    B. a diving accident
    C. crush injuries
    D. all of the above

11. The most efficient and readily available means of temporary stabilization are pairs of hands or knees. The MAIN objective of stabilization is to keep the head and neck in the _____ position.

    A. extension
    B. flexion
    C. neutral
    D. none of the above

12. The maneuver performed to open the airway in a spine-injured patient is

    A. jaw thrust
    B. chin lift
    C. jaw lift
    D. all of the above

13. Which of the following findings, if present in a male, is a characteristic sign of spinal cord injury?

    A. Hypotension
    B. Priapism
    C. Bruises of the back
    D. Tachycardia

14. If a patient with suspected spinal cord injury develops signs of shock, you should

    A. inflate the mast
    B. cover the patient with a blanket
    C. establish IV with ringer lactate solution
    D. all of the above

15. The medication which, if given within 8 hours of injury, may permit some recovery of nerve function is   15.____

    A. epinephrine   B. corticosteroids
    C. norepinephrine   D. none of the above

16. A mild, closed head injury without detectable damage to the brain is called a   16.____

    A. concussion   B. contusion
    C. laceration   D. all of the above

17. A bruised brain caused by the force of a blow to the head great enough to rupture the blood vessels is referred to as a   17.____

    A. laceration   B. contusion
    C. concussion   D. all of the above

18. The signs and symptoms indicative of possible skull fracture include   18.____

    A. blood coming from the ears
    B. clear fluid coming from the ears
    C. loss of balance as the patient attempts to position himself
    D. all of the above

19. Proper pre-hospital treatment for a victim who has clear fluid draining from the ear would be to   19.____

    A. pack the sternal ear canal
    B. apply loose sterile external dressing
    C. remove any impaled object(s)
    D. none of the above

20. The ears are responsible for   20.____

    A. hearing   B. equilibrium
    C. control of eye movement   D. A and B *only*

Questions 21-25.

DIRECTIONS: In Questions 21 through 25, match the numbered function with the lettered correlated term, listed in Column I. Place the letter of the CORRECT answer in the appropriate space at the right.

COLUMN I

21. Diaphragm   A. C_4 21.____
                      B. $S_2 - S_3$
22. Knee flexion   C. $L_5 - S_1$ 22.____
23. Bladder control   D. $C_5 - C_6$ 23.____
                      E. $C_7 - L_8 - T_1$
24. Elbow flexion   24.____

25. Finger movement   25.____

Questions 26-30.

DIRECTIONS: In Questions 26 through 30, match the numbered definition with the lettered term in Column I with which it is MOST closely correlated. Place the letter of the CORRECT answer in the appropriate space at the right.

COLUMN I

A. Decebrate posture
B. Decorticate posture
C. Herniation
D. Reticular activating system
E. Countrecoup

26. Extrusion of part of the brain through the tentorium, or foramen magnum, as a result of increased ICP.   26.___

27. Center in the brain stem that controls the state of wakefulness.   27.___

28. Injury resulting from a blow at another site.   28.___

29. Assumed by a patient with severe brain dysfunction; characterized by extension and internal rotation of the arm and extension of the legs.   29.___

30. Characterized by extension of the legs and flexion of the arm.   30.___

KEY (CORRECT ANSWERS)

1.	D	16.	A
2.	B	17.	B
3.	A	18.	D
4.	C	19.	B
5.	D	20.	D
6.	B	21.	A
7.	C	22.	C
8.	B	23.	B
9.	C	24.	D
10.	D	25.	E
11.	C	26.	C
12.	D	27.	D
13.	B	28.	E
14.	D	29.	A
15.	B	30.	B

GASTROENTEROLOGY

EXAMINATION SECTION
TEST 1

DIRECTIONS: Each question or incomplete statement is followed by several suggested answers or completions. Select the one that BEST answers the question or completes the statement. *PRINT THE LETTER OF THE CORRECT ANSWER IN THE SPACE AT THE RIGHT.*

1. The root word *chole* refers to 1.____
   A. bone   B. bile   C. gut   D. stomach

2. The root word *entero* refers to 2.____
   A. gut   B. kidney   C. lung   D. gland

3. The root word *gastro* refers to 3.____
   A. gut   B. stomach   C. liver   D. muscle

4. The root word *hepato* refers to 4.____
   A. heart   B. brain   C. liver   D. kidney

5. The MOST prominent abdominal landmark is probably the 5.____
   A. epigastrium   B. umbilicus
   C. costal arch   D. spinal column

6. The superior border of the abdominal cavity is formed by the 6.____
   A. sacrum   B. thoracic spine
   C. diaphragm   D. spleen

7. The large cavity below the diaphragm and above the pelvis is called the 7.____
   A. ovary   B. liver   C. abdomen   D. stomach

8. The term *anorexia* refers to 8.____
   A. lack of appetite
   B. absence of oxygen in tissues
   C. inequality of the size of the pupils
   D. swelling of the body

9. The term referring to the accumulation of fluid in the abdominal cavity is 9.____
   A. peritonitis   B. ascites
   C. anasarca   D. hematoma

10. The FIRST portion of large intestine, into which the small intestine empties, is called the 10.____
    A. rectum   B. cecum   C. duodenum   D. anus

11. The name given to the first 11 inches of the small intestine is

   A. duodenum   B. colon   C. cecum   D. jojumum

12. The SECOND portion of the small intestine is called the

   A. jejunum
   C. duodenum
   B. colon
   D. none of the above

13. Interference with the act of swallowing or pain or difficulty in swallowing is called

   A. dyspnea
   C. dysarthria
   B. dysphagia
   D. aphasia

14. The portion of the digestive system that lies between the pharynx and stomach is the

   A. trachea   B. larynx   C. esophagus   D. glottis

15. A thin structure, located behind the root of the tongue, that shields the entrance of the larynx during swallowing, thus preventing the aspiration of food into the trachea. This is the definition of the

   A. tonsil
   C. adenoids
   B. epiglottis
   D. pharynx

16. The upper middle region of the abdomen within the sternal angle is called

   A. epidural
   C. epigastrium
   B. hypogastric
   D. perinephric

17. The sac located just beneath the liver that concentrates and stores bile is the

   A. spleen
   C. gallbladder
   B. pancreas
   D. urinary bladder

18. The THIRD portion of the small intestine is called the

   A. ilium
   C. cecum
   B. ileum
   D. sigmoid colon

19. _____ is the organ of voice production.

   A. Larynx   B. Pharnyx   C. Trachea   D. Epiglottis

20. The large solid organ in the right upper quadrant of the abdomen that secretes bile, produces many essential proteins, detoxifies drugs, and performs many other vital functions is the

   A. pancreas   B. liver   C. kidney   D. spleen

21. The _____ is an intra-abdominal gland that secretes insulin and important digestive enzymes.

   A. adrenal gland
   C. spleen
   B. pancreas
   D. none of the above

22. The S-shaped terminal portion of the descending colon is called the _____ colon.

   A. sigmoid
   C. transverse
   B. ascending
   D. all of the above

23. The organ in the upper quadrant of the abdomen that destroys old red blood cells is the 23.____

    A. spleen   B. kidney   C. sternum   D. pancreas

24. The hollow digestive organ in the epigastrium that receives food material from the esophagus. 24.____
    This describes the

    A. duodenum   B. jejunum   C. stomach   D. colon

25. The true abdomen contains all of the following EXCEPT the 25.____

    A. small intestine   B. large intestine
    C. bladder   D. diaphragm

26. The _____ is(are) NOT among the retroperitoneal organs. 26.____

    A. aorta and inferior vena cava
    B. kidney and pancreas
    C. uterus and ovary
    D. duodenum

27. The beginning of the mechanical and enzymatic breakdown of food occurs in the 27.____

    A. mouth   B. stomach   C. duodenum   D. cecum

28. Normally, food will be emptied from the stomach within _____ (s) after its ingestion. 28.____

    A. 0 to 1   B. 1 to 3   C. 5 to 7   D. 9 to 12

29. All of the following are solid abdominal organs EXCEPT the 29.____

    A. liver   B. spleen   C. stomach   D. pancreas

30. Which of the following is NOT a hollow abdominal organ? 30.____

    A. Gallbladder   B. Kidney
    C. Small intestine   D. Ureters

KEY (CORRECT ANSWERS)

1. B	11. A	21. B
2. A	12. A	22. A
3. B	13. B	23. A
4. C	14. C	24. C
5. B	15. B	25. D
6. C	16. C	26. C
7. C	17. C	27. A
8. A	18. B	28. B
9. B	19. A	29. C
10. B	20. B	30. B

TEST 2

DIRECTIONS: Each question or incomplete statement is followed by several suggested answers or completions. Select the one that BEST answers the question or completes the statement. *PRINT THE LETTER OF THE CORRECT ANSWER IN THE SPACE AT THE RIGHT.*

1. A pocket formed by a weakened area of the wall of the colon is called a   1.___
   A. fistula B. diverticulitis
   C. diverticulum D. shunt

2. The common signs and symptoms of splenic rupture include   2.___
   A. generalized abdominal pain
   B. hypotension
   C. possible referred pain in the left shoulder
   D. all of the above

3. The MOST common cause of upper GI bleeding is   3.___
   A. gastric cancer B. esophagitis
   C. peptic ulcer D. polyp

4. The passage of dark tarry stools, signifying blood in the gastrointestinal tract, is called   4.___
   A. melanin B. melena
   C. hemoptysis D. hematochezia

5. A bright red blood passed per rectum is referred to as   5.___
   A. hematochezia B. melena
   C. hemoptysis D. hematemesis

6. The protrusion of the stomach into the mediastinum through an opening in the diaphragm forms a(n) _____ hernia.   6.___
   A. inguinal B. umbilical
   C. hiatus D. none of the above

7. Which of the following hormones is secreted by the stomach?   7.___
   A. Cholecystokine B. Gastrin
   C. Insulin D. Cortisol

8. Fat-soluble vitamins are absorbed in the small intestine with the help of   8.___
   A. gastrin B. insulin C. bile D. cortisol

9. Bloody vomitus, either of fresh, bright red blood or dark, grainy, digested blood with a *coffee grounds* appearance is called   9.___
   A. hemotochezia B. occult bleeding
   C. hematemesis D. melena

10. A protrusion of the intestine through a weakness in the abdominal muscles or through the inguinal canal forms a

    A. tumor
    B. hernia
    C. cyst
    D. none of the above

11. The telescoping of one part of the intestine into another is called

    A. intussuception
    B. torsion
    C. stenosis
    D. ileus

12. The ulcer associated with head trauma or brain surgery is the _____ ulcer.

    A. peptic   B. gastric   C. cushing   D. curling

13. _____ refers to the failure of intestinal mucosa to absorb digested nutrients.

    A. Maldigestion
    B. Malabsorption
    C. Diarrhea
    D. All of the above

14. The inflammatory disorder of gastric mucosa which erodes the surface epithelium in a diffuse, localized pattern is

    A. acute gastritis
    B. peptic ulcer disease
    C. gastric ulcer disease
    D. esophagitis

15. A break in the protective mucosal lining of the lower esophagus, stomach, or upper small intestine can expose submucosal areas to gastric secretion and autodigestion. Which of the following conditions does this situation cause?

    A. Gastritis
    B. Peptic ulcer disease
    C. Diverticulitis
    D. Diverticulosis

16. Stress ulcers that develop as a result of burn injuries are frequently called _____ ulcers.

    A. ischemic   B. cushing   C. curling   D. peptic

17. Nausea, vomiting, and anorexia following the onset of epigastric or periumbilical pain and a low-grade fever are common signs and symptoms of

    A. a tumor
    B. acute appendicitis
    C. diverticulosis
    D. none of the above

18. The yellow or greenish pigmentation of the skin caused by hyperbilirubinemia is called

    A. melanosis
    B. cyanosis
    C. jaundice
    D. hyperhydrosis

19. Inflammation of the gallbladder or cystic duct is known as

    A. cirrhosis
    B. cholelithiasis
    C. cholecystitis
    D. pancreatitis

20. The formation of gallstones is termed

    A. cirrhosis
    B. nephrolithiasis
    C. cholecystitis
    D. cholelithiasis

21. The return of stomach contents into the esophagus because of relaxation or incompetence of the lower esophageal sphincter is called

    A. gastritis
    B. gastroesophageal reflex
    C. emesis
    D. none of the above

22. Near the junction of the ileum and the colon is a short dead-end tube called the

    A. rectum   B. anus   C. appendix   D. colon

23. _____ pain occurs when nerve fibers in the peritoneum are irritated by chemical or bacterial inflammation.

    A. Visceral
    B. Somatic
    C. Referred
    D. None of the above

24. Putting stretch on the autonomic nerve fibers that surround the abdominal viscera causes _____ pain.

    A. visceral
    B. somatic
    C. neurogenic
    D. referred

25. Medications commonly prescribed to patients with gastrointestinal problems include all of the following EXCEPT

    A. antacids   B. Tagamet   C. aspirin   D. Zantac

Questions 26-30.

DIRECTIONS: In Questions 26 through 30, match the numbered definition with the lettered term, listed in Column I, that it MOST accurately describes. Place the letter of the CORRECT answer in the appropriate space at the right.

COLUMN I

A. Colostomy
B. Colic
C. Cachexia
D. Mesentery
E. Kehr's sign

26. Crampy pain associated with obstruction of hollow organs

27. Severe malnutrition and poor health as a result of disease or malnourishment

28. Establishment of an opening between the colon and the surface of the body for the purpose of providing drainage of bowel

29. Pain in the left shoulder after rupture of the spleen

30. Tissue by which the intestines are connected to the back surface of the abdominal cavity and that contain the blood vessels, lymphatics, and nerves supplying the intestines

KEY (CORRECT ANSWERS)

1.	C	11.	A	21.	B
2.	D	12.	C	22.	C
3.	C	13.	B	23.	B
4.	B	14.	A	24.	A
5.	A	15.	B	25.	C
6.	C	16.	B	26.	B
7.	B	17.	B	27.	C
8.	C	18.	C	28.	A
9.	C	19.	C	29.	E
10.	B	20.	D	30.	D

SOFT TISSUE INJURIES
EXAMINATION SECTION
TEST 1

DIRECTIONS: Each question or incomplete statement is followed by several suggested answers or completions. Select the one that BEST answers the question or completes the statement. *PRINT THE LETTER OF THE CORRECT ANSWER IN THE SPACE AT THE RIGHT.*

1. The MOST important function of the skin is　　　　　　　　　　　　　　　1.____

    A. temperature regulation
    B. service as a sense organ
    C. prevention of excessive loss of water from the body
    D. all of the above

2. The outermost layer of skin, which acts as the principle barrier against water, dust,　2.____
   microorganisms, and mechanical stress, is the

    A. dermis　　　　　　　　　　　　　　B. epidermis
    C. collagen　　　　　　　　　　　　　D. none of the above

3. The layer of connective tissue containing nerve endings, blood vessels, sweat glands,　3.____
   sebaceous glands, and hair follicles is called the

    A. epidermis　　　　　　　　　　　　　B. dermis
    C. subcutaneous layer　　　　　　　　D. endoderm

4. Nerve endings　　　　　　　　　　　　　　　　　　　　　　　　　　　　　4.____

    A. carry oxygen and nutrients to the skin
    B. produce sweat and discharge it through ducts
    C. mediate the sense of touch in terms of temperature and pain
    D. produce an oily substance called sebum

5. The average volume of sweat lost over a 24-hour period under normal conditions is　5.____
   between _____ and _____ ml.

    A. 500; 1000　　　　　　　　　　　　B. 2000; 3000
    C. 3000; 4000　　　　　　　　　　　　D. none of the above

6. The layer of tissue beneath the dermis is, by definition, the subcutaneous layer.　　　6.____
   It consists MAINLY of

    A. collagen　　　　　　　　　　　　　B. elastin
    C. adipose tissue　　　　　　　　　　D. melanin granules

7. Possible causes of red skin include all of the following EXCEPT　　　　　　　　7.____

    A. carbon dioxide poisoning
    B. hypoxia
    C. allergic reaction
    D. fever

8. A collection of blood beneath the skin, appearing as a lump with a bluish discoloration, is called a(n)

   A. hematoma
   B. ecchymosis
   C. petich
   D. none of the above

9. Treatment of a contusion would NOT include the application of

   A. ice or cold packs
   B. antibiotics
   C. firm compression over the injured area
   D. a splint to an injured extremity

10. A(n) _____ is a superficial wound that occurs when the skin is rubbed or scraped over a rough surface, causing the loss of part of the epidermis.

    A. abrasion
    B. laceration
    C. hematoma
    D. ecchymosis

11. A cut inflicted by a sharp instrument, such as a knife or razor blade, produces a clean or jagged incision through the skin's surface and underlying structures. This type of wound is a(n)

    A. abrasion
    B. laceration
    C. ecchymosis
    D. all of the above

12. The management of an impaled object includes

    A. avoiding trying to remove the impaled object
    B. avoiding trying to shorten the impaled object
    C. stabilizing the object in one place
    D. all of the above

13. To preserve an amputated part, do all of the following EXCEPT

    A. rinse it free of debris with a cool, sterile saline
    B. wrap it loosely in saline-moistened sterile gauze
    C. place it directly on ice
    D. seal it inside a plastic bag and place it in a cool container

14. Methods of controlling external bleeding include

    A. direct manual pressure and air splints
    B. mast and pressure point control
    C. splint and tourniquet
    D. all of the above

15. Always suspect respiratory tract injury in a burn victim who has experienced

    A. exposure to smoke or hot gases
    B. loss of consciousness in a burning area
    C. confinement in a closed space at the time of the burn
    D. all of the above

16. The Parkland formula states that during the first 24 hours following injury, the burned patient will need _____ ml/kg body weight per percent of body surface burned.

    A. 4   B. 8   C. 10   D. 12

17. To manage a first degree burn, one would do all of the following EXCEPT _____ the burned area.

    A. immerse in cool water or apply cold compresses
    B. place sterile dressing over
    C. use cream over
    D. avoid the use of salves, ointments, or sprays on

18. Management of a second degree burn would NOT include

    A. the application of a wet or water gel dressing within the first hour to diminish edema and provide significant pain relief
    B. an attempt to rupture the blister over the burn and then place ointment on it
    C. starting IV if the second degree burn covers more than 15 percent of the body surface area
    D. avoiding giving any narcotic until after fluid resuscitation is well-established

19. The treatment of choice for a chemical burn is

    A. flushing with water   B. antibiotics
    C. antihistamine   D. hydrocortisone cream

20. Which of the following is NOT contraindicated in the treatment of a chemical burn in the eye?

    A. Vinegar   B. Baking soda
    C. Water   D. None of the above

21. In the treatment of a chemical burn, one should

    A. remove clothing from the patient
    B. be careful not to get the chemical substance on clothing or skin
    C. flush the area with water for 20 to 30 minutes
    D. all of the above

22. Of the following statements, all are true regarding electrical burns EXCEPT:

    A. Domestic injuries are most likely to involve children.
    B. The majority of victims are found to have been electrocuted in the course of their work.
    C. Electrical burns usually do not produce internal injury.
    D. The degree of tissue injury resulting from an electrical burn is related to the resistance of various body tissues.

23. Electricity can cause _____ burns.

    A. contact   B. flash
    C. flame   D. all of the above

24. Bull's eye lesions are characteristically found in _____ burns. 24.___

   A. flash
   B. contact
   C. flame
   D. none of the above

25. Flash burns usually 25.___

   A. are associated with electricity
   B. happen when the victim is close to the flash
   C. have a crater-like appearance
   D. all of the above

26. The two MOST common causes of death from electric injury are 26.___

   A. asphyxia and cardiac arrest
   B. renal failure and stroke
   C. fractures and emboli
   D. liver failure and renal failure

27. The head and neck of an adult account for _____ percent of body surface area. 27.___

   A. 1   B. 9   C. 18   D. 27

Questions 28-30.

DIRECTIONS: In Questions 28 through 30, match the numbered features with the lettered type of burn, listed in Column I, which they characterize. Place the letter of the CORRECT answer in the appropriate space at the right.

COLUMN I

   A. First degree
   B. Second degree
   C. Third degree

28. Blistering subcutaneous edema and severe pain 28.___

29. Reddening and moderate pain 29.___

30. Charred and leathery appearance, usually dry and pale; pain is usually absent 30.___

KEY (CORRECT ANSWERS)

1.	D	11.	B	21.	D
2.	B	12.	D	22.	C
3.	B	13.	C	23.	D
4.	C	14.	D	24.	B
5.	A	15.	D	25.	D
6.	C	16.	A	26.	A
7.	B	17.	C	27.	B
8.	A	18.	B	28.	B
9.	B	19.	A	29.	A
10.	A	20.	C	30.	C

TEST 2

DIRECTIONS: Each question or incomplete statement is followed by several suggested answers or completions. Select the one that BEST answers the question or completes the statement. *PRINT THE LETTER OF THE CORRECT ANSWER IN THE SPACE AT THE RIGHT.*

1. If the cutaneous blood vessel constricts or cardiac output increases, the skin will become   1.___

   A. cool
   B. pale
   C. cyanotic
   D. all of the above

2. The MOST common facial fracture is a fracture of the   2.___

   A. nose
   B. mandible
   C. maxillary bone
   D. cheekbones

3. The MOST common complication of a fracture of the mandible is   3.___

   A. inability to talk
   B. malocclusion
   C. inability to breathe
   D. loss of upward gaze

4. The MOST common signs and symptoms of a zygoma (cheekbone) fracture include   4.___

   A. loss of sensation below the orbit
   B. palpable flattening
   C. loss of upward gaze
   D. all of the above

5. To treat a broken nose, apply   5.___

   A. pressure to control bleeding
   B. cold packs
   C. four tall bandages
   D. A and B *only*

6. Of the following, the MOST common type of orbital fracture is fracture of the _____ orbit.   6.___

   A. lateral
   B. roof of
   C. inferior
   D. medial wall of

7. Fractures of orbits may cause all of the following EXCEPT   7.___

   A. double vision
   B. malocclusion
   C. paralysis of upward gaze
   D. loss of sensation above the eyebrow

8. General management of an eyelid injury would NOT include   8.___

   A. direct pressure to stop the bleeding
   B. making sure the globe is not injured before applying pressure
   C. covering the lid with tight dressing
   D. preserving any fragments and transporting them with the patient

9. Injuries to the neck MUST be considered critical until proven otherwise because the neck houses

    A. the spinal cord
    B. major blood vessels
    C. air passages
    D. all of the above

10. A patient with a neck injury is complaining of shortness of breath and inability to lie down in the supine position. His voice is hoarse.
    The MOST likely injured structure is the

    A. thyroid gland
    B. larynx
    C. trachea
    D. spinal cord

11. The _____ is NOT a solid organ.

    A. pancreas
    B. gallbladder
    C. spleen
    D. liver

12. Which of the following organs bleeds PROFUSELY if disrupted?

    A. Stomach
    B. Ureter
    C. Spleen
    D. Large intestine

13. All of the following are true statements regarding posterior epistaxis EXCEPT:

    A. It is common among young adults.
    B. It is usually more severe than anterior epistaxis.
    C. It is usually associated with hypertension.
    D. There is sometimes no bleeding through the nares.

14. The techniques of management of electrical injuries beyond oxygen administration and monitoring cardiac rhythm include

    A. starting IV and running ringer's lactate wide open to keep the kidney flushed out
    B. sodium bicarbonate at 1 to 2 ampules, to alkalinize the urine
    C. mannitol at 0.5 to 1.0 gm/kg, to induce an osmotic diuresis
    D. all of the above

15. The BEST treatment for injury from lightning is

    A. sodium bicarbonate
    B. prevention
    C. mannitol
    D. oxygen

16. Advice for the prevention of lightning injuries may include all of the following EXCEPT:

    A. Stay low if out in the open, as in a field, lying flat on the ground.
    B. Stay near the open water.
    C. Do not hold on to fishing poles or golf clubs.
    D. If in a car, keep the windows shut.

Questions 17-21.

DIRECTIONS: In Questions 17 through 21, match the numbered description with the lettered term, listed in Column I, with which it is most closely related. Place the letter of the correct answer in the appropriate space at the right.

COLUMN I

A. Contact burn
B. Flash burn
C. Melanin
D. Myoglobin
E. First degree burn

17. Gives skin its color 17.___

18. A protein found in muscle that is released into the circulation after a crush injury or other muscle damage 18.___

19. Endothermal injury caused by the arcing of an electric current 19.___

20. Produced by touching a hot object 20.___

21. Involves only the epidermis, producing very red, painful skin 21.___

Questions 22-24.

DIRECTIONS: In Questions 22 through 24, match the numbered symptoms with the lettered disorder, listed in Column I, which they most likely signal. Place the letter of the correct answer in the appropriate space at the right.

COLUMN I

A. Acute glaucoma
B. Retinal detachment
C. Central retinal artery occlusion

22. Curtain blocking vision with light flashes or dark spots in front of the eye 22.___

23. Eye ache, headache, and seeing halves of light 23.___

24. Sudden, painless loss of vision 24.___

Questions 25-30.

DIRECTIONS: In Questions 25 through 30, match the numbered description with the lettered part of the eye, listed in Column I, which it BEST describes. Place the letter of the CORRECT answer in the appropriate space at the right.

COLUMN I

A. Iris
B. Lens
C. Cornea
D. Aqueous humor
E. Vitreous humor
F. Pupil

25. Adjustable opening within the iris 25.____

26. Fills the space between the cornea and the lens 26.____

27. Jelly-like substance that maintains the shape of the globe 27.____

28. Pigmented tissue made up of muscles and blood vessels that can contract or expand to regulate the size of the pupil 28.____

29. Transparent structure that can alter its thickness in order to focus light on the retina at the back of the eye 29.____

30. Crystal clear anterior segment of the sclera 30.____

KEY (CORRECT ANSWERS)

1. D	11. B	21. E
2. A	12. C	22. B
3. B	13. A	23. A
4. D	14. D	24. C
5. D	15. B	25. F
6. C	16. B	26. D
7. B	17. C	27. E
8. C	18. D	28. A
9. D	19. B	29. B
10. B	20. A	30. C

MUSCULOSKELETAL SYSTEM & INJURIES
EXAMINATION SECTION
TEST 1

DIRECTIONS: Each question or incomplete statement is followed by several suggested answers or completions. Select the one that BEST answers the question or completes the statement. *PRINT THE LETTER OF THE CORRECT ANSWER IN THE SPACE AT THE RIGHT.*

1. All of the following are part of the musculoskeletal system EXCEPT

    A. bones and muscles
    B. ligaments and tendons
    C. spleen and liver
    D. cartilage

    1.___

2. The musculoskeletal system is NOT responsible for

    A. support and shape
    B. clearance of waste products
    C. protection and locomotion
    D. production of red blood cells

    2.___

3. The spinal column performs all of the following functions EXCEPT

    A. protect the spinal cord
    B. support the head and trunk
    C. carry impulses from the brain to the other parts of the body
    D. more than one but not all of the above

    3.___

4. All of the following correlations of rate, area, and cause of incidence are true regarding spinal column injury EXCEPT:

    A. low; cervical and lumbar spine; good support
    B. high; cervical and lumbar spine; lack of support
    C. low; thoracic spine; support of the ribs
    D. low; sacrum; support of the pelvis

    4.___

5. Regarding the rib cage, it is NOT true that the

    A. upper seven pairs of ribs are joined in front by the sternum
    B. next three pairs of ribs are joined by cartilage attached to the sternum
    C. eleventh and twelfth pairs of ribs have no front attachment
    D. clavicle or collarbone does not support the sternum

    5.___

6. Major components of joints include all of the following EXCEPT

    A. bone ends covered with articular cartilage
    B. synovial membrane which produces a lubricating fluid
    C. capsules in a thin elastic layer
    D. ligaments or bands of connective tissue that bind the bones together, allowing some flexibility

    6.___

7. Ball and socket joints provide a range of motion which is

   A. restricted to the left side only of the joint
   B. restricted only to the right side of the joint
   C. wide in all directions
   D. all of the above

8. Pelvis hip bones consist of all of the following EXCEPT the

   A. ileum   B. carpals   C. ischium   D. pubis

9. The functions of skeletal muscles do NOT include

   A. only exerting force by contracting
   B. working in pairs
   C. not moving the bones
   D. tendons attaching the muscles to the bones

10. Among the different types of muscles in the body is (are) _____ muscles.

    A. voluntary   B. involuntary
    C. cardiac   D. all of the above

11. When a bone is broken at the point of impact, it is called a

    A. twisting injury   B. direct injury
    C. fatigue fracture   D. none of the above

12. A fracture occurring at some distance from the impact is referred to as a(n)

    A. pathologic fracture   B. direct injury
    C. indirect injury   D. twisting injury

13. Joints, such as those between the bones of the hand, which allow very subtle and delicate movement are called _____ joints.

    A. ball and socket   B. gliding
    C. pivot   D. all of the above

14. Joints, such as those of the fingers, which permit flexion and extension are called _____ joints.

    A. hinge   B. pivot
    C. gliding   D. ball and socket

15. The _____ is a bone covered by a membrane.

    A. synovial membrane   B. pericardium
    C. periosteum   D. all of the above

16. The strength and hardness of bone is due PRIMARILY to

    A. calcium   B. sodium
    C. phosphorus   D. A and C *only*

17. Smooth or involuntary muscle mostly constitutes the muscle of the internal organs. Such muscle can be found in the walls of the

    A. urinary bladder
    B. blood vessels
    C. digestive system
    D. all of the above

18. Muscle contraction requires energy, which is derived from the metabolism of glucose and results in the production of

    A. galactose
    B. lactic acid
    C. lactose
    D. none of the above

19. Of the following injuries, which one MOST frequently occurs in association with pelvic fracture?

    A. Urinary bladder injury
    B. Femoral head dislocation
    C. Popliteal artery rupture
    D. None of the above

20. The fracture which occurs in children whose bones are still pliable, is a break straight across the bone, and goes only part-way through the bone is called _____ fracture.

    A. spiral
    B. greenstick
    C. impacted
    D. comminuted

21. The injuries in which ligaments are partially torn, usually as a result of the sudden twisting of a joint beyond its normal range of motion, are

    A. strains
    B. sprains
    C. dislocations
    D. none of the above

22. Soft tissue injuries or muscle spasms around a joint characterized by pain on active movement are called

    A. strains
    B. sprains
    C. dislocations
    D. A and B *only*

23. The pre-hospital management of a victim with anterior dislocation of the sternoclavicular joint would MOST likely include a(n)

    A. cold pack sling
    B. air splint
    C. pad axilla
    D. none of the above

24. A victim who sustained a clavicle fracture as a result of a direct blow would MOST likely receive the pre-hospital treatment of a(n)

    A. cold pack sling and swath
    B. air splint
    C. board splint
    D. none of the above

Questions 25-30.

DIRECTIONS: In Questions 25 through 30, match the numbered description with the lettered classification of fracture, listed in the column below, which it BEST describes. Place the letter of the CORRECT answer in the appropriate space at the right.

CLASSIFICATION OF FRACTURES
A. Transverse
B. Spiral
C. Impacted
D. Comminuted
E. Oblique
F. Greenstick

25. Ends of broken bones are jammed into each other.   25.___

26. Break forms an angle to the shaft.   26.___

27. Break is straight across the shaft of a bone.   27.___

28. Bone is fragmented.   28.___

29. Fracture has the appearance of a spring; break twists around the shaft of the bone.   29.___

30. Fracture is incomplete and common in children whose bones are still soft and pliable.   30.___

KEY (CORRECT ANSWERS)

1.	C	16.	D
2.	B	17.	D
3.	C	18.	B
4.	A	19.	A
5.	D	20.	B
6.	C	21.	B
7.	C	22.	A
8.	B	23.	D
9.	C	24.	C
10.	D	25.	C
11.	B	26.	E
12.	C	27.	A
13.	B	28.	D
14.	A	29.	B
15.	C	30.	F

TEST 2

DIRECTIONS: Each question or incomplete statement is followed by several suggested answers or completions. Select the one that BEST answers the question or completes the statement. *PRINT THE LETTER OF THE CORRECT ANSWER IN THE SPACE AT THE RIGHT.*

1. To immobilize a fracture of the _____, use a _____. 1.____

   A. hip; full backboard
   B. foot or ankle; pillow
   C. shoulder or clavicle; sling or swathe
   D. all of the above

2. The MAJOR complication of anterior dislocation of the shoulder is _____ injury. 2.____

   A. radial damage
   B. axillary nerve
   C. subclavian artery
   D. all of the above

3. Possible complications of posterior dislocation of the sternoclavicular joint include 3.____

   A. damage to trachea
   B. damage to esophagus
   C. pneumothorax
   D. all of the above

4. One possible complication of a clavicular fracture may be 4.____

   A. subclavian artery injury
   B. axillary artery injury
   C. Volk-Mannis ischemic contracture
   D. none of the above

5. A victim involved in a motor vehicle accident sustained a fracture of the shaft of the humerus. He has ecchymosis, swelling and deformity of the area. Among the complications he may encounter is _____ nerve injury. 5.____

   A. ulner
   B. radial
   C. median
   D. all of the above

6. Pre-hospital treatment of a fracture of the shaft of the humerus includes 6.____

   A. sling and swathe
   B. padded board splint
   C. hot pack
   D. A and B *only*

7. The MOST likely complication of an elbow fracture (e.g., skateboard injury) is 7.____

   A. Volk-Mannis ischemic contracture
   B. shock
   C. wrist drop
   D. A and C *only*

8. A victim who falls on a hyperextended arm and develops locked painful elbow is MOST likely to develop which of the following complications? 8.____

   A. Ulner nerve injury
   B. Vascular injury
   C. Associated injuries to the rib
   D. All of the above

9. Pre-hospital management of a forearm fracture would include

   A. air splint
   B. padded board splint
   C. all of the above
   D. none of the above

10. The signs and symptoms of dislocation include

    A. an obvious deformity of the joint
    B. swelling at the joint and pain which increases with movement
    C. loss of use of the joint or complaint of a locked or frozen joint
    D. all of the above

11. The MOST common symptom of strain is

    A. pain
    B. discoloration
    C. hematoma
    D. all of the above

12. Among the common symptoms of a sprain is

    A. swelling
    B. discoloration
    C. pain on movement
    D. all of the above

13. Of the following, the FIRST priority of care is for fractures of the

    A. spine
    B. head, rib cage, and pelvis
    C. extremities
    D. none of the above

14. When a bone is broken or dislocated, the process of _____ supplies a substitute support and immobilization to the bone.

    A. traction
    B. splinting
    C. all of the above
    D. none of the above

15. A _____ fracture is the fracture of the wrist that gives a silverfork appearance.

    A. boxer's
    B. colles
    C. nightstick
    D. none of the above

16. A garden spade deformity occurs when a victim

    A. falls on his outstretched hand
    B. falls on his extended wrist
    C. gets his hand slammed in a car door
    D. all of the above

17. General treatment of injuries to the lower extremities includes

    A. pulse and nerve function assessment
    B. manual traction
    C. spinal protection
    D. all of the above

Questions 18-19.

DIRECTIONS: Questions 18 and 19 are to be answered on the basis of the following information.

A victim is hit by a car and suffers hematoma of the scrotum. He is complaining of pain on compression of the iliac wings. You suspect a pelvic fracture.

18. Pre-hospital treatment, after the ABCs, may include

    A. mast
    B. backboard
    C. IV fluid
    D. all of the above

19. Among the possible complications of the above patient's condition is

    A. shock
    B. bladder or urethra injury
    C. associated spinal injury
    D. all of the above

20. A victim who has a dislocated knee may also have

    A. shock
    B. sciatic nerve injury
    C. popliteal artery injury
    D. all of the above

21. A victim who sustained an angulated tibia and fibula fracture is at high risk of developing

    A. shock
    B. compartment syndrome
    C. an associated lumbar spine fracture
    D. all of the above

22. All of the following sets of bones are part of the hand EXCEPT

    A. carpals
    B. metatarsals
    C. metacarpals
    D. phalanges

23. A fracture of the fifth metacarpal MOST typically occurs in

    A. boxers
    B. duelers
    C. wrestlers
    D. none of the above

24. The proximal bony projection of the ulna at the elbow which constitutes the *funny bone* is called the

    A. olecranon
    B. patella
    C. humerus
    D. malleolus

25. The tough bands of tissue connecting bone to bone around a joint or supporting internal organs within the body are called

    A. synovial joints
    B. ligaments
    C. tendons
    D. malleolus

Questions 26-30.

DIRECTIONS: In Questions 26 through 30, match the numbered description with the lettered part of the musculoskeletal system, listed in Column I, which it BEST describes. Place the letter of the CORRECT answer in the appropriate space at the right.

COLUMN I
A. Axial skeleton
B. Appendicular skeleton
C. Tendon
D. Tibia
E. Trochanter

26. The part of the skeleton comprising the upper and lower extremities 26.

27. The part of the skeleton comprising the skull, spinal column and rib cage 27.

28. Either of the two processes below the neck of the femur 28.

29. The fibrous portion of muscle that attaches to bone 29.

30. The shin bone 30.

Questions 31-35.

DIRECTIONS: In Questions 31 through 35, match the numbered description with the lettered part of the musculoskeletal system, listed in Column I, which it BEST describes. Place the letter of the CORRECT answer in the appropriate space at the right.

COLUMN I
A. Diaphysis
B. Epiphysis
C. Periosteum
D. Acetabulum
E. Metatarsals

31. Strong, white, fibrous material which covers the bone 31

32. Portion of spongy bone covered with compact bone 32

33. Central shaft of a long bone composed of compact bone 33

34. Foot bones 34

35. Cup-shaped cavity in which the rounded head of the femur rotates 35

KEY (CORRECT ANSWERS)

1. D
2. B
3. D
4. A
5. B

6. D
7. A
8. B
9. C
10. D

11. A
12. D
13. A
14. B
15. B

16. B
17. D
18. D
19. D
20. C

21. B
22. B
23. A
24. A
25. B

26. B
27. A
28. E
29. C
30. D

31. C
32. B
33. A
34. E
35. D

MEDICAL EMERGENCIES
EXAMINATION SECTION
TEST 1

DIRECTIONS: Each question or incomplete statement is followed by several suggested answers or completions. Select the one that BEST answers the question or completes the statement. *PRINT THE LETTER OF THE CORRECT ANSWER IN THE SPACE AT THE RIGHT.*

1. The state of unresponsiveness from which a patient cannot be roused is called   1.____

    A. stupor   B. coma
    C. drowsiness   D. aura

2. Which of the following cause coma?   2.____

    A. Hypoglycemic shock   B. Epilepsy
    C. Uremia   D. All of the above

3. Management of a comatose patient may include all of the following EXCEPT   3.____

    A. ensuring an open airway, intubating if there is no gag reflex
    B. starting an IV lifeline and administering antibiotics
    C. administering thiamine followed by 50% dextrose
    D. rechecking and recording vital and neurologic signs frequently

4. The one of the following that is NOT a true statement about regulation of insulin is: 4.____

    A. Glucose has a direct effect on pancreatic activity in secreting insulin.
    B. Excess glucose in the system stimulates the pancreas.
    C. Excess glucose in the system inhibits the pancreas.
    D. The pancreas secretes insulin, causing glucose to enter into the cell until the normal level in the bloodstream returns.

5. When an insulin deficiency exists, all of the following may occur EXCEPT: 5.____

    A. Glucose cannot enter a cell fast enough to be an adequate supply; therefore, glucose accumulates in the blood, causing osmolarity to rise.
    B. The cell must burn fats and proteins to form energy.
    C. The metabolism of fats forms bases as a by product, causing alkalosis.
    D. The metabolism of fats forms acids as a byproduct, causing acidosis.

6. It is NOT an effect of hyperinsulinemia that   6.____

    A. severe hyperglycemia develops
    B. neurons require a constant supply of glucose, which is not available
    C. convulsions and coma develop if hypoglycemia is extreme
    D. the amount of glucose in the bloodstream falls below normal limits

7. Diabetic ketoacidosis occurs when the blood sugar becomes   7.____

    A. normal   B. high
    C. low   D. none of the above

8. The MAIN defect resulting from diabetes mellitus is

    A. excessive absorption of glucose from the kidneys
    B. excessive absorption of glucose from the gastrointestinal tract
    C. inability of the pancreas to secrete insulin
    D. none of the above

9. The common signs and symptoms of diabetes mellitus include all of the following EXCEPT

    A. polyuria
    B. anuria
    C. polydipsia
    D. polyphagia

10. In the initial treatment of diabetes ketoacidosis, it is NOT necessary to

    A. start intravenous therapy, usually with a normal saline solution
    B. maintain an airway and administer oxygen
    C. administer intravenous lasix
    D. draw blood samples

11. Among the common signs and symptoms of hypoglycemia are included

    A. weak and rapid pulse
    B. cold, clammy, pale skin
    C. weakness, lack of coordination, and seizures
    D. all of the above

12. One would do all of the following to manage hypoglycemia EXCEPT

    A. start an IV of dextrose in water
    B. administer intravenous insulin
    C. administer a 50% glucose IV push
    D. administer orange juice sweetened with sugar if the patient is awake, alert, and able to swallow

13. _____ is a sudden, temporary loss of consciousness usually lasting less than 5 minutes.

    A. Syncope
    B. Coma
    C. Drowsiness
    D. Stupor

14. The condition of syncope usually develops due to which of the following pathophysiologic processes?

    A. Seizure activity
    B. Inadequate glucose supply to the brain
    C. Inadequate oxygen supply to the brain
    D. All of the above

15. The common question to ask of bystanders observing a patient in the condition of syncope is:

    A. What exactly did they see happen?
    B. Did the patient make any convulsive movements?
    C. How long did it take the patient to recover consciousness?
    D. All of the above

16. The BEST position for a patient who has a syncopal episode in the sitting position is

   A. standing
   B. sitting
   C. recumbent
   D. half-sitting

17. The BEST pre-hospital management of a patient who has syncope is to

   A. keep the patient in a sitting position
   B. elevate the patient's lower extremities for 10 to 20 seconds to facilitate venous return to the heart
   C. administer furosemide
   D. administer epinephrine

18. The type of seizures characterized by momentary loss of awareness without loss of motor tone is the _____ seizure.

   A. grand mal
   B. psychomotor
   C. petit mal
   D. focal motor

19. The seizures often characterized by a sudden alteration in personality sometimes preceded by dizziness or a sensation of a peculiar, metallic taste in the mouth are _____ seizures.

   A. psychomotor
   B. grand mal
   C. focal motor
   D. petit mal

20. The seizures characterized by loss of consciousness, tonic-clonic movements, and sometimes tongue-biting, incontinence, and mental confusion are _____ seizures.

   A. psychomotor
   B. focal motor
   C. grand mal
   D. none of the above

21. A state in which a patient can be roused by a painful stimulus but not a vocal stimulus is called

   A. drowsiness
   B. stupor
   C. coma
   D. stroke

22. Of the following, the MOST common type of syncope is

   A. syncope of cardiac origin
   B. vasovagal syncope
   C. postural syncope
   D. all of the above

Questions 23-25.

DIRECTIONS: In Questions 23 through 25, match each numbered factor with the lettered type of syncope it causes, listed in Column I. Place the letter of the CORRECT answer in the appropriate space at the right.

COLUMN I

23. Phenothiazine

24. Pain

25. Aortic stenosis

   A. Simple syncope
   B. Postural syncope
   C. Syncope of cardiac origin

KEY (CORRECT ANSWERS)

1. B
2. D
3. B
4. C
5. C

6. A
7. B
8. C
9. B
10. C

11. D
12. B
13. A
14. D
15. D

16. C
17. B
18. C
19. A
20. C

21. B
22. B
23. B
24. A
25. C

———

TEST 2

DIRECTIONS: Each question or incomplete statement is followed by several suggested answers or completions. Select the one that BEST answers the question or completes the statement. *PRINT THE LETTER OF THE CORRECT ANSWER IN THE SPACE AT THE RIGHT.*

1. Causes of seizures include   1._____

   A. recent or remote stroke
   B. hypoxemia and hypoglycemia
   C. withdrawal from alcohol
   D. all of the above

2. The MOST common cause of epilepsy is   2._____

   A. meningitis
   B. idiopathic
   C. eclampsia of pregnancy
   D. space-occupying lesion

3. The FIRST phase of a seizure is the _____ phase.   3._____

   A. clonic
   B. tonic
   C. hypertonic
   D. autonomic discharge

4. The MOST serious threat of a seizure is   4._____

   A. posterior shoulder dislocation
   B. hypoxemia
   C. hypertension
   D. neck fracture

5. The occurrence of two or more seizures without a period of consciousness in between is called   5._____

   A. psychomotor seizure
   B. status epilepticus
   C. grand mal seizure
   D. none of the above

6. The drug of choice for status epilepticus is   6._____

   A. phenobarbital
   B. phenytoin
   C. diazepam
   D. carbamazepam

7. The MOST common cause of status epilepticus in adults is   7._____

   A. hypoglycemia
   B. hyponatremia
   C. failure to take prescribed anti-seizure medication
   D. overdose of anti-seizure medication

8. _____ is the relatively sudden onset of a neurologic deficit that corresponds to the distribution of a cerebral artery and lasts more than 24 hours.   8._____

   A. Syncope   B. Stroke   C. Seizure   D. Stupor

9. The MOST common type of stroke is   9._____

   A. thrombostic
   B. embolic
   C. hemorrhagic
   D. none of the above

10. The signs and symptoms of thrombotic carotid system blockage include all of the following EXCEPT

    A. hemiplegia
    B. double vision
    C. unilateral numbness
    D. aphasia

11. The common signs and symptoms of thrombotic vertebrobasilar system blockage do NOT include

    A. slurred speech
    B. difficulty in swallowing
    C. hemiparesis
    D. dizziness or vertigo

12. Embolic strokes MOST commonly occur in patients with

    A. rheumatic heart disease
    B. atrial fibrillation
    C. myocardial infarction
    D. all of the above

13. The term *pseudoseizure* refers to seizures occurring

    A. without an irritable focus in the brain
    B. with an irritable focus in the temporal lobe
    C. due to an irritable focus in the frontal lobe
    D. post-traumatically

14. The term *posticital* refers to the period _____ the convulsive stage of a seizure.

    A. prior to
    B. during
    C. after
    D. prior to and during

15. The oral hypoglycemia agents most commonly used today include all of the following EXCEPT

    A. dymelor and diabinse
    B. humulin and nevolin
    C. glucotrol and tolinase
    D. diabeta and micronase

16. The abdominal cavity as a whole is lined by a smooth membranous layer called the

    A. periosteum
    B. peritoneum
    C. endocardium
    D. pericardium

17. All of the following are hollow abdominal organs EXCEPT the

    A. gallbladder
    B. uterus
    C. spleen
    D. bladder

18. The _____ is NOT a solid abdominal organ.

    A. stomach   B. liver   C. kidneys   D. pancreas

19. Possible causes of right upper quadrant pain include all of the following EXCEPT

    A. biliary colic
    B. liver abscess
    C. diverticulitis
    D. pancreatitis

20. Intracerebral hemorrhage is nearly always the result of

    A. trauma
    B. hypertension
    C. atherosclerosis
    D. renal failure

Questions 21-25.

DIRECTIONS: In Questions 21 through 25, match the numbered description of a disorder with the lettered disorder it defines, listed in Column I. Place the letter of the CORRECT answer in the appropriate space at the right.

COLUMN I

A. Aphasia
B. Aura
C. Dysarthria
D. Hemiparesis
E. Polydipsia

21. Interferes with proper articulation of words; slurring of speech   21._____
22. Pre-monitor sensation of an impending epileptic seizure   22._____
23. Defect in speaking or in understanding speech   23._____
24. Excessive thirst and/or excessive intake of fluids   24._____
25. Weakness on one side of the body   25._____

KEY (CORRECT ANSWERS)

1.	D	11.	C
2.	B	12.	D
3.	B	13.	A
4.	B	14.	C
5.	B	15.	B
6.	C	16.	B
7.	C	17.	C
8.	B	18.	A
9.	A	19.	C
10.	B	20.	B

21. C
22. B
23. A
24. E
25. D

MEDICAL EMERGENCIES
EXAMINATION SECTION
TEST 1

DIRECTIONS: Each question or incomplete statement is followed by several suggested answers or completions. Select the one that BEST answers the question or completes the statement. *PRINT THE LETTER OF THE CORRECT ANSWER IN THE SPACE AT THE RIGHT.*

1. The possible causes of left upper quadrant pain include all of the following EXCEPT   1._____
   - A. ruptured spleen
   - B. gastric ulcer
   - C. ovarian cyst
   - D. myocardial infarction

2. The posterior boundary of the abdomen is formed by the   2._____
   - A. psoasmuscles
   - B. quadratus lumborum muscles
   - C. spine
   - D. all of the above

3. All of the following statements about esophagitis are true EXCEPT: 3._____
   - A. It results from a reflux of gastric acid into the esophagus.
   - B. It is more common among the elderly, the obese, and women.
   - C. It is more common among the young, the thin, and men.
   - D. The patient usually complains of burning substernal pain and/or difficulty swallowing.

4. The BEST pre-hospital management of esophagitis is   4._____
   - A. intravenous morphine
   - B. oral acetominophen
   - C. oral non-steroidal anti-inflammatory drugs
   - D. no treatment

5. The causes of esophageal rupture do NOT include   5._____
   - A. endotracheal intubation
   - B. ingestion of caustic substances
   - C. ingestion of a foreign body
   - D. esophageal obturator airway

6. Proper pre-hospital management of esophageal perforation would include all of the following EXCEPT   6._____
   - A. maintaining an airway
   - B. isoproterenol drip
   - C. monitoring vital signs
   - D. replacing the fluid volume

7. All of the following are among the causes of bowel obstruction EXCEPT   7._____
   - A. strangulated inguinal hernia
   - B. esophageal carcinoma

C. adhesions from previous surgery
D. intussusception

8. Of the following signs and symptoms, the one which does NOT signal acute cholecystitis is

   A. crampy right upper quadrant or epigastric pain
   B. pain radiating to the tip of the right scapula
   C. pain radiating to the buttocks
   D. tenderness in the right upper quadrant

9. If the kidney ceases to excrete the waste products of protein metabolism, the patient develops

   A. hyponamia
   B. hypokalemia
   C. uremia
   D. hyperglycemia

10. If a patient on renal dialysis develops hypotension in a pre-hospital setting, _____ should be administered.

    A. epinephrine
    B. dopamine
    C. 50 ml of normal saline IV
    D. none of the above

11. The BEST emergency treatment of hyperkalemia in a patient on renal dialysis is

    A. 10% calcium chloride IV
    B. furosemide IV
    C. epinephrine
    D. hydrochlorothiazid

12. If a dialysis patient develops sudden dyspnea and hypotension cyanosis

    A. disconnect him from the dialysis machine
    B. place him in the left lateral recumbent position with head tilted down about 10°
    C. transport him immediately
    D. all of the above

13. _____ is an exaggerated allergic reaction characterized by bronchospasm and vascular collapse.

    A. Orthostatic hypotension
    B. Anaphylaxis
    C. Status asthmaticus
    D. None of the above

14. Common causes of anaphylaxis include

    A. bee stings
    B. oral penicillin
    C. peanuts and fish
    D. all of the above

15. A protein produced in response to the presence of a specific foreign substance to destroy or inactivate that foreign substance is called a(n)

    A. allergen
    B. antigen
    C. antibody
    D. basophil

16. An agent that stimulates the formation of a specific protective protein is called a(n)   16._____

    A. antigen B. antibody
    C. mast cell D. basophil

17. The physiologic effects of histamine include all of the following EXCEPT   17._____

    A. systemic vasodilation
    B. bronchodilatation
    C. increased permeability of blood vessels
    D. decreased myocardial contractility

18. _____ is NOT a physiologic effect of a slow-reacting substance.   18._____

    A. Increased force of cardiac contraction
    B. Increased leakiness of blood vessels
    C. Dysrhythmias
    D. Decreased coronary blood flow

19. The common respiratory symptoms of anaphylaxis include   19._____

    A. laryngeal edema B. hoarseness or stridorous
    C. tightness in the chest D. all of the above

20. The one of the following which is NOT a common cardiovascular symptom of anaphylaxis is   20._____

    A. tachycardia B. hypertension
    C. dysrhythmias D. decreased cardiac output

Questions 21-25.

DIRECTIONS: In Questions 21 through 25, match the numbered definition with the lettered term, listed in Column I, which it BEST describes. Place the letter of the CORRECT answer in the appropriate space at the right.

COLUMN I
A. Diverticulosis
B. Melena
C. Retroperitoneal
D. Hematemesis
E. Hemodialysis

21. The area of the abdomen behind the peritoneum which contains the kidneys, ureter, and great vessels   21._____

22. The process of removing noxious agents and excess fluid from the blood by diffusion through a semi-permeable membrane   22._____

23. Vomiting blood   23._____

24. The passage of dark, tarry stools, signifying blood in the gastrointestinal tract   24._____

25. A cause of painless lower gastrointestinal bleeding   25._____

KEY (CORRECT ANSWERS)

1. C
2. D
3. C
4. D
5. A

6. B
7. B
8. C
9. C
10. C

11. A
12. D
13. B
14. D
15. C

16. A
17. B
18. A
19. D
20. B

21. C
22. E
23. D
24. B
25. A

TEST 2

DIRECTIONS: Each question or incomplete statement is followed by several suggested answers or completions. Select the one that BEST answers the question or completes the statement. *PRINT THE LETTER OF THE CORRECT ANSWER IN THE SPACE AT THE RIGHT.*

1. Among the following, the MOST dangerous complication of anaphylactic shock is   1.____

    A. dyspnea
    B. hoarseness or stridor
    C. urticaria
    D. wheezes

2. The FIRST priority for the management of a patient with anaphylactic shock is to   2.____

    A. treat hypotension
    B. treat dysrhythmias
    C. protect airway
    D. increase cardiac contractility

3. The drug of choice for an anaphylactic reaction is   3.____

    A. diphenhydramine
    B. aminophyline
    C. hydrocortisone
    D. epinephrine

Questions 4-7.

DIRECTIONS: In Questions 4 through 7, match the numbered definition with the lettered term, listed in Column I, which it BEST describes. Place the letter of the CORRECT answer in the appropriate space at the right.

COLUMN I
A. Allergen
B. Allergy
C. Mast cell
D. Basophil

4. A white blood cell that contains chemical mediators of the immune/inflammatory process   4.____

5. An abnormal susceptibility upon re-exposure to a substance that does not ordinarily cause adverse symptoms in the average person   5.____

6. A substance that produces an allergic reaction in a sensitive individual   6.____

7. A mobile chemical mediator factory that releases histamine and related substances in response to an antigen/antibody reaction   7.____

8. Hypertension may be caused by the ingestion of all of the following agents EXCEPT   8.____

    A. amphetamines
    B. nicotine
    C. narcotics
    D. lead

9. Possible causative agents for a burn in the mouth include   9.____

    A. iodine phenol
    B. lye and acids
    C. pine oil and silver nitrate
    D. all of the above

131

10. The common signs and symptoms of organophosphate poisoning do NOT include

   A. weakness or paralysis
   B. tremors
   C. dry mouth
   D. pulmonary edema

11. The one of the following that is NOT among the causative agents of bradycardia is

   A. cocaine   B. digitalis   C. cyanide   D. narcotics

12. A constricted pupil can be attributed to ingestion of or exposure to any of the following agents EXCEPT

   A. narcotics
   B. LSD
   C. organophosphates
   D. nutmeg and darvon

13. A dilated pupil cannot be caused by the ingestion of

   A. cyanide or carbon monoxide
   B. atropin or amphetamines
   C. jimson weed
   D. barbiturates or doriden

14. The vast majority (approximately 75%) of poisoning in the United States occur in

   A. children under 5 years of age
   B. adolescents
   C. young adults
   D. adults older than 50 years of age

15. The poisoning of children under five years of age is USUALLY caused by

   A. barbiturates
   B. nsaid
   C. alcohol
   D. household products

16. A bitter almond smell may be associated with poisoning by

   A. alcohol
   B. chloral hydrate
   C. cyanide
   D. methyl salicylate

17. A garlicky smell is associated with _____ poisoning.

   A. arsenic
   B. organophosphate
   C. phosphorous
   D. all of the above

18. Of the following, the contraindications for inducing vomiting are

   A. stupor and seizures
   B. pregnancy and acute MI
   C. corrosive and hydrocarbon ingestion
   D. tylenol and aspirin poisoning with no symptomatology

19. When no contraindications exist, the USUAL method is to administer _____ ml of _____ of Ipecac by _____.

   A. 30; syrup; mouth
   B. 10; solution; IV
   C. 2; solution; IM
   D. any of the above

20. If a patient is stuporous due to poisoning, you should NOT   20.____
    A. pass a nasogastric tube before intubation
    B. maintain an open airway
    C. administer oxygen
    D. perform endotracheal intubation to protect the airway

Questions 21-25.

DIRECTIONS: In Questions 21 through 25, match the numbered poisoning agent with the lettered odor, listed in Column I, associated with it. Place the letter of the CORRECT answer in the appropriate space at the right.

<u>COLUMN I</u>
A. Acetone
B. Pear
C. Violet
D. Camphor
E. Wintergreen

21. Methyl salicylate   21.____

22. Turpentine   22.____

23. Camphor   23.____

24. Aspirin   24.____

25. Chloral hydrate   25.____

KEY (CORRECT ANSWERS)

1. B
2. C
3. D
4. D
5. B

6. A
7. C
8. C
9. D
10. C

11. A
12. B
13. C
14. A
15. D

16. C
17. D
18. D
19. A
20. A

21. E
22. C
23. D
24. A
25. B

MEDICAL EMERGENCIES
EXAMINATION SECTION
TEST 1

DIRECTIONS: Each question or incomplete statement is followed by several suggested, answers or completions. Select the one that BEST answers the question or completes the statement. *PRINT THE LETTER OF THE CORRECT ANSWER IN THE SPACE AT THE RIGHT.*

1. The BEST pre-hospital management of an alert patient who swallowed a caustic agent is 1.____

    A. a neutralizing substance
    B. charcoal
    C. milk
    D. ipecac

2. All of the following contain alkalis EXCEPT 2.____

    A. purex bleach
    B. slate cleaners
    C. hair dyes
    D. washing powders

3. All of the following contain acids EXCEPT 3.____

    A. paint removers
    B. swimming pool cleaners
    C. toilet bowl cleaners
    D. bleach disinfectants

4. The drug of choice for organophosphate poisoning is 4.____

    A. penicillamine
    B. BAL
    C. atropin
    D. amyl nitrate

5. Effective treatment of an envenomed snake bite would include all of the following EXCEPT 5.____

    A. splinting the bitten extremity
    B. allowing the victim to walk on the bitten leg
    C. not permitting the victim to drink alcohol
    D. getting a description of the snake

6. Compared to dog bites, human bites are _____ dangerous. 6.____

    A. less
    B. more
    C. equally
    D. none of the above

7. The treatment of choice for a human bite is to 7.____

    A. clean the wound as thoroughly as possible with lots of soap and water
    B. administer antibiotic immediately
    C. administer tetanus toxoid
    D. all of the above

8. A physiological state of adaptation to a drug, usually characterized by tolerance to the drug's effects and a withdrawal syndrome if the drug is stopped, is called 8.____

    A. tolerance
    B. physical dependence
    C. psychologic dependence
    D. drug addiction

9. _____ is the emotional state of craving a drug to maintain a feeling of well-being.

   A. Drug abuse
   B. Withdrawal syndrome
   C. Psychologic dependence
   D. Physical dependence

10. The form of alcohol consumed by humans in alcoholic beverages is

    A. ethanol
    B. methanol
    C. ethylene glycol
    D. all of the above

11. Poisoning due to _____ may cause blindness.

    A. ethanol
    B. methanol
    C. ethylene glycol
    D. none of the above

12. Ethylene glycol poisoning may cause renal damage, which usually occurs after _____ hours.

    A. 2 to 4
    B. 4 to 8
    C. 12 to 24
    D. 24 to 72

13. Pre-hospital management of methanol poisoning includes

    A. activated charcoal by IV
    B. milk
    C. whiskey
    D. all of the above

14. The toxicity of carbon monoxide is due PRIMARILY to its affinity for

    A. destroying the bone
    B. hemoglobin in red blood cells
    C. the kidney
    D. the heart

15. Treatment of carbon monoxide poisoning may include

    A. removal of the patient from the exposure environment
    B. administration of 100% oxygen by tight-fitting, non-rebreathing mask
    C. sodium thiosulfate
    D. all of the above

16. Among the following, the drug of choice for treatment of cyanide poisoning is

    A. BAL
    B. amyl nitrate
    C. sodium carbonate
    D. epinephrine

Questions 17-20.

DIRECTIONS: In Questions 17 through 20, match the numbered symptoms with the lettered snake or spider listed in Column I whose bite would be MOST likely to induce those symptoms. Place the letter of the CORRECT answer in the appropriate space at the right.

COLUMN I

A. Black widow spider
B. Brown recluse spider
C. Coral snake
D. Pit viper

17. Muscular rigidity in the abdomen and shoulder ptosis; eyelid edema   17.____

18. Metallic or rubber taste in mouth; fasciculation; syncope; shock   18.____

19. Absence of pain and swelling; muscular incoordination; difficulty in swallowing and phonation   19.____

20. Lesion appears as bullseye; hemolysis; thrombocytopenia; kidney failure; death   20.____

Questions 21-25.

DIRECTIONS: In Questions 21 through 25, match the numbered plant with the lettered poison, listed in Column I, which it may contain. Place the letter of the CORRECT answer in the appropriate space at the right.

COLUMN I

A. Cyanide
B. Atropine
C. Tyramine
D. LSD
E. Calcium oxalate

21. Philodendron, jack-in-the-pulpit; dieffenbachia   21.____

22. Mistletoe   22.____

23. Apricot   23.____

24. Morning glory   24.____

25. Jimson weed, deadly nightshade   25.____

KEY (CORRECT ANSWERS)

1. C
2. B
3. A
4. C
5. B

6. B
7. A
8. B
9. C
10. A

11. B
12. D
13. C
14. B
15. D

16. B
17. A
18. D
19. C
20. B

21. E
22. C
23. A
24. D
25. B

TEST 2

DIRECTIONS: Each question or incomplete statement is followed by several suggested, answers or completions. Select the one that BEST answers the question or completes the statement. *PRINT THE LETTER OF TEE CORRECT ANSWER IN THE SPACE AT THE RIGHT.*

1. Nerve cells contain a special enzyme whose job is to inactivate acetylcholine after it has crossed the synapse from one nerve cell to another.
   This enzyme is

   A. atropin
   B. cholinesterase
   C. methylene chloride
   D. tetrachloroethylene

   1.____

2. A chronic disorder characterized by the compulsive use of a substance that results in physical, psychologic, or social harm to the user is

   A. tolerance
   B. drug abuse
   C. drug addiction
   D. none of the above

   2.____

3. When carrying out the physical assessment of a patient known or suspected to be under the influence of drugs, the MOST important thing to evaluate is the patient's

   A. state of consciousness
   B. heart rate
   C. blood pressure
   D. temperature

   3.____

4. All of the following are common street names of amphetamines EXCEPT

   A. dexies, footballs, oranges
   B. bonita, bambita
   C. blue cheers, California sunshine
   D. benzies, cartwheels, hearts, peaches, rose

   4.____

5. Of the following, the MOST common street names of cocaine are

   A. bernice, big c, blow, burese, nose candy
   B. dama blanca, gold dust, happy dust, zoom
   C. speed ball, liquid lady, paradise
   D. all of the above

   5.____

6. Yellow jackets, blue devils, blue birds, and blue heaven are the common street names for

   A. barbiturates   B. LSD   C. heroin   D. marijuana

   6.____

7. _____ is commonly referred to as china white, horse, harry, smack, and bianco.

   A. Cocaine
   B. PCP (phencyclidine)
   C. Heroin
   D. Mescaline

   7.____

8. Among the following, the drug of choice to treat narcotic overdose is

   A. atropine   B. naloxone   C. epinephrine   D. BAL

   8.____

9. The initial management of barbiturate overdose may include all of the following EXCEPT

   A. sodium bicarbonate
   B. activated charcoal
   C. atropine sulphate
   D. IV lifeline with lactated ringer's

   9.____

10. A patient has an unwarranted sense that people have hostile intentions towards him. He is in a state of

   A. schizophrenia
   B. paranoia
   C. hallucination
   D. dementia

11. Among the following, which is NOT a sign or symptom of amphetamine toxicity?

   A. Hyperpyresia
   B. Paranoia
   C. Miosis
   D. Hypertension

12. Important clues to alcoholism include all of the following EXCEPT

   A. an unexplained history of repeated gastrointestinal problems
   B. green tongue syndrome
   C. cigarette burns on clothing from falling asleep with a lit cigarette
   D. needle track marks on the forearm

13. Wernicke's encephalopathy is NOT characterized by

   A. persistent seizures
   B. cranial nerve palsy
   C. dementia
   D. ataxia

14. The most IMMEDIATE danger to an acutely intoxicated person due to alcohol is

   A. seizures
   B. subdural hematoma
   C. death from respiratory depression
   D. dysrhythmias

15. One of the MOST serious syndromes resulting from alcohol withdrawal is

   A. esophageal varices
   B. delirium tremens
   C. green tongue syndrome
   D. pancreatitis

16. French _____ levine tubes (nasogastric) should be used for an adult.

   A. 10   B. 12   C. 16   D. 24

17. The MOST reliable indication that the tube has reached the right place is when

   A. it is down about 20 inches
   B. a rapid return of gastric contents occurs upon aspiration with a syringe
   C. a rapid return of air bubbles occurs upon aspiration with a syringe
   D. all of the above

18. Objects that harbor microorganisms and can transmit them to others are called

   A. fomites
   B. reservoirs
   C. carriers
   D. none of the above

19. The disease characterized by fever, conjunctivitis, cough, and a blotchy red rash is

   A. measles
   B. rubella
   C. mumps
   D. chickenpox

Questions 20-25.

DIRECTIONS: In Questions 20 through 25, match the numbered definition with the lettered term from the list below that it MOST accurately describes. Place the letter of the CORRECT answer in the appropriate space at the right.

COLUMN I

A. Reservoir
B. Carrier
C. Communicable period
D. Intubation period
E. Contagious
F. Nosocomial infection

20. Person who harbors an infectious agent and, although not himself ill, can transmit the infection to another person. 20.____

21. Disease that is readily transmissible from one person to another. 21.____

22. Place where germs live and multiply. 22.____

23. Period during which an infected person is capable of transmitting his illness to someone else. 23.____

24. Period from infection until the appearance of the first symptoms of a disease. 24.____

25. Infection acquired from a health-care setting. 25.____

KEY (CORRECT ANSWERS)

1. B
2. C
3. A
4. C
5. D

6. A
7. C
8. B
9. C
10. B

11. C
12. D
13. A
14. C
15. B

16. C
17. B
18. A
19. A
20. B

21. E
22. A
23. C
24. D
25. F

MEDICAL EMERGENCIES
EXAMINATION SECTION
TEST 1

DIRECTIONS: Each question or incomplete statement is followed by several suggested answers or completions. Select the one that BEST answers the question or completes the statement. *PRINT THE LETTER OF THE CORRECT ANSWER IN THE SPACE AT THE RIGHT.*

1. The MOST common mode of transmission of measles is   1.____

   A. sexual contact
   B. blood transfusion
   C. aerosolized droplets
   D. food-borne

2. The disease that occurs MOST commonly in winter and spring and is characterized by fever along with swelling and tenderness of one of the salivary glands is   2.____

   A. mumps
   B. rubella
   C. roseola
   D. chickenpox

3. Painful inflammation of the testicles (orchitis) in as many as 25 percent of cases, with sterility as a possible result is a complication of   3.____

   A. german measles
   B. mumps
   C. roseola
   D. varicella

4. Rubella may cause severe abnormalities in the developing fetus, including   4.____

   A. deafness
   B. cataracts
   C. heart defect
   D. all of the above

5. A young patient with fever, severe headache, stiff neck, change in state of consciousness, and bluish rash PROBABLY has   5.____

   A. subdural hematoma
   B. meningococcal meningitis
   C. streptococcal meningitis
   D. infectious mononucleosis

6. An EMT transferring a patient with suspected meningococcal infection should   6.____

   A. wear a surgical mask
   B. place all disposable material in a plastic bag after finishing the call
   C. disinfect any articles that have come in contact with the patient's secretions
   D. all of the above

7. When an EMT has close contact with a patient with meningococcal meningitis, he may be required to take _____ prophylactically.   7.____

   A. erythromycin
   B. rifampin
   C. penicillin
   D. gentamicin

143

8. Signs and symptoms of hepatitis includes

   A. fever, anorexia, nausea, and vomiting
   B. sudden distaste for cigarettes among smokers
   C. dark urine and jaundice
   D. all of the above

9. What precaution should be taken when dealing with a patient with HIV?

   A. Wear gloves
   B. Wear a gown
   C. Universal precaution
   D. Barrier protection

10. The immunizations recommended for paramedics in general include

    A. DPT in childhood and tetanus booster every 10 years
    B. MMR and polio
    C. hepatitis
    D. all of the above

11. The communicable period of AIDS is

    A. not known
    B. 3 weeks after exposure
    C. 5 weeks after exposure
    D. 10 weeks after exposure

12. The normal physiologic changes in the cardiovascular systems of the elderly include all of the following EXCEPT

    A. heart atrophy
    B. hypertension
    C. decline in cardiac output
    D. bradycardia

13. The normal physiologic changes in the respiratory systems of the elderly do NOT include

    A. increased residual volume
    B. declining arterial PO_2
    C. increased vital capacity
    D. decreased cough and gag reflexes

14. The one of the following that is NOT a normal physiologic change in the renal system of an elderly person is

    A. loss of functioning nephron units
    B. hypokalemia
    C. decreased renal blood flow
    D. all of the above

15. All of the following statements are true regarding the digestive system of the elderly EXCEPT:

    A. A decrease in the number of taste buds with age along with changes in olfactory receptors lead to reduced ability to taste and smell.
    B. A decrease in appetite can lead, over a period of time, to various degrees of malnutrition.
    C. Dental loss is a normal result of the aging process.
    D. Gastric secretions are reduced with age.

16. Anatomists and physiologists examining the brains of the elderly report that brain weight can decline as much as _____ percent by age 80.

    A. 5   B. 17   C. 25   D. 50

17. Aging brings about widespread changes in the musculo-skeletal system, including a decrease in

    A. bone mass
    B. height
    C. muscle mass
    D. all of the above

18. The MOST common cause of drug toxicity in the elderly is

    A. digitalis
    B. diuretics
    C. phenothiazines
    D. steroids

19. _____ is a chronic deterioration of mental functions.

    A. Delirium
    B. Dementia
    C. Amnesia
    D. Delusion

20. A pathologic reduction of bone mass to the degree that the skeleton can no longer perform its supportive function is called

    A. hypertrophy
    B. osteoporosis
    C. spondylosis
    D. all of the above

21. Elderly patients should be considered SERIOUSLY ill if they experience

    A. acute confusion or any other sudden change in mental state
    B. the acute onset or worsening of chest pain and/or dyspnea
    C. a fall or any significant trauma
    D. all of the above

22. The INITIAL infection of syphilis produces an ulcerative lesion called

    A. chancroid
    B. chancre
    C. granuloma
    D. guma

Questions 23-25.

DIRECTIONS: In Questions 23 through 25, match the numbered description with the lettered disease, listed in Column I, to which it is related. Place the letter of the CORRECT answer in the appropriate space at the right.

COLUMN I

    A. Gonorrhea
    B. Herpes simplex type II
    C. Syphilis

23. Treponema pallidum is a causative organism.

24. There is usually a purulent discharge from the urethra and often pain on urination starting a few days after the exposure.

25. In women, the vesicle occurs initially on the cervix, and in men lesions are more common on the penis.

Questions 26-30.

DIRECTIONS: In Questions 26 through 30, match the numbered precautions with the lettered disease, listed in Column I, which they can prevent. Place the letter of the CORRECT answer in the appropriate space at the right.

COLUMN I

A. Mumps
B. Rubella
C. Chickenpox
D. AIDS
E. Meningitis

26. Mask if not immune; PEI advised for all female paramedics. 26.___
27. Mask if not immune; PEI advised for all male paramedics. 27.___
28. Mask and antibiotic prophylaxis for some types. 28.___
29. Shower and change clothes. 29.___
30. Mask, gloves, gown, wash hands, extreme care with needles. 30.___

KEY (CORRECT ANSWERS)

1. C	11. A	21. D
2. A	12. A	22. B
3. B	13. C	23. C
4. D	14. B	24. A
5. B	15. C	25. B
6. D	16. B	26. B
7. B	17. D	27. A
8. D	18. A	28. E
9. C	19. B	29. C
10. D	20. B	30. D

TEST 2

DIRECTIONS: Each question or incomplete statement is followed by several suggested answers or completions. Select the one that BEST answers the question or completes the statement. *PRINT THE LETTER OF THE CORRECT ANSWER IN THE SPACE AT THE RIGHT.*

1. Factors that increase internal heat production include all of the following EXCEPT   1.____

    A. physical exertion
    B. radiation
    C. response to infection
    D. hyperthyroidism

2. Heat absorption is NOT increased by   2.____

    A. locking children in parked automobiles in the summer
    B. working in hot conditions (bakeries, steel mills)
    C. working in an air-conditioned office
    D. living in confined, unventilated, hot quarters

3. To treat heat cramps, do all of the following EXCEPT   3.____

    A. move the patient to a cool environment and have him lie down if he feels faint
    B. massage the cramping muscles
    C. if the patient is not nauseated, give him one or two glasses of a salt-containing solution
    D. if the patient is nauseated, start IV with normal saline

4. To manage heat exhaustion, it is NOT necessary to   4.____

    A. move the patient into a cool environment and take off his excess clothing
    B. if the patient's temperature is elevated, sponge him with tepid water
    C. give dextrose water by mouth
    D. monitor cardiac rhythm and vital signs

5. Common signs and symptoms of heat stroke include   5.____

    A. confused, delirious, or even comatose state
    B. tremors, seizures, fixed and dilated pupils
    C. elevated temperature above 40.6°C
    D. all of the above

6. Management of heat stroke may include all of the following EXCEPT   6.____

    A. establishing an airway and administering oxygen
    B. cooling the patient as rapidly as possible
    C. monitoring axillary temperature every 5 minutes
    D. being prepared to treat seizures

7. Among the people at greatest risk of suffering hypothermia are included all of the following EXCEPT   7.____

    A. the elderly
    B. young adults
    C. alcoholics
    D. people with chronic illnesses

8. To treat frostbite

   A. rub snow on the frostbitten part
   B. massage or rub the frostbitten area
   C. rewarm the patient with water
   D. allow the victim to smoke

9. The suggested radiation kit for ambulances includes

   A. Geiger-Mueller instrument
   B. dosimeter badge for each paramedic and EMT
   C. several sets of surgical hoods, gowns, and shoe covers
   D. all of the above

10. Pneumonia is a respiratory disease caused by

    A. virus
    C. fungus
    B. bacteria
    D. all of the above

11. Spray paint often includes

    A. trichloethylene
    C. toluene
    B. carbon tetrachloride
    D. benzene

12. Among the following, which is considered a common trigger of ventricular fibrillation in a hypothermia victim?

    A. Endotracheal intubation
    B. Metabolic alkalosis from sodium bicarbonate administration
    C. Unwarranted cardiopulmonary resuscitation
    D. All of the above

Questions 13-17.

DIRECTIONS: In Questions 13 through 17, match the numbered description to the lettered term, listed in Column I, which it MOST accurately describes. Place the letter of the CORRECT answer in the appropriate space at the right.

COLUMN I

A. Core
B. Shell
C. Frostbite
D. Frostnip
E. After-drop

13. Characterized by numbness and pallor without significant tissue damage.

14. In reference to the human body, comprises the skin, subcutaneous tissues, skeletal muscles, and extremities.

15. In reference to the human body, comprises the heart, lungs, brain, and abdominal viscera.

16. Continued fall in core temperature after a victim of hypothermia has been removed from the cold environment due at least in part to the return of cold blood from the body surface to the body core.

16._____

17. Localized damage to tissues resulting from prolonged exposure to extreme cold.

17._____

Questions 18-20.

DIRECTIONS: In Questions 18 through 20, match the numbered definition to the lettered process, listed in Column I, which it BEST describes. Place the letter of the CORRECT answer in the appropriate space at the right.

COLUMN I

A. Conduction
B. Convection
C. Radiation

18. Body heat is picked up and carried away by moving air currents.

18._____

19. Transfer of heat to a solid object or a liquid.

19._____

20. Emission of heat from an object into colder surrounding air.

20._____

Questions 21-25.

DIRECTIONS: In Questions 21 through 25, match the numbered definition with the lettered term, listed in Column I, which it BEST describes. Place the letter of the CORRECT answer in the appropriate space at the right.

COLUMN I

A. Proprioception
B. Residual volume
C. Vital capacity
D. Spondylosis
E. Hypertrophy

21. Volume of air remaining in the lungs after a maximal exhalation.

21._____

22. Ability to perceive the position and movement of one's body or its limbs.

22._____

23. Enlargement of an organ, caused by an increase in the size of its constituent cells.

23._____

24. Abnormal immobility and consolidation of vertebral joints.

24._____

25. Volume of air that can be forcefully exhaled from the lungs following a full inhalation.

25._____

Questions 26-30.

DIRECTIONS: In Questions 26 through 30, match the numbered definition with the lettered term, listed in Column I, that it BEST describes. Place the letter of the CORRECT answer in the appropriate space at the right.

COLUMN I

A. Roentgen
B. Gamma rays
C. Radiation
D. Alpha particle
E. Beta particle

26. Positively-charged subatomic particle corresponding to the nucleus of a helium atom, with his ionizing ability but low penetration. 26.___

27. Negatively-charged subatomic particle corresponding to the electron of an atom, with moderate penetration ability. 27.___

28. Radioactive emission from the nucleus of an atom, with very high penetration ability. 28.___

29. Unit of measurement for radioactive emissions. 29.___

30. Transmission of energy in the form of waves or particles. 30.___

KEY (CORRECT ANSWERS)

1.	B	11.	C	21.	B
2.	C	12.	D	22.	A
3.	B	13.	D	23.	E
4.	C	14.	B	24.	D
5.	D	15.	A	25.	C
6.	C	16.	E	26.	D
7.	B	17.	C	27.	E
8.	C	18.	B	28.	B
9.	D	19.	A	29.	A
10.	D	20.	C	30.	C

OBSTETRIC/GYNECOLOGICAL EMERGENCIES
EXAMINATION SECTION
TEST 1

DIRECTIONS: Each question or incomplete statement is followed by several suggested answers or completions. Select the one that BEST answers the question or completes the statement. *PRINT THE LETTER OF THE CORRECT ANSWER IN THE SPACE AT THE RIGHT.*

1. The female reproductive system includes all of the following EXCEPT the   1.____
   - A. uterus
   - B. ureter
   - C. ovaries
   - D. fallopian tubes

2. In the right and left lower quadrants of the abdomen are two walnut-sized organs that produce the female sex hormone. These organs are the   2.____
   - A. uteri
   - B. fallopian tubes
   - C. ovaries
   - D. none of the above

3. At the distal end of the uterus is a narrow opening called the   3.____
   - A. cervix
   - B. clitoris
   - C. vagina
   - D. fallopian tube

4. Each ovary contains APPROXIMATELY _____ follicles.   4.____
   - A. 50,000
   - B. 200,000
   - C. 1,000,000
   - D. 2,000,000

5. All of the following are external female genitalia EXCEPT the   5.____
   - A. vulva
   - B. labia minor
   - C. ovaries
   - D. labia majora

6. The two hormones produced by the anterior pituitary gland and important in the menstrual cycle are   6.____
   - A. estrogen and progesterone
   - B. follicle stimulating hormone and luteinizing hormone
   - C. growth hormone and thyroid hormone
   - D. all of the above

7. FSH stimulates the ovarian follicle to develop into a mature egg. The growing follicle, in turn, produces another hormone called   7.____
   - A. estrogen
   - B. progesterone
   - C. thyroid hormone
   - D. none of the above

8. The _____ is the name for the lining of the uterus as the follicle starts developing and pumping out hormones.   8.____
   - A. cervia
   - B. fallopian tube
   - C. endometrium
   - D. perineum

9. The phase of the menstrual cycle under estrogen control, when the endometrium is increasing in thickness, is called the _____ phase.

   A. secretory
   B. neutral
   C. proliferative
   D. all of the above

10. Which of the following phases is MAINLY influenced by progesterone? _____ phase.

    A. Secretory
    B. Neutral
    C. Proliferative
    D. Initial

11. _____ is secreted by the corpus luteum.

    A. Progesterone
    B. Estrogen
    C. FSH
    D. Prolactin

12. The vaginal, rectal, and urethral orifices open into the

    A. endometrium
    B. perineum
    C. myometrium
    D. none of the above

13. The muscular tube connecting the uterus to the external genitalia is called the

    A. cervix
    B. vagina
    C. ovaries
    D. fallopian tubes

14. Fallopian tubes

    A. are pear-shaped
    B. have their larger portion close to the ovaries and their narrow end attached to the uterus
    C. contain cilia and draw the egg into them when ovulation occurs
    D. all of the above

15. The name for the developing structure from 4 weeks to 5 weeks after fertilization is

    A. ovum
    B. embryo
    C. fetus
    D. none of the above

16. From 8 weeks after fertilization until birth, the developing structure is called

    A. blastocyst
    B. embryo
    C. fetus
    D. large ovum

17. Approximately fourteen days after ovulation, what special structure of pregnancy begins to develop?

    A. Placenta
    B. Amniotic sac
    C. Umbilical cord
    D. All of the above

18. The special hormone of pregnancy produced by the placenta to maintain the pregnancy and stimulate changes in the mother's breasts, vagina, and cervix is called

    A. estrogen
    B. progesterone
    C. chorionic gonadotrophin
    D. luteinizing hormone

19. The _____ is a specialized structure of pregnancy which connects the placenta to the fetus via the fetal navel.

    A. umbilical cord
    B. amniotic sac
    C. amniotic fluid
    D. none of the above

20. The umbilical cord contains _____ artery (ies) and _____ vein(s).

    A. two; two   B. two; one   C. one; one   D. one; no

21. *A membranous bag that encloses the fetus in a watery fluid* defines the

    A. placenta
    B. endometrium
    C. amniotic sac
    D. none of the above

22. The fetus weighs about 170 gm, there is a good heartbeat, and the sex can be distinguished at _____ weeks.

    A. 4   B. 8   C. 10   D. 16

23. The fetus weighs about 400 gm, the fetal heart sounds are audible, and the mother can feel fetal movements at _____ weeks.

    A. 12
    B. 16
    C. 20
    D. all of the above

24. The fetus is fully developed and well-insulated with subcutaneous fat and the skin is not wrinkled at _____ weeks.

    A. 30   B. 36   C. 40   D. 44

25. The expulsion of the fetus from ANY cause before the twentieth week of gestation is called

    A. abortion
    B. gestation
    C. implantation
    D. pregnancy

KEY (CORRECT ANSWERS)

1. B
2. C
3. A
4. B
5. C
6. B
7. A
8. C
9. C
10. A
11. A
12. B
13. A
14. D
15. B
16. C
17. A
18. C
19. A
20. B
21. C
22. D
23. C
24. C
25. A

TEST 2

DIRECTIONS: Each question or incomplete statement is followed by several suggested answers or completions. Select the one that BEST answers the question or completes the statement. *PRINT THE LETTER OF THE CORRECT ANSWER IN THE SPACE AT THE RIGHT.*

1. An abortion that occurs naturally and is often referred to by laypeople as a miscarriage is called a _____ abortion. 1.___

    A. threatened
    B. therapeutic
    C. spontaneous
    D. all of the above

2. An abortion characterized by vaginal bleeding during the first half of the pregnancy is called a(n) _____ abortion. 2.___

    A. spontaneous
    B. septic
    C. threatened
    D. induced

3. An abortion in which there is prolonged retention in the uterus of a fetus that died during the first 20 weeks of gestation is called a(n) _____ abortion. 3.___

    A. septic
    B. missed
    C. incomplete
    D. none of the above

4. Premature separation of a normally implanted placenta from the wall of the uterus during the last trimester of pregnancy is referred to as 4.___

    A. placenta previa
    B. placenta abruptio
    C. uterine rupture
    D. none of the above

5. The placenta is implanted low in the uterus so that it partially or completely covers the cervical canal.
   This describes 5.___

    A. placenta previa
    B. placenta abruptio
    C. uterine rupture
    D. all of the above

6. Signs and symptoms of placenta abruptio include 6.___

    A. vaginal bleeding
    B. abdominal bleeding
    C. tachycardia
    D. all of the above

7. Pre-hospital management of third trimester bleeding would include all of the following EXCEPT 7.___

    A. administering oxygen
    B. an internal vaginal exam
    C. immediate transport
    D. large bore IV

8. A ruptured uterus typically occurs in a patient who has had previous 8.___

    A. uterine surgery
    B. cesarean section
    C. twin pregnancy
    D. all of the above

9. All of the following statements regarding preeclampsia are true EXCEPT: It

   A. is unique to pregnancy.
   B. only occurs beyond 20 weeks.
   C. is frequently accompanied by seizures.
   D. produces generalized vasospasms of unknown origin.

10. _____ is NOT among the signs and symptoms of preeclampsia.

    A. Edema
    B. Blurring of vision
    C. Hypotension
    D. Hypertension

11. Which of the following is the BEST position for patient with eclampsia?

    A. Supine
    B. Recumbent on her left side
    C. Sitting
    D. Standing

12. The MAJOR causes of injury to pregnant women include

    A. motor vehicle accidents
    B. falls
    C. penetrating injuries
    D. all of the above

13. Possible physiologic changes of pregnancy include all of the following EXCEPT

    A. increased vascular volume
    B. decreased vascular volume
    C. increased pulse rate
    D. increased cardiac output

14. A woman who has had two or more pregnancies, regardless of their outcomes, is called

    A. primipara
    B. nullipara
    C. multigravida
    D. multipara

15. A woman who has had two or more deliveries is known as

    A. primipara
    B. multipara
    C. multigravida
    D. primigravida

16. A woman who has never delivered is

    A. nullipara
    B. primipara
    C. multigravida
    D. multipara

17. The first stage of labor is NOT normally characterized by

    A. contractions coming at 2 minute intervals
    B. contractions coming at 5 to 15 minute intervals
    C. effacement
    D. progressive cervical dilatation

18. The average duration of the first stage of labor in a nullipara woman is _____ hours.

    A. 1-2
    B. 8-12
    C. 24-48
    D. none of the above

19. A woman who is pregnant for the first time is

    A. primigravida
    B. primipara
    C. multigravida
    D. multipara

20. Intermittent contractions of the uterus after the third month of pregnancy are called

    A. effacement
    B. Braxton Hicks contractions
    C. abortion
    D. none of the above

KEY (CORRECT ANSWERS)

1.	C	11.	B
2.	C	12.	D
3.	B	13.	B
4.	B	14.	C
5.	A	15.	B
6.	D	16.	A
7.	B	17.	A
8.	D	18.	B
9.	C	19.	A
10.	C	20.	B

OBSTETRIC/GYNECOLOGICAL EMERGENCIES
EXAMINATION SECTION
TEST 1

DIRECTIONS: Each question or incomplete statement is followed by several suggested answers or completions. Select the one that BEST answers the question or completes the statement. *PRINT THE LETTER OF THE CORRECT ANSWER IN THE SPACE AT THE RIGHT.*

1. The stage of birth during which the presenting part of the baby becomes visible at the vaginal opening is

    A. effacement
    B. dilatation
    C. crowning
    D. A and B *only*

2. The term referring to the FIRST recognizable movements of the fetus in the uterus, usually occurring around the sixteenth to twentieth week of pregnancy, is

    A. crowning
    B. quickening
    C. implantation
    D. all of the above

3. *Transverse lie* is MOST frequently associated with

    A. placenta previa
    B. placenta abruptio
    C. uterine rupture
    D. toxemia of pregnancy

4. The second stage of labor

    A. begins as the baby's head enters the birth canal
    B. is when the cervix becomes fully dilated and effaced
    C. is when crowning occurs
    D. all of the above

5. The MOST important factor for distinguishing false from true labor is

    A. continuous contraction
    B. effacement
    C. dilatation
    D. bleeding

6. If the mother dies, a cesarean MAY save the baby if performed within _____ minutes after the mother's death.

    A. 10 to 15   B. 60   C. 180   D. 240

7. What conditions should an EMT look for when examining the abdomen?

    A. With each contraction, it becomes hard.
    B. Between contractions, the uterus is soft.
    C. Fetal heart tones are present.
    D. All of the above

8. An EMT should inspect the vagina for

    A. crowning
    B. amount of bleeding
    C. preparation for a vaginal exam
    D. color of discharge

9. If it is decided that a patient should be transported, the EMT should

    A. prepare the mother
    B. notify the delivery room
    C. prepare himself for possible delivery during transport
    D. all of the above

10. When an EMT prepares the mother, he must do all of the following EXCEPT

    A. transport her in a reclining position
    B. remove any underclothing that might obstruct the delivery
    C. attempt to delay or restrain a delivery
    D. not allow the mother to go to the toilet

11. If the judgment call is to deliver the baby, the EMT should

    A. place the mother on a bed, sturdy table, or ambulance cot
    B. place a sheet under the mother's buttocks and lower back
    C. protect everything but the vaginal area
    D. all of the above

12. After the baby has been fully delivered, the EMT does NOT have to

    A. wipe away blood and mucous from the baby's mouth and nose with sterile gauze
    B. take a rubber bulb aspirator and suction both the mouth and nose of the baby
    C. immediately intubate with an endotracheal tube
    D. let the baby breathe spontaneously after suctioning

13. The cord should be clamped _____ inches away from the infant's navel.

    A. 2   B. 8   C. 18   D. 24

14. All of the following statements regarding placenta delivery are true EXCEPT:

    A. Delivery usually occurs within 20 minutes.
    B. Delivery usually occurs after 30 minutes.
    C. Bleeding may be expected as the placenta separates.
    D. The placenta should be saved in a basin or plastic bag and transported with the mother.

15. During the delivery of the placenta, the EMT should

    A. never pull on the cord to deliver the placenta
    B. examine the perineum for lacerations and apply pressure to any tears
    C. add 10 units of pitocin to the IV bottle and drip slowly
    D. all of the above

16. If the placenta is not delivered within 30 minutes, the EMT should

    A. add 10 units of pitocin to the IV bottle
    B. add 20 units of pitocin to the IV bottle
    C. transport the mother and the baby to the hospital
    D. all of the above

17. If the baby is not breathing within 30 seconds after delivery, the EMT should do which of the following?

    A. Clean the airway again, using suctioning
    B. Slap the feet or rub the back
    C. Begin mouth-to-mouth resuscitation
    D. All of the above

18. When cutting the cord,

    A. place the baby on his side on a sterile sheet or blanket
    B. wait for pulsating in the cord to cease
    C. clamp the cord 8 inches from the infant's navel
    D. all of the above

19. If a patient has excessive bleeding after delivery, the EMT should do all of the following EXCEPT

    A. perform vaginal packing
    B. have the mother close her legs and lower them
    C. look for a mass in the lower abdomen, the uterus
    D. add 10 units of pitocin to an IV bottle

20. Risk factors for postpartum hemorrhaging include

    A. prolonged labor
    B. retained products of conception
    C. placenta previa
    D. all of the above

21. The MOST common cause of amenorrhea is

    A. pelvic inflammatory disease (PID)
    B. pregnancy
    C. endometriosis
    D. ovarian tumor

22. The term for very heavy menstrual flow is

    A. amenorrhea   B. menorrhagia
    C. metrorrhagia   D. oligomenorrhea

23. Pelvic inflammatory disease is MOST often

    A. viral   B. parasitic
    C. bacterial   D. fungal

24. Signs and symptoms of PID include

    A. fever and chills   B. lower abdominal pain
    C. vaginal discharge   D. all of the above

25. The MOST common potentially life-threatening gynecologic emergency is   25.___
    A. ectopic pregnancy
    B. pelvic inflammatory disease
    C. placenta abruptio
    D. none of the above

KEY (CORRECT ANSWERS)

1. C
2. B
3. A
4. D
5. C

6. A
7. D
8. C
9. D
10. C

11. D
12. C
13. B
14. B
15. D

16. C
17. D
18. D
19. A
20. D

21. B
22. B
23. C
24. D
25. A

TEST 2

DIRECTIONS: Each question or incomplete statement is followed by several suggested answers or completions. Select the one that BEST answers the question or completes the statement. *PRINT THE LETTER OF THE CORRECT ANSWER IN THE SPACE AT THE RIGHT.*

1. The MOST common cause of maternal death in the first trimester is   1.____
   - A. abortion
   - B. ectopic pregnancy
   - C. ovarian tumor
   - D. uterine rupture

2. 95% of cases of ectopic implantation occur in a(n)   2.____
   - A. ovary
   - B. fallopian tube
   - C. abdominal cavity
   - D. cervical canal

3. Among the common signs and symptoms of ectopic pregnancy is   3.____
   - A. hemoperitoneum
   - B. vaginal bleeding
   - C. hypotension
   - D. all of the above

4. Pre-hospital management of suspected ectopic pregnancy should include all of the following EXCEPT   4.____
   - A. ensuring an adequate airway and administering oxygen
   - B. keeping the patient recumbent, preferably lying on her left side
   - C. giving a lot of fluid by mouth
   - D. keeping the patient warm

Questions 5–9.

DIRECTIONS: In Questions 5 through 9, match the numbered description with the lettered type of abortion, listed in the column below, that it BEST describes. Place the letter of the CORRECT answer in the appropriate space at the right.

TYPES OF ABORTIONS
- A. Inevitable
- B. Incomplete
- C. Missed
- D. Therapeutic
- E. Septic

5. Occurs when part of the products of conception remain in the uterus.   5.____

6. A spontaneous abortion that cannot be prevented.   6.____

7. Occurs when the uterus becomes infected following any type of abortion.   7.____

8. A prolonged retention in the uterus of a fetus that died during the first 20 weeks of gestation.   8.____

9. Induced for justifiable medical reasons and carried out in an authorized medical setting.   9.____

Questions 10–15.

DIRECTIONS: In Questions 10 through 15, match the numbered definition with the lettered condition, listed in the column below, that it MOST accurately describes. Place the letter of the CORRECT answer in the appropriate space at the right.

COLUMN I
A. Antepartum hemorrhage
B. Postpartum hemorrhage
C. Ectopic pregnancy
D. Menarche
E. Metorrhagia
F. Hemoperitoneum

10. Vaginal bleeding between menstrual periods 10.___

11. Pregnancy in which the ovum is implanted somewhere other than the uterine endometrium 11.___

12. Blood in the peritoneal cavity 12.___

13. When blood loss exceeds 500 ml during the first 24 hours after giving birth 13.___

14. Bleeding before delivery 14.___

15. The onset of menstrual period 15.___

Questions 16–18.

DIRECTIONS: In Questions 16 through 18, match the numbered description with the lettered presentation, listed in the column below, that it BEST describes. Place the letter of the CORRECT answer in the appropriate space at the right.

COLUMN I
A. Transverse lie
B. Footling breach presentation
C. Vertex presentation
D. Face presentation

16. The chin, a prominent and identifiable facial landmark, is used as a point of reference. 16.___

17. The position is determined by the relation of the fetal occiput to the mother's right or left side. 17.___

18. The fetus is crosswise in the uterus. 18.___

Questions 19-20.

DIRECTIONS: In Questions 19 and 20, match the numbered definition with the lettered process, listed in the column below, that it BEST describes. Place the letter of the CORRECT answer in the appropriate space at the right.

COLUMN I
A. Ovulation
B. Implantation

19. The fertilized egg attaches to the endometrium. 19.____

20. An ovum is released from an ovarian follicle; usually occurs once a month in a non-pregnant woman of child-bearing age. 20.____

KEY (CORRECT ANSWERS)

1. B
2. B
3. D
4. C
5. B

6. A
7. E
8. C
9. D
10. E

11. C
12. F
13. B
14. A
15. D

16. D
17. C
18. A
19. B
20. A

PEDIATRIC & NEONATAL EMERGENCIES
EXAMINATION SECTION
TEST 1

DIRECTIONS: Each question or incomplete statement is followed by several suggested answers or completions. Select the one that BEST answers the question or completes the statement. *PRINT THE LETTER OF THE CORRECT ANSWER IN THE SPACE AT THE RIGHT.*

1. General guidelines for dealing with children include: 1.____
   A. Stay calm and do not tower over the child.
   B. Identify yourself and smile a lot.
   C. Be patient and gentle, and do not separate a child from his parents.
   D. All of the above

2. Special considerations in physical assessment include all of the following EXCEPT the child's 2.____
   A. general appearance and level of consciousness
   B. race
   C. position and movement
   D. degree of distress

3. An infant or child may be content to be held by a stranger and takes a rather indiscriminating interest in faces up to the age of _____ month(s). 3.____
   A. 1   B. 6   C. 12   D. 24

4. At what age is a child USUALLY difficult to deal with? 4.____
   A. 2 to 3 years   B. 4 to 5 years
   C. 8 to 10 years   D. Adolescence

5. It is important to check the nostrils to make sure they are not obstructed by secretions because infants are obligate nose-breathers, sometimes up to the age of 5.____
   A. 6 years   B. 6 months   C. 10 years   D. 15 years

6. It is important to remember that, in children, the vital signs are 6.____
   A. constant throughout childhood
   B. not of any importance
   C. age-specific
   D. none of the above

7. Throughout the physical assessment of a child, it is important to follow general guidelines. 7.____
   These guidelines include all of the following EXCEPT:
   A. Respect the child's modesty; undress only the part you are examining and cover that part up when you finish examining it.
   B. Postpone the use of instruments as long as possible.
   C. Stabilize the intravenous line before examining the child.
   D. Examine the injured or painful area last.

8. The treatment of complete obstruction in a child utilizes

    A. back blows
    B. abdominal thrusts
    C. chest thrusts
    D. both A and C

9. The pathophysiology of an asthmatic attack does NOT include

    A. reversible spasm and constriction of the bronchi
    B. permanent damage of bronchi
    C. edema and congestion of lining membrane of bronchi
    D. hypersecretion of mucus

10. In an acute asthmatic attack, the child struggles more and more to breathe with less and less to show for it.
    The net effect is increasing

    A. hypoxemia
    B. hypercarbia
    C. acidosis
    D. all of the above

11. Among the following, the FIRST line of drugs to treat acute asthmatic attacks was

    A. albuterol
    B. steroids
    C. cromolyn sodium
    D. all of the above

12. Specific protocols for the treatment of acute asthmatic attacks vary from place to place. All treatment regimens, however, are based on certain principles, which attempt to

    A. improve oxygenation
    B. correct dehydration
    C. reverse the processes that are inhibiting air flow within the lungs
    D. all of the above

13. If a patient fails to respond to _____, then he is, by definition, in status asthmaticus.

    A. aminphylline
    B. epinephrine
    C. steroids
    D. oxygen

14. Bronchiolitis, an inflammation of the bronchioles, is MOST commonly caused by the _____ virus.

    A. respirator syncytial
    B. para influenza
    C. echo
    D. rhino

15. The HIGHEST incidence of bronchiolitis occurs in an infant or child _____ years of age during _____.

    A. under 2; winter and spring
    B. 4 to 5; fall
    C. 8 to 10; spring
    D. none of the above

16. Regarding croup, it is TRUE that

    A. the infection leads to airway obstruction by causing edema beneath the glottis
    B. a child with croup is hoarse, with a high-pitched strider and a whooping sound on inspiration
    C. it usually occurs in children 6 months to 4 years of age
    D. all of the above

17. Effective treatment of a child with croup would include all of the following EXCEPT

   A. positioning the child in the most comfortable position
   B. immediate tracheostomy
   C. administering humidified oxygen
   D. racemic epinephrine via nebulizer

18. The one of the following that is NOT a feature of epiglottitis is

   A. high fever
   B. drooling
   C. most patients under 1 year of age
   D. difficulty swallowing

19. Epiglottitis is MOST likely caused by

   A. bacteria
   B. viruses
   C. parasites
   D. foreign bodies

20. Pre-hospital treatment of epiglottitis would NOT require

   A. placement of the child in a position in which he is most comfortable and administration of humidifier oxygen
   B. visualized throat with a tongue blade
   C. availability of a laryngoscope and endotracheal tube of the appropriate sizes immediately at hand
   D. transport without delay to the hospital

21. Common causes of seizures in children include

   A. head trauma
   B. meningitis
   C. hypoglycemia
   D. all of the above

22. All of the following statements regarding febrile seizures are true EXCEPT:

   A. Incidence is highest in children between 6 months and 3 years of age.
   B. It is usually focal in nature.
   C. Often, there is a family history of similar seizures.
   D. It usually lasts up to 15 minutes.

23. Most deaths due to seizures occur because of

   A. fever
   B. hypoxia
   C. hypertension
   D. all of the above

24. The drug of choice for status epilepticus is

   A. phenobarbital
   B. phenytoin
   C. diazepam
   D. carbamazepine

25. Important clues to the identification of a battered child can exist in the medical history of the child.
Possible clues include

    A. significant delay in seeking medical care
    B. discrepancy between different people's versions of the story
    C. discrepancy between the history and the observed injuries
    D. all of the above

26. The parent or caretaker who abuses a child is often

    A. a person who was her or himself abused as a child
    B. associated with a rich family
    C. one of only a few people living in the family
    D. all of the above

27. Which of the following conditions should elicit suspicion of a battered child? A child who has

    A. multiple extremity fractures
    B. multiple bruises and abrasions, especially on the trunk and buttocks
    C. burns, especially cigarette or scald burns
    D. all of the above

28. The indications for intubation of a child with burns include

    A. stridor   B. wheezing
    C. respiratory distress   D. all of the above

29. The head and neck account for _____ percent of the body surface area of a child.

    A. 9   B. 18   C. 30   D. 40

30. The proper treatment of a child with salicylate overdose, provided the child is fully alert and you arrived within 15 to 20 minutes of ingestion, is

    A. intubation   B. sodium bicarbonate
    C. syrup of ipecac   D. all of the above

31. What is the MOST likely danger due to acetaminophen poisoning in a child?

    A. Renal failure   B. Fatal liver damage
    C. Gastric ulcer   D. All of the above

32. The antidote for acetominophen poisoning is

    A. N-acetylcysteine B. BAL
    C. pencillamine   D. none of the above

33. A child's pulse should be checked in the _____ position.

    A. radial   B. popliteal
    C. brachial   D. none of the above

34. Correct defibrillation dosage in children weighing 12 kg is about

    A. 25 to 50
    B. 100 to 150
    C. 100 to 200
    D. 200 to 300

35. A fractured left femur, ruptured spleen, and injury to the right side of the head in a child struck by a car while crossing the street signal

    A. Waddelk's triad
    B. Murfy's sign
    C. William's triad
    D. none of the above

KEY (CORRECT ANSWERS)

1.	D	16.	D
2.	B	17.	B
3.	A	18.	C
4.	A	19.	A
5.	B	20.	B
6.	B	21.	D
7.	C	22.	B
8.	D	23.	B
9.	B	24.	C
10.	D	25.	D
11.	A	26.	A
12.	D	27.	D
13.	B	28.	D
14.	A	29.	B
15.	A	30.	C

31. B
32. A
33. C
34. A
35. A

TEST 2

DIRECTIONS: Each question or incomplete statement is followed by several suggested answers or completions. Select the one that BEST answers the question or completes the statement. *PRINT THE LETTER OF THE CORRECT ANSWER IN THE SPACE AT THE RIGHT.*

1. The CORRECT compression point for the infant during resuscitation (CPR) is 1.___

    A. upper half of the sternum
    B. just below the midsternum
    C. lower half of the sternum
    D. lower third of the sternum

2. The CORRECT compression point for the child during resuscitation (CPR) is 2.___

    A. upper half of the sternum
    B. just below the midsternum
    C. lower half of the sternum
    D. lower third of the sternum

3. The recommended INITIAL energy dose for defibrillation of a 10 kg child is _____ joules. 3.___

    A. 5   B. 20   C. 50   D. 100

4. During resuscitation of a child, compressions should be applied using 4.___

    A. two hands, one on top of the other
    B. the heel of one hand
    C. two fingers
    D. none of the above

5. During resuscitation of an infant, compressions should be applied using 5.___

    A. two fingers
    B. the heel of one hand
    C. two hands, one on top of the other
    D. all of the above

6. The compression rate in children is _____ per minute. 6.___

    A. 50 - 60   B. 70 - 80   C. 80 - 100   D. 100 - 120

7. The compression rate in infants is _____ per minute. 7.___

    A. 50   B. 60   C. 80   D. 100

8. For external chest compression to be effective in a child, the sternum must be depressed _____ cm. 8.___

    A. 1.5 to 2.5   B. 2.5 to 3.5
    C. 4.5 to 6.5   D. 6.5 to 10

9. The compression depth in an infant during CPR should be _____ cm.

   A. 1.5 - 2.5
   B. 2.3 - 3.5
   C. 4 - 5
   D. 5 - 6

10. What is the NORMAL ratio of chest compression to ventilation in children and infants during CPR?

    A. 2:1   B. 5:1   C. 15:2   D. 20:2

11. The INITIAL recommended dose of epinephrine for asystole in an infant is 1: _____ at _____ ml per kilogram by IV push.

    A. 1000; 0.05
    B. 1000; 0.1
    C. 10,000; 0.1
    D. 10,000; 0.5

12. You should use a size _____ laryngoscope blade for newborns up to 8 months of age.

    A. zero   B. one   C. two   D. three

13. The infant in need of chest compression has a heart rate

    A. of 80 and a respiratory rate in the 60's
    B. below 60, not increasing after 15-30 seconds of ventilation with 100% oxygen
    C. of 100 with a respiratory rate of 10
    D. all of the above

14. If the tube is CORRECTLY placed in the mid-tracheal region, there should be

    A. bilateral breath sound
    B. equal breath sound
    C. a slight rise of the chest with each ventilation
    D. all of the above

15. If an endotracheal tube is incorrectly placed in a mainstem and bronchus, the signs you would expect include all of the following EXCEPT

    A. unilateral breath sound
    B. gastric distension
    C. unequal breath sound
    D. no air heard entering stomach

16. If an endotracheal tube is incorrectly placed in the esophagus, you would expect all of the following EXCEPT

    A. no breath sound
    B. air heard entering stomach
    C. gastric distension
    D. slight rise of the chest with each ventilation

17. Do NOT spend more than _____ seconds on any one intubation attempt in an infant.

    A. 20   B. 40   C. 60   D. 80

18. A _____ percent solution of sodium bicarbonate should be used in a newborn.

    A. 4.2   B. 9   C. 12.6   D. none of the above

19. Abdominal thrust is NOT recommended for children under _____ year(s) of age.

    A. 1   B. 2   C. 3   D. 4

20. A 5-year-old, 25 kg child is in shock.
    You should INITIALLY give him _____ cc/kg of normal saline.

    A. 10   B. 20   C. 40   D. 60

21. The drug of choice for status epilepticus in children is

    A. phenobarbital
    B. valium
    C. dilantin
    D. all of the above

Questions 22-25.

DIRECTIONS: In Questions 22 through 25, match the numbered definition with the lettered term, listed in Column I, that it BEST describes. Place the letter of the CORRECT answer in the appropriate space at the right.

COLUMN I
A. Intraosseous
B. Hygroscopic
C. Waddell's triad
D. Osteomyelitis

22. Inflammation or infection of the bone

23. Within the bone

24. The syndrome indicated by a fractured left femur, ruptured spleen, and injury to the right side of the head of a child struck by a car while crossing the street

25. Tending to absorb water

Questions 26-30.

DIRECTIONS: In Questions 26 through 30, match the numbered definition with the lettered term, listed in Column I, that it BEST describes. Place the letter of the CORRECT answer in the appropriate space at the right.

COLUMN I
A. Peripheral cyanosis
B. Central cyanosis
C. Pericardial effusion
D. Pericardiocentesis
E. Pericardial tamponade

26. Excess fluid within the pericardial sac

27. Accumulation of excess fluid or blood in the pericardial sac to the point that it interferes with cardiac functions

28. Aspiration of blood or fluid from the pericardium

29. Cyanosis including only the hands and feet

30. Cyanosis involving the entire body

KEY (CORRECT ANSWERS)

1.	B	16.	D
2.	C	17.	A
3.	B	18.	A
4.	B	19.	A
5.	A	20.	B
6.	C	21.	B
7.	D	22.	D
8.	B	23.	A
9.	A	24.	C
10.	B	25.	B
11.	C	26.	C
12.	B	27.	E
13.	B	28.	D
14.	D	29.	A
15.	B	30.	B

EXAMINATION SECTION
TEST 1

DIRECTIONS: Each question or incomplete statement is followed by several suggested answers or completions. Select the one that BEST answers the question or completes the statement. *PRINT THE LETTER OF THE CORRECT ANSWER IN THE SPACE AT THE RIGHT.*

1. The causes of abnormal behavior include 1.____
   A. alcohol and drugs
   B. head injuries and severe infection
   C. diabetes and psychiatric problems
   D. all of the above

2. All of the following are common reactions to anxiety EXCEPT 2.____
   A. depression
   B. flight of ideas
   C. denial
   D. regression

3. Of the following infections, the one which does NOT produce psychotic syndrome is 3.____
   A. chancroid
   B. brain abscess
   C. syphilis
   D. toxoplasmosis

4. In dealing with emotionally disturbed patients, an EMT should 4.____
   A. not assess the patient's needs
   B. intervene in the situation to the extent to which he feels capable
   C. overreact to the patient's behavior or emotional attacks
   D. none of the above

5. Crisis situations, including periods of _____, may affect the paramedic adversely. 5.____
   A. anxiety
   B. anger
   C. impatience
   D. all of the above

6. A professional attitude MUST be maintained while the paramedic is dealing with emotionally disturbed patients. This attitude can be characterized by all of the following EXCEPT 6.____
   A. anger
   B. warmth
   C. sensitivity
   D. compassion

7. The common emotional difficulties of the paramedic may be managed by 7.____
   A. discussing problems and anxieties with co-workers
   B. developing a regular discussion rap session with peers to discuss good and bad experiences
   C. discussing problems with the supervisor
   D. all of the above

8. There are certain general guidelines for dealing with any patient with a psychiatric problem.
   The one of the following which is NOT among these guidelines is:
   A. Be prepared to spend time with the disturbed patient.
   B. Be as calm and direct as possibl
   C. You do not need to identify yoursel
   D. Assess the patient wherever the emergency occurs.

9. Disorders of motor activity include all of the following EXCEPT
   A. agitation   B. compulsion
   C. perservation   D. restlessness

10. A repetitive action carried out to relieve the anxiety of obsessive thought is called
    A. compulsion   B. delirium
    C. confrontation   D. confabulation

11. The invention of experiences to cover over gaps in memory, seen in patients with certain organic brain syndromes, is
    A. dementia   B. confabulation
    C. psychosis   D. delusion

12. Among the following, which is NOT a symptom of a panic attack?
    A. Shortness of breath or a sensation of being smothered
    B. Feeling of unreality or of stepping apart from oneself
    C. Constant fatigue and no motivation to do anything
    D. Fear of dying and of being crazy

13. Risk factors for violence do NOT include
    A. any place where alcohol is being consumed
    B. natural death in the family
    C. crowd incidents
    D. incidents where violence has already occurred (e.g., shooting, stabbing)

14. Disorders of thinking include all of the following EXCEPT
    A. flight of ideas   B. retardation of thought
    C. compulsions   D. perseveration

15. All of the following are disorders of consciousness EXCEPT
    A. amnesia   B. delirium
    C. fugue stage   D. stupor and coma

16. A repetition of movements that don,t seem to serve any useful purpose is called
    A. compulsion   B. echolalia
    C. stereotyped activity   D. all of the above

17. The definition of *compulsion* is:

    A. A repetitive action carried out to relieve the anxiety of obsessive thought
    B. The situation in which a patient cannot sit still
    C. Condition in which the patient echoes the words of the examiner
    D. None of the above

18. The MOST profound disorder of memory is

    A. confabulation
    B. amnesia
    C. illusion
    D. hallucination

19. An acute state of confusion characterized by global impairment of thinking, perception, and memory is called

    A. delusion   B. delirium   C. psychosis   D. dementia

20. Proper pre-hospital management of the manic patient includes

    A. not arguing or getting into a power struggle with the patient
    B. talking to a patient in a quiet place, away from other people
    C. consulting medical command if the patient refuses transport
    D. all of the above

Questions 21-25.

DIRECTIONS: In Questions 21 through 25, match the numbered definition with the lettered disorder, listed in Column I, that it MOST accurately describes. Place the letter of the CORRECT answer in the appropriate space at the right.

COLUMN I
A. Echolalia
B. Illusion
C. Delusion
D. Hallucination
E. Mood

21. Misinterpretation of sensory stimuli

22. False belief

23. Meaningless echoing of the interviewer's words by the patient

24. Sustained and pervasive emotional state

25. Sense of perception not founded on objective reality

KEY (CORRECT ANSWERS)

1.	D		11.	B
2.	B		12.	C
3.	A		13.	B
4.	B		14.	C
5.	D		15.	A
6.	A		16.	C
7.	D		17.	A
8.	C		18.	B
9.	C		19.	B
10.	A		20.	D

21. B
22. C
23. A
24. E
25. D

TEST 2

DIRECTIONS: Each question or incomplete statement is followed by several suggested answers or completions. Select the one that BEST answers the question or completes the statement. *PRINT THE LETTER OF THE CORRECT ANSWER IN THE SPACE AT THE RIGHT.*

1. The depressed patient can often be readily identified by

    A. a sad expression
    B. bouts of crying
    C. expression of feelings of worthlessness
    D. all of the above

2. The third leading cause of death among the 15- to 25 year-old age group is

    A. diabetes mellitus
    B. rheumatoid arthritis
    C. suicide
    D. congenital heart disease

3. The assessment of every depressed person MUST include an evaluation of

    A. schizophrenia
    B. suicide risk
    C. chronic debilitating illness
    D. anxiety

4. When caring for a patient who is displaying typical stress reactions, you should

    A. act in a calm manner, giving the patient time to gain control of his emotions
    B. quietly and carefully evaluate the situation
    C. stay alert for sudden changes in behavior
    D. all of the above

5. The patient in a psychiatric emergency is far more out of reach and out of control than the person in an emotional emergency.
   In a psychiatric emergency, the patient may do all of the following EXCEPT

    A. try to hurt himself
    B. try to seek help for protection
    C. withdraw, no longer responding to people or to his environment
    D. continue to act depressed, sometimes crying and expressing feelings of worthlessness

6. When a patient is acting as if he may hurt himself or another, you should do all of the following EXCEPT

    A. alert the police
    B. not isolate yourself from your partner or other sources of help
    C. try to restrain the patient by yourself
    D. always be on the watch for weapons

7. A mental disorder characterized by loss of contact with reality is called

    A. psychosis
    B. dementia
    C. phobia
    D. none of the above

8. Anti-psychotic drugs are also called

   A. antidepressants
   B. neuroleptics
   C. anxiolytics
   D. antiepileptics

9. The patient who hears voices commanding him to hurt himself or others must be considered

   A. normal
   B. safe
   C. dangerous
   D. none of the above

10. When in a state of *conversion hysteria,* a person's

    A. reaction may move from extreme anxiety to relative calmness
    B. may transform anxiety to some bodily function
    C. often becomes hysterically blind, deaf, or paralyzed
    D. all of the above

11. Repeating the same idea over and over again is called

    A. perseveration
    B. compulsion
    C. obsession
    D. facilitation

12. _____ is the interviewing technique in which the interviewer encourages the patient to proceed by noncommittal words and gestures.

    A. Echolalia
    B. Facilitation
    C. Affect
    D. None of the above

13. The CHRONIC deterioration of mental function is referred to as

    A. dementia
    B. psychosis
    C. delirium
    D. schizophrenia

14. A persistent idea that a person CANNOT dismiss from his thought is a(n)

    A. affect
    B. obsession
    C. compulsion
    D. delusion

15. An interviewing technique in which the interviewer points out to the patient something of interest in his conversation or behavior is

    A. facilitation
    B. confabulation
    C. confrontation
    D. perseveration

16. It is important for paramedics to be aware of one particular syndrome that may occur in patients taking anti-psychotic medication.
    This condition is

    A. acute diuresis
    B. acute dystonic reaction
    C. hypertensive crises
    D. none of the above

17. An acute dystonic reaction can be rapidly corrected by

    A. chlorpromazine
    B. prolixin
    C. diphenhydramine
    D. tindal

18. Tranquilizers are also called 18.____

   A. neuroleptics B. anxiolytics
   C. chinergics D. stimulants

19. The COMMON symptoms of antipsychotic drugs include 19.____

   A. blurred vision B. dry mouth
   C. cardiac dysrhythmias D. all of the above

20. Uncontrolled, disconnected thoughts characterize a disorganized patient who may be 20.____

   A. incoherent or rambling in his speech
   B. wandering aimlessly
   C. dressed inappropriately
   D. all of the above

Questions 21-25.

DIRECTIONS: In Questions 21 through 25, match the numbered definition with the lettered disorder, listed in Column I, that it MOST accurately describes. Place the letter of the CORRECT answer in the appropriate space at the right.

COLUMN I
A. Agitation
B. Agoraphobia
C. Flight of ideas
D. Neologism
E. Confabulation

21. Fear of the marketplace 21.____

22. An invented word that has meaning only to its inventor 22.____

23. The invention of experiences to cover over gaps in memory 23.____

24. Extreme restlessness and anxiety 24.____

25. Accelerated thinking in which the mind skips very rapidly from one thought to the next 25.____

KEY (CORRECT ANSWERS)

1. D
2. C
3. B
4. D
5. B

6. C
7. A
8. B
9. C
10. D

11. A
12. B
13. A
14. B
15. C

16. B
17. C
18. B
19. D
20. D

21. B
22. D
23. E
24. A
25. C

EXAMINATION SECTION
TEST 1

DIRECTIONS: Each question or incomplete statement is followed by several suggested answers or completions. Select the one that BEST answers the question or completes the statement. *PRINT THE LETTER OF THE CORRECT ANSWER IN THE SPACE AT THE RIGHT.*

1. The paramedic's PRIMARY responsibility is to provide   1.____

   A. protection to the patient
   B. emergency medical care
   C. guidance for prevention of injuries
   D. none of the above

2. How many stages are there in any extrication?   2.____

   A. One   B. Two   C. Three   D. Five

3. Essential rescue equipment for ambulances include   3.____

   A. manila ropes   B. triangular reflectors
   C. shoring blocks   D. all of the above

4. Personal safety of rescue personnel requires the use of   4.____

   A. protective headgear   B. protective coats
   C. eye protector   D. all of the above

5. Of the following, the FIRST stage of extrication is   5.____

   A. assessing the scene and controlling hazards
   B. gaining access to the patient
   C. providing urgent medical care
   D. disentangling the patient

6. At the scene of an automobile accident, the EASIEST way to enter an automobile is through   6.____

   A. the roof   B. the window
   C. the door   D. breaking the windshield

7. The FINAL stage of rescue is   7.____

   A. providing emergency care
   B. controlling the hazards
   C. disentangling the patient
   D. packaging the patient and removal

8. Which of the following human factors INCREASE the potential for an EMT to be injured at a collision site?   8.____

   A. A careless attitude toward personal safety
   B. Lack of skill in tool use
   C. Physical problems that impede strenuous effort
   D. All of the above

9. Unsafe and improper acts during rescue that cause injuries include all of the following EXCEPT

   A. failure to eliminate or control hazards
   B. using safe tools
   C. failure to select the proper tool for the task
   D. lifting heavy objects improperly

10. When placing flares, you should do all of the following EXCEPT

    A. look for spilled fuel and dry vegetation
    B. position a few flares at the edge of the danger zone
    C. position a flare every 2 feet
    D. do not throw flares out of moving vehicles

11. If you discover that a utility pole is broken and wires are down,

    A. park the ambulance outside the danger zone
    B. before you leave the ambulance, be sure that no portion of the vehicle, including the radio antenna, is contacting any sagging conductors
    C. discourage occupants of the collision vehicle from leaving the wreckage
    D. prohibit traffic flow through danger zone

12. If you find an unconscious victim during rescue, you should FIRST

    A. apply a cervical collar
    B. open an airway
    C. assess circulation
    D. stop external bleeding

13. The EMT should be able to recognize and manage situations that pose a threat to the patient, the EMT, or bystander.
    This would include which of the following hazardous conditions?

    A. Fire
    B. Explosive materials
    C. Radioactive material
    D. All of the above

14. During rescue, a victim develops hypotension. Which would be the BEST vein for infusion? _____ vein.

    A. Internal jugular
    B. Subclavian
    C. Antecubital
    D. Popliteal

15. A block of wood placed in front or behind a wheel to prevent the vehicle from rolling is called a

    A. chock
    B. cribbing
    C. disentanglement
    D. all of the above

KEY (CORRECT ANSWERS)

1. B
2. D
3. D
4. D
5. A

6. C
7. D
8. D
9. B
10. C

11. C
12. B
13. D
14. C
15. A

EXAMINATION SECTION
TEST 1

DIRECTIONS: Each question or incomplete statement is followed by several suggested answers or completions. Select the one that BEST answers the question or completes the statement. PRINT THE LETTER OF THE CORRECT ANSWER IN THE SPACE AT THE RIGHT.

1. Which carrying device is BEST suited for passage through narrow halls?
   A. Long board
   B. Short board
   C. Scoop-type stretcher
   D. Stair-chair
   E. Portable stretcher

2. The ambulance's floor is _____ inches from ground level.
   A. 18   B. 24   C. 36   D. 2   E. 30

3. Which of the following is standard ambulance equipment?
   I. Wheeled cot
   II. Wheel chair
   III. Portable stretcher
   IV. Long backboard
   V. Portable incubator

   The CORRECT answer is:
   A. I, II, V
   B. I, II, III
   C. I, III, IV
   D. II, III, IV
   E. II, III, V

4. The selection of an appropriate transfer method is determined by the
   A. age of the patient
   B. patient's medical condition
   C. patient's weight
   D. carrying device
   E. location of the patient

5. In using the direct-carry method, how should the stretcher be positioned to the bed?
   A. Parallel, head to head
   B. Parallel, head to foot
   C. Perpendicular, head to foot
   D. Parallel, foot to head
   E. Perpendicular, head to head

6. How do the EMT's proceed once the patient is secure and they are in a full standing position?
   A. The head-end EMT takes one step back.
   B. The foot-end EMT takes one step back.
   C. Both EMTs take one step to the left or right, depending upon the stretcher's position.
   D. Both EMTs take one step back.
   E. Both EMTs take one step forward.

7. In the direct-carry method, the EMTs should be positioned on _____ to lift a bed-level patient.

    A. the same side of the bed, one at head, one at foot
    B. opposite sides of the bed, one at head, one at foot
    C. opposite sides of the bed, both at head
    D. opposite sides of the bed, both at mid-section
    E. adjacent sides of the bed, one at head, one at midsection

8. In using the direct-carry method, both attendants should place their right foot on the lower bar of a multi-level wheeled stretcher in order to

    A. reduce the risk of back strain
    B. lock the wheels of the stretcher
    C. balance themselves before lowering the patient
    D. raise the stretcher to its proper height
    E. ensure the, stretcher is not jarred while lowering the patient

9. Prior to placing the patient on the stretcher, using the direct-carry method, both attendants should be

    A. standing
    B. kneeling on one knee
    C. kneeling on both knees
    D. crouched over the stretcher
    E. standing with one foot on the base of the stretcher

10. In using the direct-carry method, which of the following are proper patient procedures.
    I. Remove cover during transfer
    II. Place in supine position
    III. Keep anatomically straight
    IV. Position in center of stretcher mattress
    V. Release neck and head as soon as patient is secure on stretcher

    The CORRECT answer is:
    A. I, II, III
    B. I, IV, V
    C. II, III, IV
    D. I, III, IV
    E. I, II, III, V

11. The _____ is(are) NOT directly supported during transfer, using the direct-carry method.

    A. neck and shoulders
    B. calves
    C. hips
    D. thighs
    E. lower back

12. The _____ method is the EASIEST method for lifting and carrying a patient at ground level.

    A. draw sheet
    B. direct carry
    C. slide transfer
    D. extremity transfer
    E. patient roll

13. The _____ has the MOST significant effect on the procedures for proper positioning, covering, and securing the patient on the stretcher.

    A. size of the patient
    B. patient's medical condition
    C. transfer method used
    D. type of stretcher used
    E. weather condition

14. The safety straps should be placed across the _____ on a portable stretcher.
    I. chest
    II. waist
    III. shoulders
    IV. legs
    V. ankles

    The CORRECT answer is:
    A. I, II, V
    B. I, IV
    C. II, V
    D. II, III, V
    E. II, III, IV

15. _____ are the MOST common fastening devices for wheeled stretchers.

    A. Wheel cups
    B. Wall brackets
    C. Slide bars
    D. Post cups
    E. U-hooks

16. The MAIN difficulty associated with moving a spine-injured patient is that

    A. the patient cannot be positioned anatomically straight
    B. the patient must be secured to a backboard
    C. danger to the spinal cord does not occur at the point of injury
    D. the spine cannot be immobilized
    E. two men are inadequate

17. What carrying device is BEST suited to transporting a patient with a fractured extremity?

    A. Portable stretcher
    B. Wheeled stretcher
    C. Scoop-type stretcher
    D. Stair chair
    E. Short backboard

18. The proper procedure to carry a patient with a cardiopulmonary resuscitation unit is to

    A. keep patient and unit covered
    B. maintain head lower than feet
    C. place unit resting on stretcher frame of head rest under mattress
    D. keep head elevated approximately 30°
    E. transfer patient to wheeled stretcher by means of a scoop-type stretcher

19. Which of the following procedures does NOT require both EMTs to face the patient?

    A. Wheeling a wheeled stretcher
    B. Loading a portable stretcher
    C. Carrying a loaded stair chair
    D. Carrying a wheeled stretcher
    E. Adjusting the height of a multi-level stretcher

20. What is the STANDARD ambulance cot? 20.____

    A. Scoop-type stretcher
    B. U-frame portable stretcher
    C. Squad bench
    D. Standard pole portable stretcher
    E. Wheeled stretcher

21. Stair chairs are typically combined with 21.____

    A. scoop-type stretchers
    B. short backboards
    C. portable stretchers
    D. long backboards
    E. wheeled stretchers

22. What will help prevent the pillow from sliding off the stretcher in transit? 22.____

    A. Buckle safety strap
    B. Lift head rest one notch
    C. Tuck head end of folded blanket under mattress
    D. Place lengthwise on mattress
    E. Place under mattress

23. A wrap-around sheet is ESPECIALLY useful for 23.____

    A. a portable stretcher
    B. a wheeled stretcher
    C. inclement weather protection
    D. an out-of-control patient
    E. cold weather protection

24. What part of the patient's body is NOT directly supported 2 by the EMTs during a slide transfer? 24.____

    A. Neck
    B. Calves
    C. Right shoulder
    D. Buttocks
    E. Left shoulder

25. It is NOT recommended to 25.____

    A. suspend litters by wall brackets
    B. use floor-mounted crash stable fasteners
    C. transport more than one person
    D. use wall-mounted crash stable fasteners
    E. use floor wells for storage of items

KEY (CORRECT ANSWERS)

1. D
2. B
3. C
4. E
5. C

6. D
7. A
8. E
9. B
10. C

11. D
12. D
13. B
14. B
15. A

16. E
17. A
18. B
19. C
20. E

21. C
22. B
23. A
24. B
25. A

TEST 2

DIRECTIONS: Each question or incomplete statement is followed by several suggested answers or completions. Select the one that BEST answers the question or completes the statement. PRINT THE LETTER OF THE CORRECT ANSWER IN THE SPACE AT THE RIGHT.

1. The PRIMARY objective of moving stretcher patients is to 1.____

    A. quickly transfer the patient to ambulance
    B. maintain an acceptable body temperature
    C. secure the patient on the stretcher
    D. make the patient comfortable
    E. ensure the patient's privacy

2. Which of the following are PROPER procedures for the end carry? 2.____
    I. Both EMTs face the same direction.
    II. A palms-down grip is used with arms extended carry position.
    III. The head-end EMT initiates movement.
    IV. Allow the patient to see where he is going.
    V. Grip should be with hands toward corners of the end.

    The CORRECT answer is:
    A. I, II, IV   B. I, III, IV   C. I, III, V
    D. I, IV, V   E. II, IV, V

3. The EMT enters the patient compartment while loading a portable stretcher 3.____

    A. after the stretcher is supported by the floor and other EMT
    B. after the stretcher frame is rolled into half-ring hook
    C. before the stretcher is secured
    D. after the stretcher is secured
    E. after the doors are closed

4. A short backboard is usually removed from a spine-injured patient 4.____

    A. after the patient is on the carrying device
    B. after the patient is loaded into the ambulance
    C. before x-rays are taken
    D. after the examination and x-rays
    E. before medical attention is rendered

5. The PRIMARY objective when handling an unconscious patient is to 5.____

    A. maintain adequate support during handling and transport
    B. keep the airway free of obstruction
    C. correctly positioning the patient
    D. maintain adequate body temperature
    E. prevent additional injury

6. A patient that requires a third attendant as a necessity is a(n) 6._____
   A. patient receiving oxygen
   B. patient attached to IV apparatus
   C. infant patient
   D. patient with heart-lung resuscitation unit
   E. patient with urine-collecting tube and bag

7. A wheeled stretcher may be safely wheeled 7._____
   A. outdoors
   B. over thresholds
   C. over rugs
   D. all of the above
   E. none of the above

8. The two-man seat carry requires EMTs to link arms at the patient's 8._____
   A. shoulder and buttocks
   B. back and knees
   C. shoulders and thighs
   D. back and thighs
   E. waist and knees

9. How does lifting a patient onto a stair chair by the direct-carry method differ from the procedure used for a wheeled stretcher? 9._____
   A. The patient's thighs are supported.
   B. The head is not cradled.
   C. The lower back is supported.
   D. The shoulders are not supported.
   E. The lift does not begin with the patient in a supine position.

10. Additional personnel are MOST needed when transfer involves a(n) 10._____
    I. unconscious patient
    II. spine-injured patient
    III. patient needing ancillary equipment
    IV. hard to handle patient
    V. patient with injured extremity

    The CORRECT answer is:
    A. I, II, III
    B. I, II, IV
    C. II, III
    D. II, III, V
    E. I, II

11. How many people are required to properly secure a short backboard to a long backboard by a patient roll? 11._____
    A. 5   B. 4   C. 2   D. 3   E. 6

12. To unload a wheeled stretcher, both EMTs 12._____
    A. remain in the compartment facing the patient
    B. wheel or lift the stretcher to the rear of the ambulance
    C. release the hooks from the stretcher frame
    D. remain in the compartment facing the rear door
    E. grasp the stretcher while standing on the ground outside the compartment

13. Prior to loading, a wheeled stretcher should be placed perpendicular to the rear door within _____ foot(feet).
    A. 6   B. 1   C. 4   D. 3   E. 2

14. The patient's head can be BEST protected from drafts and cold weather by
    A. drawing a sheet over the head
    B. drawing a blanket over the head
    C. wrapping a blanket around the head
    D. surrounding the head with two pillows
    E. wrapping a towel around the head

15. The slide transfer of a ground level patient is useful when the
    A. EMTs have a portable stretcher higher than 2 to 3 inches
    B. patient is unconscious
    C. patient is very heavy
    D. patient has a suspected spine injury
    E. EMTs have access to only one side of the patient

16. Emergency calls USUALLY involve
    A. a patient in need of ancillary equipment
    B. a patient in a confined area
    C. an unconscious patient
    D. a floor/ground level patient
    E. multiple patients

17. Accessory equipment should be
    A. left in the vehicle
    B. transported by a third person
    C. carried between the two EMTs
    D. secured to the stretcher
    E. carried during a second trip

18. Special transfer sheets are typically constructed of
    A. linen   B. nylon   C. polyester   D. cotton   E. silk

19. The advantages of a short backboard are that it
    I. provides a firm surface for administering external cardiac compression
    II. immobilizes the supine patient
    III. has a narrower width than the long backboard
    IV. permits x-rays to be taken without removing backboard
    V. is designed to fold widthwise

    The CORRECT answer is:
    A. I, IV
    B. I, II, IV
    C. I, III, IV
    D. II, IV, V
    E. III, V

20. Scoop-type stretchers are well suited to patients   20.____

    A. in need of special airway care
    B. with suspected arm or leg injuries
    C. at a floor or ground level location
    D. of advanced age
    E. with suspected spine injuries

21. What is the key to transferring a patient in confined areas and over obstacles?   21.____

    A. Positioning the patient on the stretcher
    B. Maintaining a level stretcher position
    C. Securing the patient to the stretcher
    D. Using proper carry procedures
    E. Patient comfort

22. The patient that requires more care and thought by the EMTs than any other   22.____
    type patient is the

    A. hard to control patient
    B. vomiting patient
    C. unconscious patient
    D. patient attached to life-support equipment
    E. spine-injured patient

23. Where should body straps be placed on spine-injured patients transported by a long   23.____
    backboard?

    A. Shoulders - waist – ankles   B. Shoulders - hips - ankles
    C. Chest - waist – knees   D. Chest - hips - knees
    E. Shoulders - waist - knees

24. Which of the following is a safety regulation for a portable stretcher having no   24.____
    legs or wheels?

    A. Secure it at floor level
    B. Suspend it by ceiling-mounted brackets
    C. Strap it on the squad bench
    D. Position the patient's head toward the rear of the ambulance
    E. None of the above

25. All of the following are characteristics of standard ambulances EXCEPT: 25.____

    A. They are large enough to accommodate two patients
    B. They have doors at the rear of the vehicle
    C. They have level floors
    D. The floor is close to the ground
    E. They have securing devices

KEY (CORRECT ANSWERS)

1. E
2. E
3. A
4. D
5. B

6. B
7. A
8. D
9. A
10. C

11. B
12. E
13. D
14. E
15. E

16. D
17. D
18. B
19. A
20. E

21. C
22. A
23. D
24. C
25. A

EXAMINATION SECTION
TEST 1

DIRECTIONS: Each question or incomplete statement is followed by several suggested answers or completions. Select the one that BEST answers the question or completes the statement. PRINT THE LETTER OF THE CORRECT ANSWER IN THE SPACE AT THE RIGHT.

1. What are the PRINCIPAL objectives to covering the patient on the stretcher?   1.____
   - I. Maintain an acceptable body temperature
   - II. Avoid exposure to drafts
   - III. Ensure patient's privacy
   - IV. Help secure patient on stretcher
   - V. Avoid excessive soiling of bedding

   The CORRECT answer is:
   - A. I, II, IV
   - B. I, II, III
   - C. I, II
   - D. I, II, V
   - E. I, IV, V

2. Where is the stretcher located for a direct carry transfer of a patient at ground level if the EMTs are facing the patient's right side?   2.____
   - A. Perpendicular to patient's head
   - B. Along patient's left side
   - C. Perpendicular to patient's feet
   - D. Behind EMTs
   - E. Between EMTs

3. Where should a lightweight chair mattress be placed when transferring a bed-level patient?   3.____
   - A. At waist level between the two EMTs
   - B. On the floor next to the bed
   - C. On the stair chair
   - D. On the bed
   - E. Perpendicular to the bed

4. What is the MOST popular transfer method used by ambulance personnel?   4.____
   - A. Slide transfer
   - B. Extremity transfer
   - C. Patient roll
   - D. Seat carry
   - E. Arm-lift-chest carry

5. What is the key task of the EMT?   5.____
   - A. Loading the ambulance
   - B. Preparing and positioning patient-carrying devices
   - C. Carrying the patient-loaded stretcher
   - D. Transferring the patient to the stretcher
   - E. Unloading the ambulance

6. The advantages of the portable stretcher are
   I. easy maneuverability
   II. less bending for the EMT
   III. lightweight
   IV. easy immobilization of the patient
   V. compactness

   The CORRECT answer is:
   A. I, II, III
   B. II, III, V
   C. I, III, V
   D. I, III, IV, V
   E. I, II, V

7. The _____ should be stored in a ready state.
   A. wheeled cot
   B. portable stretcher
   C. stair chair
   D. all of the above
   E. none of the above

8. The specific application of the transfer method selected depends MOST upon the
   A. age of the patient
   B. patient's medical condition
   C. patient's weight
   D. carrying device
   E. patient's location

9. Using the draw sheet method, the _____ supports much of the patient's weight during transfer.
   A. portable stretcher
   B. mattress
   C. EMT's arms
   D. sheet
   E. EMT's legs

10. Using the draw sheet method, the patient should be positioned
    A. supine with arms folded across chest, legs straight and close together
    B. supine with arms straight at sides, legs straight and close together
    C. supine with arms folded across chest, legs crossed - at ankles
    D. on his side, arms bent against chest, knees drawn up and together
    E. on his side, arms folded across chest, one knee drawn up

11. When using a low-level stretcher, the EMTs should position themselves
    A. on the side of the stretcher nearest the bed
    B. on the side of the stretcher opposite the bed
    C. at opposite short ends of the stretcher
    D. at opposite long sides of the stretcher
    E. adjacent, one at the short end, one at the long side

12. When using a bed-level stretcher, the ambulance attendants should position themselves
    A. on the side of the stretcher nearest the bed
    B. on the side of the stretcher opposite the bed
    C. at opposite short ends of the stretcher
    D. at opposite long sides of the stretcher
    E. adjacent, one at short end, one at long side

13. What parts of the patient's body are supported by the ambulance attendants during the transfer? 13.____
    I. Head   II. Shoulders   III. Hips
    IV. Knees   V. Feet

    The CORRECT answer is:
    A. I, II, III
    B. I, II, IV
    C. I, V
    D. II, III
    E. III, IV, V

14. The MAIN difference between transferring a bed-level patient and a ground-level patient by means of the direct-carry method is the 14.____

    A. type of equipment used
    B. placement of EMTs' arms
    C. placement of the stretcher
    D. method of positioning patient
    E. position of EMTs in relation to the patient

15. Once the wheeled stretcher is secured in the ambulance, the back rest may be elevated to 15.____

    A. 45°-60°   B. 15°-30°   C. 30°-45°   D. 5°-15°   E. 0°-10°

16. The side carry is typically reserved for 16.____

    A. lifting and moving a portable stretcher
    B. carrying the stretcher over any distance
    C. lifting and moving the stretcher over adverse terrain conditions
    D. tasks of loading and unloading the ambulance
    E. navigating stairs

17. The EMT enters the patient compartment while loading a wheeled stretcher 17.____

    A. after the stretcher is supported by the floor and the other EMT
    B. after the stretcher frame is rolled into a half-ring hook
    C. before the stretcher is secured
    D. after the stretcher is secured
    E. after the rear doors are closed

18. What is the BEST carrying device for patients with serious fractures? 18.____

    A. Wheeled stretchers
    B. Portable stretchers
    C. Scoop-type stretchers
    D. Stair chairs
    E. Long backboards

19. All of the following are procedures for positioning the unconscious patient EXCEPT 19.____

    A. rolling on the left side
    B. bending the uppermost leg
    C. positioning the lower arm parallel to the back
    D. bending the upper arm with palm in line with face
    E. bending the head and neck forward until the chin falls to the chest

4 (#1)

20. An infant is placed on his back when 20._____
    A. his head should be exposed
    B. he is premature
    C. he is carried in an incubator
    D. he is suffering any respiratory difficulties
    E. at no time

21. Suggested EMT dress excludes all of the following EXCEPT 21._____
    A. long overcoats   B. pocket pens   C. neckties
    D. watches   E. boots

22. A(n) _____ is NOT a reusable item. 22._____
    A. pillow   B. blanket   C. unsoiled linen
    D. mattress   E. all of the above

23. The slide transfer differs from the draw sheet method by the 23._____
    A. patient's position
    B. stretcher's position
    C. number of EMTs required
    D. amount of direct contact required
    E. fact that no sheet is used

24. Why is the bed-level patient easier to transfer than a floor or ground-level patient? 24._____
    I.   The patient can be positioned in comfort.
    II. The patient is conscious.
    III. The EMTs can work in a comfortable position.
    IV. It is not an emergency situation.
    V.   Clean work surfaces are accessible.

    The CORRECT answer is:
    A. I, II, III, IV   B. III, V   C. I, III, IV
    D. I, II, III   E. II, IV, V

25. The MOST common device for lifting a patient from the floor is the 25._____
    A. wheeled stretcher   B. short backboard
    C. long backboard   D. portable stretcher
    E. scoop-type stretcher

KEY (CORRECT ANSWERS)

1. B	6. C	11. C	16. D	21. E
2. B	7. A	12. E	17. D	22. C
3. D	8. D	13. B	18. E	23. E
4. E	9. D	14. C	19. E	24. B
5. D	10. A	15. C	20. D	25. E

TEST 2

DIRECTIONS: Each question or incomplete statement is followed by several suggested answers or completions. Select the one that BEST answers the question or completes the statement. PRINT THE LETTER OF THE CORRECT ANSWER IN THE SPACE AT THE RIGHT.

1. What are the BASIC procedures for positioning a patient on a wheeled stretcher? 1.____
   - I. Place the patient's head on a flat pillow
   - II. Position feet against footrest
   - III. Position legs flat against mattress
   - IV. Position backrest in level position
   - V. Adjust patient's body to form a straight line

   The CORRECT answer is:
   - A. I, II, V
   - B. I, IV, V
   - C. II, III, IV, V
   - D. II, III, V
   - E. II, IV, V

2. The advantage of the side carry is its 2.____
   - A. good weight distribution
   - B. easy maneuvering of stretcher position
   - C. near natural walking manner
   - D. all of the above
   - E. none of the above

3. The second EMT enters the patient compartment while loading a portable stretcher 3.____
   - A. after the stretcher is secured
   - B. after the stretcher is parallel to its transport position
   - C. before the stretcher is secured
   - D. after the stretcher is in its transport position
   - E. after the first EMT has entered

4. The _____ carrying device is generally used for spine-injured patients who have been secured to a short backboard. 4.____
   - A. long backboard
   - B. portable stretcher
   - C. stair chair
   - D. scoop-type stretcher
   - E. chair mattress

5. What is the recommended patient-handling procedure for the patient with an injured extremity? 5.____
   - A. Move patient as little as possible
   - B. Avoid proximity to the injured extremity
   - C. Maintain adequate support of the injured extremity
   - D. Splint or bandage the injured extremity.
   - E. All of the above

6. Where is an IV bottle USUALLY placed?

   A. Hand carried
   B. Between patient's legs
   C. On stretcher beside the patient
   D. Resting on stretcher frame of head rest under mattress
   E. On rail opposite loading side of the stretcher

7. The height of a two-level stretcher is typically adjusted by a

   A. slide bar
   B. foot release bar
   C. frame release handle
   D. hand release bar
   E. hand wheel

8. The head-end EMT drops to one knee after the ground-level patient has been raised to a sitting position during an extremity transfer to a stair chair in order to

   A. steady' the stair chair
   B. grasp the patient's wrists
   C. support the patient's back
   D. position himself for the two-man seat carry
   E. cradle the patient's head

9. When difficult maneuvers are anticipated, the stair chair patient is secured by safety belts around all of the following EXCEPT the

   A. waist
   B. chest
   C. lower legs
   D. thighs
   E. shoulders

10. The stair chair should NOT be used to transfer
    I.   spine-injured patients
    II. patients receiving oxygen
    III. patients with fracture of lower extremities
    IV. vomiting patients
    V.   unconscious patients

    The CORRECT answer is:
    A. I, II, IV
    B. I, III, V
    C. II, IV, V
    D. II, IV
    E. II, V

11. What type patients are positioned in a prone position on the stretcher?
    I.   Patient with injured extremity
    II. Spine-injured patient (with short backboard)
    III. Vomiting patient
    IV. Unconscious patient
    V.   Hard to control patient

    The CORRECT answer is:
    A. I, II, V
    B. I, IV
    C. I, V
    D. III, IV, V
    E. II, IV, V

12. The oxygen cylinder is usually NOT placed   12.____
    A. on the patient's lap
    B. on the stretcher beside the patient
    C. resting on the stretcher frame of head rest under mattress
    D. on the cot-mounted cylinder holder
    E. on the rail opposite the loading side of the stretcher

13. What patient arm position is used to transport a spine-injured patient on a long   13.____
    backboard?
    A. Across chest   B. Across stomach
    C. Straight at sides   D. Bent toward shoulders
    E. Across pelvis

14. The _____ should be removed from a wheeled stretcher being prepared to   14.____
    receive a patient-loaded scoop-type stretcher.
    A. pillow   B. sheets   C. blanket
    D. all of the above   E. none of the above

15. The first ambulance attendant leaves the patient compartment while unloading a   15.____
    non-wheeled portable stretcher
    A. after the ambulance has stopped
    B. after the stretcher is lowered to the floor
    C. after the securing device is removed
    D. before the securing device is removed
    E. after the ambulance driver enters the compartment

16. What patient condition demands the MOST care in handling?   16.____
    A. Unconscious
    B. Psychiatric
    C. Spine-injured
    D. Patient requiring life support equipment
    E. Limb fracture

17. It is necessary to load a patient into an ambulance supported only by a portable   17.____
    stretcher when
    A. the wheeled stretcher was not used in transfer
    B. there is more than one stretcher patient
    C. there is ancillary equipment
    D. a spine injury is suspected
    E. emergency conditions exist

18. The side carry carrying procedure recommends attendants   18.____
    A. grasp the upper bar of the stretcher frame
    B. use an extended arm position
    C. grasp bar with one palm up, one palm down
    D. grasp bar with both palms up
    E. grasp bar with both palms down

19. Which of the following is NOT a recommended procedure for applying a foul weather pouch?　　19.____
    A. Place unzipped section toward the head
    B. Tuck top section over pillow
    C. Zip top section close over patient's face during transport
    D. Tuck pouch around frame of the stretcher
    E. All of the above

20. The _____ restraint is NOT a special restraint strap used to secure patients.　　20.____
    A. wrist　　B. ankle　　C. knee　　D. head　　E. waist

21. What part of the attendant's body should be kept rigid during the direct carry of a ground-level patient?　　21.____
    A. Legs　　B. Arms　　C. Back　　D. Neck　　E. Wrists

22. A portable canvas stretcher can substitute for a　　22.____
    A. draw sheet　　　　B. backboard　　　　C. stair chair
    D. splint　　　　　　E. mattress chair

23. What transfer method is inappropriate for a floor/ground level patient?　　23.____
    A. Use of hinged scoop-type stretcher　　B. Extremity transfer
    C. Slide transfer　　　　　　　　　　　　D. Direct carry
    E. Draw sheet

24. What approach is preferred if the patient is bed-ridden and CANNOT be handled directly?　　24.____
    A. Arm-lift-chest carry　　　　B. Draw sheet method
    C. Patient roll　　　　　　　　D. Slide transfer
    E. Extremity transfer

25. Which of the following procedures are relatively similar for various transfer methods and carrying devices?　　25.____
    I.   Positioning equipment
    II. Lifting patient
    III. Positioning patient
    IV. Carrying patient to the stretcher
    V.   Placing patient on the stretcher

    The CORRECT answer is:
    A. I, III. V　　　　　　B I, V　　　　　　C. III, IV, V
    D. II, III, IV　　　　　E. I, IV, V

KEY (CORRECT ANSWERS)

1. A
2. E
3. B
4. A
5. E

6. A
7. B
8. C
9. E
10. B

11. D
12. E
13. C
14. D
15. B

16. C
17. B
18. C
19. D
20. C

21. C
22. A
23. E
24. B
25. C

EXAMINATION SECTION
TEST 1

DIRECTIONS: Each question or incomplete statement is followed by several suggested answers or completions. Select the one that BEST answers the question or completes the statement. *PRINT THE LETTER OF THE CORRECT ANSWER IN THE SPACE AT THE RIGHT.*

1. The transmission of signals by electromagnetic waves is referred to as　　1.____
    - A. biotelemetry
    - B. radio
    - C. noise
    - D. all of the above

2. The transmission of physiologic data, such as an ECG, from the patient to a distant point of reception is called　　2.____
    - A. biotelemetry
    - B. simplex
    - C. landline
    - D. none of the above

3. The assembly of a transmitter, receiver, and antenna connection at a fixed location creates a　　3.____
    - A. transceiver
    - B. radio
    - C. biotelemetry
    - D. base station

4. The portion of the radio frequency spectrum between 30 and 150 mhz is called　　4.____
    - A. very high frequency (VHF)
    - B. ultrahigh frequency (UHF)
    - C. very low frequency (VLF)
    - D. all of the above

5. A _____ is a miniature transmitter that picks up a radio signal and rebroadcasts it, thus extending the range of a radiocommunication system.　　5.____
    - A. transceiver
    - B. repeater
    - C. simplex
    - D. duplex

6. The portion of the radio frequency spectrum falling between 300 and 3,000 mhz is called　　6.____
    - A. ultrahigh frequency (UHF)
    - B. very high frequency (VHF)
    - C. very low frequency (VLF)
    - D. none of the above

7. One cycle per second equals one _____ in units of frequency.　　7.____
    - A. hertz
    - B. kilohertz
    - C. megahertz
    - D. gigahertz

8. The sources of noise in ECG telemetry include　　8.____
    - A. loose ECG electrodes
    - B. muscle tremors
    - C. sources of 60-cycle alternating current such as transformers, power lines, and electric equipment
    - D. all of the above

9. The method of radio communications called _____ utilizes a single frequency that enables either transmission or reception of either voice or an ECG signal, but is incapable of simultaneous transmission and reception.

   A. duplex
   B. simplex
   C. multiplex
   D. none of the above

10. A terminal that receives transmissions of telemetry and voice from the field and transmits messages back through the base is referred to as a

    A. transceiver
    B. remote control
    C. remote console
    D. ten-code

11. The role of dispatcher includes

    A. reception of requests for help
    B. arrangements for getting the appropriate people and equipment to a situation which requires them
    C. deciding upon and dispatching of the appropriate emergency vehicles
    D. all of the above

12. A dispatcher should NOT

    A. maintain records
    B. scope a problem by requesting additional information from a caller
    C. direct public safety personnel
    D. receive notification of emergencies and call for assistance from both individual citizens and public safety units

13. The professional society of public safety communicators has developed a standard set of ten codes, the MOST common of which is 10-

    A. 1   B. 4   C. 12   D. 18

14. What is the meaning of 10-33?

    A. Help me quick
    B. Arrived at scene
    C. Reply to message
    D. Disregard

15. One of the MAIN purposes of ten-codes is to

    A. shorten air time
    B. complicate the message
    C. increase the likelihood of misunderstanding
    D. none of the above

Questions 16-20.

DIRECTIONS: In Questions 16 through 20, match each translation of a commonly used ten-code with its appropriate code, listed in Column I.

COLUMN I
A. 10-1
B. 10-9
C. 10-18
D. 10-20
E. 10-23

16. What is your location? 16.____
17. Urgent. 17.____
18. Signal weak. 18.____
19. Arrived at the scene. 19.____
20. Please repeat. 20.____

KEY (CORRECT ANSWERS)

1. B 11. D
2. A 12. C
3. D 13. B
4. A 14. A
5. B 15. A

6. D 16. D
7. A 17. C
8. D 18. A
9. B 19. E
10. C 20. B

TEST 2

DIRECTIONS: Each question or incomplete statement is followed by several suggested answers or completions. Select the one that BEST answers the question or completes the statement. *PRINT THE LETTER OF THE CORRECT ANSWER IN THE SPACE AT THE RIGHT.*

1. FCC rules prohibit

    A. deceptive or unnecessary messages
    B. profanity
    C. dissemination or use of confidential information transmitted over the radio
    D. all of the above

2. Penalties for violations of FCC rules and regulations range from

    A. prison to death
    B. $20,000 to $100,000
    C. $100 to $10,000 and up to one year in prison
    D. up to 10 years in prison

3. Which of the following is NOT true about base stations?

    A. The terrain and location do not affect the function.
    B. A good high-gain antenna improves transmission and reception efficiency.
    C. Multiple frequency capability is available at the base station.
    D. Antenna should be as close as possible to the base station transmitter/receiver.

4. Radio frequencies are designated by cycles per second. 1,000,000 cycles per second equals one

    A. kilohertz   B. megahertz   C. gigahertz   D. hertz

5. The Federal Communications Commission (FCC) is the agency of the United States government responsible for

    A. licensing and frequency allocation
    B. establishing technical standards for radio equipment
    C. establishing and enforcing rules and regulations for the operation of radio equipment
    D. all of the above

6. Information relayed to the physician should include all of the following EXCEPT

    A. patient's age, sex, and chief complaint
    B. pertinent history of present illness
    C. detailed family history
    D. pertinent physical findings

7. True statements regarding UHF band may include all of the following EXCEPT:
   A. It has better penetration in the dense metropolitan area
   B. Reception is usually quiet inside the building
   C. It has a longer range than VHF band
   D. Most medical communications occur around 450 to 470 mhz

8. Which of the following statements is NOT true regarding VHF band?
   A. Low band frequency may have ranges up to 2000 miles, but are unpredictable.
   B. VHF band may cause *skip interference,* with patchy losses in communication.
   C. High band frequency is wholly free of skip interference.
   D. High band frequencies for emergency medical purposes are in the 300 to 3000 mhz range.

9. 1000 cycles per second is equal to one
   A. hertz   B. kilohertz   C. megahertz   D. gigahertz

10. _____ achieves simultaneous transmission of voice and ECG signals over a single radio frequency.
    A. Duplex
    C. Channel
    B. Multiplex
    D. None of the above

11. Radio equipment used for both VHF and UHF band is
    A. frequency modulated
    B. amplitude modulated
    C. double amplitude modulated
    D. all of the above

12. ECG telemetry over UHF frequencies is confined to _____ of a 12 lead ECG.
    A. 1   B. 2   C. 6   D. 12

13. All of the following further clarity and conciseness EXCEPT
    A. understandable rate of speaking
    B. knowing what you want to transmit after transmission
    C. clear presentation of numbers, names, and dates
    D. using phrases and words which are easy to copy

14. The LEAST preferred of the following words is
    A. check   B. desire   C. want   D. advise if

15. All of the following are techniques useful during a call EXCEPT
    A. answering promptly
    B. identifying yourself and your department
    C. speaking directly into the mouthpiece
    D. none of the above

Questions 16-20.

DIRECTIONS: In Questions 16 through 20, match each definition with the term it describes, listed in Column I.

> COLUMN I
> A. Frequency
> B. Noise
> C. Patch
> D. Duplex
> E. Transceiver

16. A radio transmitter and receiver housed in a single unit; a two-way radio 16.____

17. The number of cycles per second of a radio signal, inversely related to the wavelength. 17.____

18. Interference in radio signals. 18.____

19. A radio system employing more than one frequency to permit simultaneous transmission and reception. 19.____

20. Connection between a telephone line and a radio communication system, enabling a caller to get *on the air* by special telephone. 20.____

KEY (CORRECT ANSWERS)

1.	D	11.	A
2.	C	12.	A
3.	A	13.	B
4.	B	14.	C
5.	D	15.	D
6.	C	16.	E
7.	C	17.	A
8.	D	18.	B
9.	B	19.	D
10.	B	20.	C

EXAMINATION SECTION
TEST 1

DIRECTIONS: Each question or incomplete statement is followed by several suggested answers or completions. Select the one that BEST answers the question or completes the statement. *PRINT THE LETTER OF THE CORRECT ANSWER IN THE SPACE AT THE RIGHT.*

1. In a case in which a person is unconscious, or for some other reason unable to give actual consent, and you believe a life-threatening illness or injury exists, the law assumes that the patient, if able to do so, would want to receive treatment.
   This is known as _____ consent. 1.____
   A. informed
   B. implied
   C. involuntary
   D. none of the above

2. At the EMT level, the failure to provide expected care at the standard of care, leading to injury or death of the patient, is called 2.____
   A. negligence
   B. abandonment
   C. failure to act
   D. duty to act

3. A victim found lying on his stomach, facedown, is in the _____ position. 3.____
   A. supine
   B. erect
   C. prone
   D. left recumbent

4. All of the following are anterior body cavities EXCEPT the _____ cavity. 4.____
   A. cranial   B. thoracic   C. pelvic   D. abdominal

5. The system which produces chemicals called hormones that help regulate most body activities and functions is the _____ system. 5.____
   A. integumentary
   B. endocrine
   C. immune
   D. nervous

6. _____ is a rotation of the forearm so that the palm is facing forward. 6.____
   A. Pronation
   B. Supination
   C. Superior
   D. Proximal

7. As an EMT, you will have to consider many factors before you will know what is wrong with a patient and what course of emergency care you will take.
   For example, on arrival you MUST 7.____
   A. state your name and rank or classification and the organization you represent
   B. identify yourself as an emergency medical technician
   C. ask the patient if you may help
   D. all of the above

8. Yellow-colored skin represents the possibility of abnormality in the 8.____
   A. heart
   B. liver
   C. renal system
   D. brain

213

9. If a victim has deep, gasping, and labored respiration, the possible cause may be

   A. airway obstruction   B. heart failure
   C. asthma   D. all of the above

10. Among the following, the MOST likely cause of unequal pupil size is

    A. amphetamines   B. heroin
    C. stroke   D. cardiac arrest

11. Priapism in a male patient is a possible sign of

    A. spinal injury
    B. central nervous system injury
    C. cardiac arrest
    D. liver failure

12. Coarse *popping* or snoring noises heard during expiration are called

    A. wheezing   B. rales   C. rhonchi   D. stridor

Questions 13-14.

DIRECTIONS: Questions 13 and 14 are to be answered on the basis of the following information.

A victim of an automobile accident has a respiratory rate of 36 breaths per minute, retractive chest movements, a systololic blood pressure of 80 mmHg, and delayed capillary refill. The patient also shows no eye opening, no verbal response, and an extension reaction to pain.

13. The TOTAL Glasgow coma score of the above patient is

    A. 2   B. 4   C. 5   D. 6

14. The Champion Sacco trauma score of the above patient is

    A. 3   B. 5   C. 7   D. 10

15. The trapdoor-like structure at the entrance to the trachea is the

    A. larynx   B. pharynx
    C. epiglottis   D. none of the above

16. A manual thrust to the abdomen to force bursts of air from the lungs to dislodge an airway obstruction is referred to as

    A. Murphy's sign   B. Heimlich maneuver
    C. Cooly's sign   D. all of the above

17. Cardiopulmonary resuscitation (CPR) is the basic life support measure applied when a patient's heart and lung actions have stopped.
    While performing CPR, you will have to

    A. maintain an open airway
    B. breathe for the patient
    C. perform chest compressions to force the patient's blood to circulate
    D. all of the above

18. Among the following, which is NOT an indication of effective CPR? 18._____

    A. Dilated pupils
    B. Improved skin color
    C. Spontaneous gasping respiration
    D. Attempted swallowing

19. The MOST common complication of CPR is 19._____

    A. laceration of the liver   B. clavicular fracture
    C. ribcage injury   D. laceration of the lung

20. The PRIMARY electrical disturbance resulting in cardiac arrest is called 20._____

    A. electromechanical dissociation
    B. ventricular fibrillation
    C. ventricular tachycardia
    D. none of the above

21. In 20% to 25% of cardiac arrest victims, the heart has altogether ceased generating electrical impulses, and there is no repetitive electrical stimulus to cause the heart muscle to contract. 21._____
    This condition is called

    A. ventricular fibrillation
    B. asystole
    C. atrial fibrillation
    D. electromechanical dissociation

Questions 22-25.

DIRECTIONS: In Questions 22 through 25, match the described condition with the appropriate lettered level of priority, listed in Column I, indicated by the condition. Place the letter of the CORRECT answer in the appropriate space at the right.

COLUMN I
A. Priority 1
B. Priority 2
C. Priority 3
D. Priority 4

22. Dead or fatally injured. 22._____

23. Correctable life-threatening illness or injury. 23._____

24. Walking wounded; non-serious illness or injury. 24._____

25. Serious but not life-threatening illness or injury. 25._____

KEY (CORRECT ANSWERS)

1. B
2. A
3. C
4. A
5. B

6. B
7. D
8. B
9. D
10. C

11. A
12. C
13. B
14. C
15. C

16. B
17. D
18. A
19. C
20. B

21. B
22. D
23. A
24. C
25. B

TEST 2

DIRECTIONS: Each question or incomplete statement is followed by several suggested answers or completions. Select the one that BEST answers the question or completes the statement. *PRINT THE LETTER OF THE CORRECT ANSWER IN THE SPACE AT THE RIGHT.*

1. A 40-year-old patient with sinus bradycardia develops hypotension on the way to the hospital.
   The drug of choice for this condition is
   - A. atropin sulfate
   - B. amyl nitrite
   - C. diphenhydramine
   - D. bretylium tosylate

2. The therapeutic effects of vaporole include all of the following EXCEPT
   - A. oxidizes hemoglobin to methemoglobin
   - B. causes vasodilation
   - C. causes coronary artery spasms
   - D. can relieve spasms of the biliary tract

3. The common trade name of albuterol is
   - A. proventil
   - B. solumedrol
   - C. vaporole
   - D. adrenalin

4. A 10-year-old boy who is a known asthmatic develops nausea, vomiting, palpitations, excitement, and confusion. He is on multiple medications for asthma.
   Among the following, the medication MOST likely causing the above symptoms is
   - A. prednisone
   - B. theophylline
   - C. cromolyn sodium
   - D. oxygen

5. The patient suffering from poisoning by atropine or other anticholinergics is CLASSICALLY described as
   - A. hot as a hare
   - B. blind as a bat
   - C. red as a beet
   - D. all of the above

6. The drug used to relieve muscle spasms and pain from the bite of a black widow spider is
   - A. sodium bicarbonate
   - B. magnesium sulfate
   - C. calcium gluconate
   - D. verapamil

7. A 20-year-old patient who becomes unconscious upon the administration of insulin requires 50 ml of _____ % solution of glucose slowly by IV.
   - A. 5
   - B. 10
   - C. 25
   - D. 50

8. All of the following contraindicate adrenalin use EXCEPT
   - A. angina
   - B. cardiac arrest
   - C. hyperthyroidism
   - D. hypertension

9. Vaponefrin was administered to a child with severe croup. The common side effects you should look for include

   A. dysrhythmias
   B. paradoxical bronchospasm
   C. angina
   D. all of the above

10. A 60-year-old man with a known cardiac problem develops dyspnea. On auscultation, the patient was noted to have bilateral rales. You suspect congestive heart failure. The medication which will help you decrease fluid overload in this condition is

    A. propranolol
    B. lasix
    C. verapamil
    D. aramine

11. You respond to a 911 call. On arrival, a 40-year-old male is having crushing chest pain. You suspect acute myocardial infarction.
    The drug of choice to relieve the pain of this condition is

    A. tylenol
    B. morphine sulfate
    C. a non-steroidal anti-inflammatory drug
    D. aspirin

12. Among the following, the CONTRAINDICATION to inderal use is

    A. supraventricular tachyarrhythmias
    B. ventricular tachycardia
    C. congestive heart failure
    D. atrial fibrillation

13. A patient with known hypertension who is taking spironolactone along with other medications develops ascending paralysis.
    When you put him on a cardiac monitor, you noticed a peaked T wave, which is indicative of

    A. hypokalemia
    B. hyperkalemia
    C. hyponatremia
    D. hypomagnessemia

14. A *U wave* on an EKG is suggestive of

    A. hypokalemia
    B. hyperkalemia
    C. hyponatremia
    D. hypernatremia

15. A persistent idea that a person cannot dismiss from his thoughts is known as a(n)

    A. obsession
    B. compulsion
    C. confabulation
    D. perseveration

16. All of the following are examples of neuroleptic (antipsychotic) drugs EXCEPT

    A. droperidol
    B. haloperidol
    C. alprazolam
    D. perphenazine

17. _____ is NOT among the drugs commonly used to treat depression.

    A. Amitriptyline
    B. Doxepin
    C. Triazolam
    D. Imipramine

18. Which of the following is NOT a disorder of mood and affect? 18._____

    A. Euphoria B. Confabulation
    C. Panic   D. Ambivalence

19. _____ is NOT a disorder of thought content. 19._____

    A. Delusion   B. Compulsion
    C. Obsession D. Phobia

20. Drugs which induce psychoses include 20._____

    A. steroids B. digitalis
    C. LSD   D. all of the above

Questions 21-25.

DIRECTIONS: In Questions 21 through 25, match the numbered definition with the lettered term, listed in Column I, that it BEST describes. Place the letter of the CORRECT answer in the appropriate space at the right.

COLUMN I
A. Medullary canal
B. Occipital
C. Plaque
D. Spinous processes
E. Vernix

21. The slippery protective coating that covers a baby when it is born. 21._____

22. The cavity of a long bone; it contains the bone marrow. 22._____

23. The bony extensions of the posterior vertebrae. 23._____

24. Fatty deposits on the interior walls of arteries. 24._____

25. The posterior portion of the brain in which the vision center is located. 25._____

KEY (CORRECT ANSWERS)

1. A
2. C
3. A
4. B
5. D

6. C
7. D
8. B
9. D
10. B

11. B
12. C
13. B
14. A
15. A

16. C
17. C
18. B
19. B
20. D

21. E
22. A
23. D
24. C
25. B

TEST 3

DIRECTIONS: Each question or incomplete statement is followed by several suggested answers or completions. Select the one that BEST answers the question or completes the statement. *PRINT THE LETTER OF THE CORRECT ANSWER IN THE SPACE AT THE RIGHT.*

1. Charcoal therapy is useful in treating a patient with

    A. lithium overdose
    B. iron poisoning
    C. aspirin overdose
    D. methanol poisoning

2. If a victim has chemical burns on his face, including the eyes, you should

    A. cover the eyes with loose, moist dressing
    B. cover the eyes with dark patches
    C. hold the face under running water, with the eyes open, for at least 20 minutes
    D. all of the above

3. A 30-year-old has heat burn to the eyes. On examination, you find that the eyelids are burned and the patient's eyes are closed.
What will you do?

    A. Apply a loose, moist dressing
    B. Try to inspect the eyes first
    C. Wash the eyes with running water
    D. Cover the eyes with dark patches

4. The fluid that fills the lens of the eye is

    A. vitreous humor
    B. aqueous humor
    C. CSF
    D. none of the above

5. When a penetrating or blunt injury to the heart causes blood to flow into the surrounding pericardial sac, what condition is produced?

    A. Myocardial infarction
    B. Myocardial rupture
    C. Cardiac tamponade
    D. Myocardial aneurysm

6. When a weakened section of the lung ruptures and releases air into the thoracic cavity, the resulting condition is called

    A. hemothorax
    B. pneumothorax
    C. hemopneumothorax
    D. pleural effusion

7. The _____ is a large, multifunctional gland in the right upper quadrant, protected by the lower ribs.

    A. kidney B. spleen C. liver D. pancreas

8. The highly vascularized organ located behind the stomach and protected by the lower ribs on the left side of the body is the

    A. spleen B. pancreas C. kidney D. stomach

9. If a victim receives blunt trauma of the erect penis, you should

   A. apply direct pressure dressing
   B. give a padded ice pack and transport him
   C. treat him for shock
   D. apply a triangular bandage

Questions 10-11.

DIRECTIONS: Questions 10 and 11 are to be answered on the basis of the following information.

A 50-year-old male patient calls 911 because he is experiencing pain originating behind the sternum and radiating to both upper arms, shoulders, the neck, and the jaw. The patient also complains of shortness of breath. The pain usually lasts 3 to 5 minutes, and it is not influenced by movement. He has had 3 attacks over the last 6 hours.

10. The MOST likely diagnosis is

    A. congestive heart failure
    B. angina pectoris
    C. heartburn
    D. acute gastritis

11. The BEST treatment for the above condition is

    A. furosemide IV   B. nitroglycerin sublingual
    C. mylanta   D. zantac

12. The common signs and symptoms of alcohol abuse include

    A. slowed reaction time   B. blurred vision
    C. lack of memory   D. all of the above

13. The placenta is formed in an abnormal location, usually low in the uterus and close to or over the cervical opening, which will not allow a normal delivery of a fetus. As the cervix dilates, the placenta tears.
    This condition is called

    A. abruptio placentae   B. placenta previa
    C. prolapse cord   D. uterine rupture

14. The condition in which the placenta separates from the uterine wall is

    A. abruptio placentae   B. placenta previa
    C. uterine atony   D. none of the above

15. Eclampsia is distinguished from pre eclampsia by

    A. edema
    B. excessive weight gain
    C. elevated blood pressure
    D. onset of convulsions or coma

16. The organ of pregnancy where the exchange of oxygen, foods, and wastes occurs between mother and fetus is the   16.____

    A. amniotic sac   B. placenta
    C. perineum   D. none of the above

17. The *rule of palm* is a method for estimating the extent of a burn.   17.____
    The palm of the hand equals APPROXIMATELY _____ % of the body surface area.

    A. 1   B. 2   C. 5   D. 10

Questions 18-19.

DIRECTIONS: Questions 18 and 19 are to be answered on the basis of the following information.

An 18-year-old boy is found on the ground unconscious after playing football on a hot summer day. He has shallow breathing, a rapid, strong pulse, dry, hot skin, dilated pupils, and muscular twitching.

18. The MOST likely diagnosis is heat   18.____

    A. exhaustion   B. cramps
    C. stroke   D. all of the above

19. What emergency care procedure should be taken?   19.____

    A. Cool the patient
    B. Treat for shock and administer 100% oxygen
    C. Transport as soon as possible
    D. All of the above

Questions 20-25.

DIRECTIONS: In Questions 20 through 25, match the numbered definition with the lettered term, listed in Column I, that it BEST describes. Place the letter of the CORRECT answer in the appropriate space at the right.

COLUMN I

20. Inflammation of the brain.   A. Effacement   20.____
                                      B. Ductus arteriosus
21. End of a long bone.   C. Ductus venosus   21.____
                                      D. Emaciation
22. Thinning of the cervix as the lower segment of the   E. Encephalitis   22.____
    uterus retracts during the first stage of labor.   F. Epiphysis

23. Muscular tube through which the umbilical vein   23.____
    enters the fetal abdomen.

                                                          24.____
24. Excessive leanness.
                                                          25.____
25. Direct communication between the pulmonary artery
    and the aorta in fetal circulation.

223

KEY (CORRECT ANSWERS)

1. C
2. C
3. A
4. B
5. C

6. B
7. C
8. A
9. B
10. B

11. B
12. D
13. B
14. A
15. D

16. B
17. A
18. C
19. D
20. E

21. F
22. A
23. C
24. D
25. B

EXAMINATION SECTION
TEST 1

DIRECTIONS: Each question or incomplete statement is followed by several suggested answers or completions. Select the one that BEST answers the question or completes the statement. *PRINT THE LETTER OF THE CORRECT ANSWER IN THE SPACE AT THE RIGHT.*

1. Upon arrival in response to 911, the paramedics found the victim lying facedown. Among the following, the appropriate medical terminology to describe the EXACT position of the patient is

    A. supine
    B. prone
    C. left recumbent
    D. distal

2. The FIRST thing the EMT should do if the victim has acute laryngeal edema due to an allergic reaction, manifested by a hoarse voice, is

    A. administer oxygen
    B. administer epinephrine
    C. establish an airway
    D. cricothyrotomy

3. Abdominal compression techniques should NOT be used in infants and small children for the management of choking because

    A. the abdominal space is very small
    B. they are ineffective in all ages
    C. of the vulnerability of the liver and other abdominal organs to serious injury
    D. all of the above

4. If you suspect laryngeal edema in a victim of allergic reaction, you should use a 1:_____ concentration and a dose of _____ ml subcutaneously of epinephrine.

    A. 1000; 0.3 to 0.5
    B. 1000; 1 to 2
    C. 10,000; 0.3 to 0.5
    D. none of the above

5. The very FIRST step an EMT should take upon reaching the scene of any emergency is to

    A. perform a primary survey
    B. survey the scene
    C. perform a secondary survey
    D. establish definitive field management

6. On the scene of an emergency, the FIRST step in the primary survey of every patient is to determine whether the patient is

    A. conscious or unconscious
    B. in respiratory distress
    C. in shock
    D. bleeding

7. The IMPORTANT signs of choking include:

    A. Victim cannot speak or make any sound
    B. Dusky or cyanotic skin

225

C. Exaggerated but ineffective breathing movements
D. All of the above

8. Upon arrival in response to 911, you find a conscious choking victim with complete obstruction. You perform four back blows in quick succession, but they are not effective. Your NEXT step should be to

   A. finger sweep
   B. apply 6 to 10 manual thrusts
   C. apply 10 to 12 manual thrusts
   D. all of the above

9. When the unrestrained front-seat occupant slides forward, the first impact is often that of the knees against the dashboard.
   This impact may produce a fracture of the

   A. tibia   B. fibula   C. patella   D. hip

10. On the primary survey of a victim of a motor vehicle accident, you find bruises of the anterior neck.
    You should consider

    A. pneumothorax   B. tracheal fracture
    C. pericardial tamponade D. none of the above

11. Upon arriving on the scene of a motor vehicle accident, you find a deformed side of a car, but on primary survey of the victim you find only a bruised shoulder.
    You should look for a _____ fracture.

    A. clavicular   B. humerus
    C. multiple rib D. all of the above

12. When a pedestrian rebounds off of the car onto the ground, which of the following injuries MOST commonly occurs?

    A. Open fracture of tibia and fibula
    B. Fracture of pelvis and femur
    C. Head injury
    D. Fracture of the wrist

13. Of the following, _____ mm ET tubes should be used in 7 to 12 month old infants.

    A. 2.5   B. 4   C. 6   D. 7

14. The conditions that preclude the use of a drug are called

    A. biotransformation B. cumulative action
    C. contraindication   D. none of the above

15. The fine crackling sounds that ALWAYS indicate the presence of fluid in the alveoli are termed

    A. rhonchi   B. rales   C. wheezes   D. strider

16. A patient is bleeding from his forearm. 16.____
    Of the following, the pressure point MOST helpful in slowing the bleeding would be the
    _____ artery.

    A. brachial   B. radial   C. ulnar   D. femoral

17. You can approximate the amount of fluid a burned patient needs by using the Parkland 17.____
    formula.
    This formula states that in the first 24 hours, the burned patient will need

    A. 2 ml/kg body weight/percent of body surface burned
    B. 4 ml/kg body weight/percent of body surface burned
    C. 150 ml per hour
    D. all of the above

18. An infant who has burns on his entire lower extremities, genitalia, and entire left arm, by 18.____
    using the rule of nine, has burned _____ percent of his body surface area.

    A. 20   B. 30   C. 38   D. 47

19. A 35-year-old patient has burns on his entire lower extremities, genitalia, and back of the 19.____
    trunk.
    By using the rule of nine, this patient has burned _____ percent of his body surface
    area.

    A. 25   B. 35   C. 45   D. 55

20. Among the following, the degree of burn which will NOT require analgesic treatment is a 20.____
    _____ degree burn.

    A. first   B. second
    C. third   D. all of the above

Questions 21-25.

DIRECTIONS: In Questions 21 through 25, match the numbered definition with the lettered
term, listed in Column I, that it MOST accurately describes. Place the letter of
the CORRECT answer in the appropriate space at the right.

21. The portion of the tidal volume that does not   COLUMN I   21.____
    participate in gas exchange   A. Diaphragm
                                                   B. Pleura
22. A large skeletal muscle that plays a major role in C. Dead space   22.____
    breathing and separates the chest cavity from the D. Cyanosis
    abdominal cavity   E. Hypoxemia

23. Inadequate oxygen in the blood   23.____

24. Blueness of the skin which can be caused by methemo-globulonimia   24.____

25. The membrane lining the outer surface of the lungs   25.____

KEY (CORRECT ANSWERS)

1. B
2. C
3. C
4. A
5. B

6. A
7. D
8. B
9. C
10. B

11. D
12. C
13. B
14. C
15. B

16. A
17. B
18. C
19. D
20. C

21. C
22. A
23. E
24. D
25. B

TEST 2

DIRECTIONS: Each question or incomplete statement is followed by several suggested answers or completions. Select the one that BEST answers the question or completes the statement. *PRINT THE LETTER OF THE CORRECT ANSWER IN THE SPACE AT THE RIGHT.*

1. A 28-year-old male was involved in a motor vehicle accident. On primary survey, the patient had paradoxical movement of the chest and multiple bruises on both sides of the chest.
   The MOST likely diagnosis is

   A. hemothorax
   B. flail chest
   C. pneumothorax
   D. none of the above

2. You receive a call from 911 for a stab wound. Upon arrival on the scene, your primary survey finds the patient actively bleeding on the left side of the chest, with mild respiratory distress. While you are stopping the bleeding, the patient suddenly gets dyspnic with engorged neck vein.
   The MOST likely diagnosis is

   A. pneumothorax
   B. hemothorax
   C. pericardial tamponade
   D. all of the above

3. If you want to check the motor function of a radial nerve in a patient with an injured upper extremity, you should

   A. ask the patient to dorsiflex his wrist
   B. check pinprick over the dorsal web space
   C. ask the patient to touch his fingertips with the thumb of the same hand
   D. all of the above

4. If a patient is unable to dorsiflex his great toe, the nerve MOST likely severed is the _____ nerve.

   A. tibial
   B. perineal
   C. ulnar
   D. none of the above

5. You ask a patient to spread his fingers wide apart, then make a cup with his hand. He is not able to do it.
   Of the following, the nerve MOST likely severed is the _____ nerve.

   A. radial   B. median   C. ulnar   D. tibial

6. An abnormal breathing pattern characterized by rhythmic waxing and waning of the depth of respiration with regularly occurring periods of apnea.
   This defines

   A. Cheyne-Stokes respiration
   B. central neurogenic hyperventilation
   C. kussmaul breathing
   D. none of the above

7. The word *otalgia* refers to pain in the

   A. nose   B. ear   C. eyes   D. jaw

8. A 30-year-old male patient has an object impaled in his forearm. The CORRECT treatment is to

   A. apply direct pressure at the wound's edges to control the bleeding
   B. cut a hole through several layers of gauze and gently slip them over the impaled object
   C. use triangular bandages to build a doughnut around the object
   D. all of the above

9. Before you splint any injured extremity, you should check the

   A. pulse
   B. sensation
   C. motor function
   D. all of the above

10. A 30-year-old patient has a severely angulated fracture of the right forearm. Pulse and function are intact.
    Before splinting, you should

    A. straighten the fracture
    B. not try to straighten the fracture
    C. use extra force if needed
    D. none of the above

11. A 35-year-old victim fell backward on an outstretched hand. On primary survey, you suspect anterior dislocation of the shoulder.
    Your NEXT step is to

    A. correct the dislocation and then splint the shoulder
    B. splint the shoulder in the same position in which you found it
    C. try to stretch the shoulder before splinting
    D. all of the above

12. You respond to a call to 911. On arrival, you find a 50-year-old, unconscious victim lying on the floor.
    What will you do FIRST?

    A. Establish an airway
    B. Place an IV
    C. Start chest compression
    D. Defibrillate

13. If you are able to palpate only a carotid pulse in an unconscious victim, his systolic pressure is AT LEAST _____ mmHg.

    A. 60
    B. 70
    C. 80
    D. 100

14. The commonly used trade name for digitoxin is

    A. lanoxin
    B. crystodigin
    C. tridil
    D. sectral

15. A 40-year-old male patient has chronic congestive heart failure, for which he was undergoing therapy. He was also complaining about vomiting, headaches, and yellow vision. Among the following, the one which will MOST likely cause the above symptoms is

    A. nitroglycerin
    B. digoxin
    C. tenormin
    D. sectral

16. If you are unsure whether a patient in a diabetic coma is suffering from hyperglycemia or hypoglycemia, it is always SAFER to assume

    A. normoglycemin
    B. hyperglycemia
    C. hypoglycemia
    D. none of the above

17. A 20-year-old patient with known diabetes is found to have warm, dry, flushed skin, hypotension and kussmaulis breathing.
    The MOST likely diagnosis is

    A. diabetic ketoacidosis
    B. hypoglycemic reaction
    C. hyperosmolar coma
    D. none of the above

18. The COMMON causes of seizures in adults include

    A. withdrawal from alcohol
    B. hypoglycemia
    C. hypoxemia
    D. all of the above

19. A 25-year-old patient is having grand mal seizures.
    After establishing an airway, your NEXT step should be to

    A. try to retain the patient
    B. administer oxygen
    C. administer 50 ml of D5O IV
    D. give IV diazepam

20. You respond to a call for a patient suffering persistent seizures for the last 15 minutes. If the victim dies before your arrival, the MOST probable cause of death is

    A. head trauma
    B. hypertension
    C. hypoxia
    D. none of the above

Questions 21-25.

DIRECTIONS: In Questions 21 through 25, match the numbered definition with the lettered term, listed in Column I, that it MOST accurately describes. Place the letter of the CORRECT answer in the appropriate space at the right.

COLUMN I

A. Manubrium
B. Malleolus
C. Malocclusion
D. Medulla oblongata
E. Menorrhagia

21. Excessive flow during menstrual period

22. Upper portion of the sternum to which the clavicles are attached

23. Improper alignment of the upper and lower teeth

24. Large, rounded, bony protuberance on either side of the ankle joint

25. Lower portion of the brain stem, containing the center for control of respiration

KEY (CORRECT ANSWERS)

1. B
2. C
3. A
4. B
5. C

6. D
7. B
8. D
9. D
10. A

11. B
12. A
13. A
14. B
15. B

16. C
17. A
18. D
19. B
20. C

21. E
22. A
23. C
24. B
25. D

TEST 3

DIRECTIONS: Each question or incomplete statement is followed by several suggested answers or completions. Select the one that BEST answers the question or completes the statement. *PRINT THE LETTER OF THE CORRECT ANSWER IN THE SPACE AT THE RIGHT.*

1. A victim is experiencing double vision, numbness of the face, slurred speech, and difficulty in swallowing.
   The MOST likely affected system is the

   A. carotid system
   B. vertebrobasilar system
   C. internal carotid artery
   D. all of the above

   1.____

2. A 50-year-old patient with known hypertension is experiencing hemiparesis, unilateral numbness, aphasia, and convulsions.
   The MOST likely affected system is the _____ system.

   A. subclavian
   B. vertebrobasilar
   C. carotid
   D. femoral

   2.____

3. *Dysarthria* refers to

   A. slurred speech
   B. blurred vision
   C. difficulty walking
   D. difficulty swallowing

   3.____

4. A 60-year-old renal dialysis patient develops hypotension. You will give him _____ ml of _____ IV.

   A. 50; D5W
   B. 50; normal saline
   C. 500; ringer's lactate
   D. 500; D5W

   4.____

5. If you suspect an air embolism in a patient who is on renal dialysis, you should

   A. transport the patient
   B. turn off the machine
   C. put the patient in the left lateral recumbent position in about 10 degrees of head-down tilt
   D. put the patient in the sitting position and make rapid transport to a dialysis facility

   5.____

6. A 32-year-old victim develops anaphylaxis after eating shellfish.
   Among the following, the drug of choice to treat an anaphylactic reaction is

   A. epinephrine
   B. atropine
   C. prednisone
   D. aminophyline

   6.____

7. The role of epinephrine in the treatment of anaphylaxis is to

   A. stop the process of mast cell degranulation
   B. elevate the diastolic pressure and improve coronary blood flow
   C. relieve bronchospasms in the lungs and increase the strength of cardiac contractions
   D. all of the above

   7.____

8. The MOST common route through which poisons gain access to the body is

   A. inhalation
   B. ingestion
   C. across the skin
   D. injection

9. You receive a call through 911 for a young patient who attempted to commit suicide. On arrival, you find an unconscious patient who has an acetone smell on her breath. Among the following, the MOST likely causative agent is

   A. cyanide
   B. alcohol
   C. aspirin
   D. organophosphates

10. A patient has constricted pupils, excessive salivation, and excessive sweating. The possible causative agent which caused these signs and symptoms is

    A. atropin
    B. organophosphates
    C. barbiturates
    D. carbon monoxide

11. *Orchitis* refers to

    A. painful urination
    B. swelling of the jaw
    C. swelling of the testicles
    D. swelling and tenderness of the salivary glands

12. The MOST common presenting symptom of myocardial infarction in patients age 85 and over is

    A. syncope
    B. dyspnea
    C. confusion
    D. chest pain

13. Delirium in the elderly MAY be associated with

    A. myocardial infarction
    B. congestive heart failure
    C. electrolyte imbalance
    D. all of the above

14. Many elderly people suffer chronically from confusion and diminished mental function; that is to say, they suffer from

    A. dementia
    B. delirium
    C. hallucination
    D. delusion

15. All of the following drugs commonly cause toxic reactions in the elderly patient EXCEPT

    A. digitalis
    B. diuretics
    C. penicillin
    D. analgesics

16. The ability to perceive the position and movement of one's body or its limbs is called

    A. hallucination
    B. proprioception
    C. delusion
    D. neuralgia

17. A 3-year-old child who is a known asthmatic develops difficulty in breathing. On auscultation, the patient has bilateral wheezing and subcostal retraction. The drug of choice to treat this patient is

    A. aminophylline
    B. albuterol
    C. solu-medrol
    D. all of the above

18. A child awake with a hoarse voice with high-pitched stridor and a so-called *seal bark* MOST likely has

    A. croup   B. asthma
    C. epiglottitis   D. tracheitis

19. What is the MOST common cause of sudden infant death syndrome?

    A. Unknown   B. Cardiogenic
    C. Central nervous system   D. Renal

20. The incidence for febrile seizures is HIGHEST in children between _____ of age.

    A. 1 month and 6 months   B. 6 months and 3 years
    C. 3 years and 5 years   D. 5 years and 10 years

21. A child who is 1 to 3 years old is called a(n)

    A. neonate   B. infant
    C. toddler   D. preschooler

22. A 2-year-old child is having continuous seizures on the way to the hospital. Of the following medications, the one you should administer FIRST is

    A. dilantin   B. phenobarbital
    C. valium   D. carbamezepan

23. Common causes of seizures in children include

    A. hypoglycemia   B. meningitis
    C. hypoxia   D. all of the above

24. You respond to a call from 911 for a patient in respiratory distress. On arrival, you find a 3-year-old child who has a history of sudden development of a fever of 105° F, stridor, and drooling.
The MOST likely diagnosis is

    A. epiglottitis   B. pharyngitis
    C. peritonsilar abscess   D. bacterial tracheitis

25. In what position should you transport the above child?

    A. Supine
    B. Standing
    C. Sitting
    D. The position in which the child is most comfortable

KEY (CORRECT ANSWERS)

1. B
2. C
3. A
4. B
5. C

6. A
7. D
8. B
9. C
10. B

11. C
12. B
13. D
14. A
15. C

16. B
17. B
18. A
19. A
20. B

21. C
22. C
23. D
24. A
25. D

TEST 4

DIRECTIONS: Each question or incomplete statement is followed by several suggested answers or completions. Select the one that BEST answers the question or completes the statement. *PRINT THE LETTER OF THE CORRECT ANSWER IN THE SPACE AT THE RIGHT.*

1. Among the following, the MOST severe side effect of acetaminophen poisoning is   1._____

    A. vomiting and diarrhea
    B. fatal liver damage
    C. metabolic acidosis
    D. seizures

2. Which of the following is NOT part of the glasgow coma scale?   2._____

    A. Eye opening
    B. Best motor response
    C. Verbal response
    D. Best sensory response

3. A 58-year-old male is found unconscious during a snowstorm. His rectal temperature is 84° F (about 29° C). His skin is ice cold, his muscles are rigid, and his heart sound is almost inaudible.
You should AVOID   3._____

    A. maintaining the airway by manual methods
    B. always using the oropharyngeal airway
    C. keeping the ventilator rate slow
    D. administering warmed, humidified oxygen

4. A 30-year-old patient who has shivering, tachycardia, elevated blood pressure, blank stare, and extremely violent self-destructive behavior is MOST likely having toxicity due to   4._____

    A. cocaine
    B. hallucinogens
    C. barbiturates
    D. narcotics

5. Common side effects of morphine overdose may include   5._____

    A. pinpoint pupil
    B. marked respiratory depression
    C. hypotension
    D. all of the above

6. What is (are) the common symptoms of impending burnout?   6._____

    A. Chronic fatigue and irritability
    B. Cynical, negative attitudes
    C. Lack of desire to report to work
    D. All of the above

7. The condition in which a person unconsciously translates an emotional conflict into a physical symptom, such as paralysis, is called   7._____

    A. conversion hysteria
    B. displacement
    C. projection
    D. regression

8. _____ is the redirection of an emotion from the original object to a substitute object more acceptable to the patient.

   A. Denial
   B. Displacement
   C. Regression
   D. All of the above

9. The root word *myelo* refers to the

   A. brain
   B. veins
   C. spinal cord
   D. heart

10. The steps for insertion of an oropharyngeal airway include all of the following EXCEPT

    A. orient the airway with tip upward
    B. advance tip
    C. rotate airway 90 degrees
    D. rotate airway 180 degrees

11. A 45-year-old unconscious male was intubated with an endotracheal tube. On auscultation, breath sound was absent bilaterally.
    NEXT

    A. continue ventilation through the tube
    B. push the tube further; then ventilate
    C. pull the tube ICM; then ventilate
    D. immediately remove the endotracheal tube

12. A multitrauma victim is intubated. On auscultation, breath sounds are audible on only one side of the chest. What will you do NEXT?

    A. Continue ventilation and pull the tube back very slowly
    B. Push the tube in
    C. Insert chest tube
    D. None of the above

13. *Hyperpnea* refers to

    A. slow breathing
    B. rapid breathing
    C. very deep breathing
    D. shortness of breath

14. It is customary to replace an oxygen cylinder with a fresh one when the pressure falls to _____ psi.

    A. 200
    B. 400
    C. 600
    D. 800

15. You are doing CPR by the side of the road, ventilating the patient with a pocket mask into which you are running 10 liters per minute of oxygen from a portable cylinder. The pressure gauge on the cylinder reads 1,200 psi.
    How long can you continue before the pressure reaches the safe residual and you have to go back to the ambulance for a fresh oxygen cylinder?
    _____ minutes.

    A. 18
    B. 28
    C. 38
    D. 68

16. Among the following, the device you do NOT use on a comatose patient is the   16.____

    A. venturi mask
    B. nasal catheter
    C. partial rebreathing mask
    D. nonrebreathing mask

17. The HIGHEST concentration of oxygen can be delivered to the patient by using   17.____

    A. nasal cannula
    B. venturi mask
    C. partial rebreathing mask
    D. nonrebreathing mask

18. Among the following, gastric distention is MOST likely caused by ventilation through a(n)   18.____

    A. mask   B. endotracheal tube
    C. tracheostomy tube   D. none of the above

19. The indication for terbutaline use is   19.____

    A. angina   B. asthma
    C. hypertension   D. cardiac dysrhythmias

20. The COMMON indication of streptokinase is   20.____

    A. active internal bleeding
    B. acute myocardial infarction within the first 6 hours
    C. uncontrolled hypertension
    D. recent trauma surgery

Questions 21-25.

DIRECTIONS: In Questions 21 through 25, match the numbered definition with the lettered term, listed in Column I, that it MOST accurately describes. Place the letter of the CORRECT answer in the appropriate space at the right.

COLUMN I
A. Miosis
B. Micturition syncope
C. Necrosis
D. Palate
E. Paresthesia

21. The roof of the mouth   21.____

22. Abnormal sensation indicating disturbance in nerve function   22.____

23. Pupillary constriction   23.____

24. Death of tissue, usually caused by cessation of its blood supply   24.____

25. Fainting during urination   25.____

KEY (CORRECT ANSWERS)

1. B
2. D
3. B
4. B
5. D

6. D
7. A
8. B
9. C
10. C

11. D
12. A
13. C
14. A
15. B

16. B
17. D
18. A
19. B
20. B

21. D
22. E
23. A
24. C
25. B

BASIC FUNDAMENTALS OF PATIENT HANDLING

Contents

	Page
FOREWORD	vi

Chapter 1:
INTRODUCTION 1

A. Objectives and Scope of Patient-Handling 1
B. Objectives, Scope and Organization of the Manual ... 1
C. The Basics of Lifting and Moving 3

Chapter 2:
PATIENT-HANDLING EQUIPMENT 7

A. Introduction 7
B. Equipment for Carrying Patient 8
   1. Wheeled Stretchers 8
   2. Portable Stretchers 10
   3. Stair Chairs 13
   4. Backboards 13
   5. Scoop Type Stretchers 14
   6. Incubators 14
C. Ambulance Vehicles 15
   1. Design of Access and Egress Doors 16
   2. Height of Vehicle Floor from Ground Level 16
   3. Size of Interior Compartment 16
   4. Presence or Absence of a Fixed Ambulance Bench . 17
   5. Type of Fastening Device for Cot 17
   6. Stretcher Storage Space 18
D. Ambulance Stretcher Supplies 18
   1. Bedding 18
   2. Foul Weather Accessories 19
   3. Restraining Devices 19

Chapter 3:
EQUIPMENT SELECTION AND PREPARATION ... 21

A. Selecting Appropriate Equipment 21
B. Preparing Stretcher for Patient 22
   1. General Procedures 22
   2. Procedures for Preparing the Wheeled Stretcher . 25

C. Unloading and Carrying Equipment from Ambulance to Patient . 29
   1. Evaluate Situation 29
   2. Plan Exit Route 29
   3. Avoid Taking Wheeled Cot Up or Down Stairs 30
   4. Roll Wheeled Stretcher Wherever Possible 30

Chapter 4
TRANSFER OF PATIENT TO STRETCHER 31

A. Introduction to the Transfer Task 31
B. Transfer of Bed-Level Patient 33
   1. Transfer by Direct Carry Method 34
      • Procedures for Direct Carry Method 44
   2. Transfer by Draw Sheet Method (and Slide Transfers) . 49
      • Procedures for Draw Sheet (and Slide Transfer) Method . 50
   3. Transfer by Other Methods 55
C. Transfer of Floor-/Ground-Level Patient 56
   1. Transfer by Direct Carry Method 57
      • Modified Procedures for Direct Carry Method . 58
   2. Transfer by Other Methods 61

Chapter 5:
MOVING STRETCHER PATIENTS 63

A. Preparation of Patient on Stretcher 63
   1. Positioning Patient on Stretcher 64
      • Basic (Usual) Procedures for Positioning Patient . 64
   2. Covering Patient on Stretcher 66
      • Procedures for Covering Patient 67
   3. Securing Patient on Stretcher 70
B. Lifting and Moving the Loaded Stretcher 71
   1. Procedures for Moving Stretcher by End Carry ... 72

Chapter 6:
LOADING AND UNLOADING AMBULANCE 75

A. Introduction to the Tasks 75
B. Loading the Ground Ambulance 76
   • Procedures for Loading Ambulance with Wheeled Stretcher (includes procedures for Side Carry) . 76
   • Procedures for Loading Ambulance with Portable Stretcher . 81
C. Unloading the Ground Ambulance 84
   • Procedures for Unloading Ambulance with Wheeled Stretcher . 84

iii

	Page
• Procedures for Unloading Ambulance with Portable Stretcher	86

Chapter 7: SPECIAL PROBLEMS FOR PATIENT-HANDLING

A. Introduction to Chapter	89
B. Patient with Suspected Spine Injury	89
1. Use of Backboards	91
2. Use of Scoop Type Stretcher	93
• Procedures for Transfer by Scoop Type Stretcher	95
C. Patient with Injured Extremity	96
D. Unconscious (or Vomiting) Patient	97
• Procedures for Positioning Unconscious (or Vomiting) Patient	98
E. Handling the Psychiatric or Hard-to-Control Patient	100
• Transfer Procedures for the Hard-to-Control Patient	101
F. Transfers Involving Ancillary Equipment	103
1. Patient Receiving Oxygen	103
2. Patient in Heart-Lung Resuscitation Unit	105
3. Patient Attached to I.V. Apparatus	106
G. Handling the Infant Patient	107
H. Patient-Handling in Confined Areas	108
1. Patient Transfer to Stair Chair	109
• Procedures for Extremity Transfer to Stair Chair	110
2. Positioning/Covering/Securing Patient on Stair Chair	114
3. Carrying the Loaded Stair Chair	115
• Procedures for Chair Carry	115

Appendix A: EQUIPMENT ADJUSTMENT AND OPERATING PROCEDURES

A. Procedures for Adjusting Height of Multi-Level Stretcher	117
B. Procedures for Adjusting Head Elevation of Stretcher	118
C. Procedures for Rolling Wheeled Stretcher	119

Appendix B: SUGGESTIONS FOR PERIPHERAL TASKS

A. Introduction	121
B. Suggestions for EMT Dress	121
C. Suggestions for Meeting Patient	122

iv

Photographs and Diagrams

Photo No.		Page
1	Multi-level wheeled stretcher (in elevated position)	9
2	Two-level wheeled stretcher (in high position)	9
3	Single-level wheeled stretcher	9
4	Break-away pole stretcher	11
5	Portable stretcher with fold-away legs and wheels	11
6	Combination stretcher chair	12
7, 8	Long backboard and short backboard	12
9	Scoop type stretcher	12
10	Wheeled stretcher with bedding prepared	27
11	Stretcher/bed configuration options (see Step 1)	42
12	Patient and equipment positioned and prepared for transfer by Direct Carry method	35
13	EMT's positioning arms for Direct Carry transfer (see Steps 11-15)	36
14	Close-up of EMT's arm positions	36
15	EMT's transferring patient by Direct Carry method	37
16	EMT's ready to lower patient to low-level stretcher	37
17	EMT's placing patient on low-level stretcher	38
18	EMT tucking draw sheet under patient's back	38
19	Patient has been rolled to his other side and EMT is pulling draw sheet through	39
20	EMT's roll in both sides of draw sheet	39
21	EMT's have "hammock hold" on draw sheet to lower patient to low-level stretcher (see Steps a-e)	40
22	EMT's ready to draw patient onto bed-level stretcher	40
23	EMT's ready to slide patient onto bed-level stretcher	41
24	EMT's and stretcher positioned for Direct Carry transfer of floor-level patient	41
25	EMT's assume alternative position on both knees	42
26	Direct Carry lift on floor-level patient	42
27	EMT's ready to drop to one knee and place patient on low-level stretcher	43

28	EMT's ready to "draw" or slide patient onto floor-level portable stretcher ... 43
29	EMT folding head-piece (see Steps 3-5) ... 66
30	Patient covered for cold weather ... 69
31	Patient prepared for foul weather (see Steps a-g) ... 69
32	Patient covered and secured on a portable stretcher ... 70
33	End Carry of stretcher at waist-level with palms-up grip ... 73
34	End Carry of stretcher with arms extended and palms-down ... 73
35	EMT's loading ambulance using Side Carry method for wheeled stretcher ... 79
36	Securing wheeled stretcher with ambulance slide bar ... 79
37	Placing head-end of portable stretcher on compartment floor (see Steps 3-5) ... 82
38	Loading ambulance with portable stretcher by End Carry method (see Steps 6-9) ... 82
39	EMT's grasp stretcher frame with outside arms to unload ambulance by Side Carry (see Step 6) ... 85
40	EMT's positioning scoop type stretcher (see Step 4) ... 93
41	EMT's guide scoop stretcher to fasten around patient without moving him ... 94
42	Patient secured to scoop type stretcher and EMT's ready to lift by End Carry ... 94
43	Unconscious or vomiting patient position ... 99
44	Optional position for an unconscious or vomiting patient ... 99
45	Hard-to-control patient secured with soft ties in supine position ... 102
46	Hard-to-control patient secured with soft ties in prone position ... 102
47	Oxygen cylinder fastened alongside patient ... 104
48	Smaller oxygen cylinder may be secured under stretcher head rest ... 104
49	I.V. bottle holder in position ... 106
50	Incubator attached to wheeled stretcher for transport ... 107
51	EMT's ready to raise patient to sitting position for Extremity Transfer ... 109
52	Patient raised to sitting position for Extremity Transfer ... 110
53	EMT's ready to lift patient by Extremity Transfer method ... 112
54	EMT's lowering patient into stair chair ... 112
55	EMT's placing patient into stair chair ... 113
56	Extremity Transfer method may be used with other carrying devices, too ... 113

Foreword

There has been much effort in recent years to establish a body of knowledge and good practice for providing care and transportation of the sick or injured. This effort has concentrated, and justifiably so, on defining proper emergency medical care techniques, training emergency ambulance personnel, and generally upgrading the standards of the ambulance profession. Interest in these vital activities emerged in numerous sectors of society and resulted in broad participation by many dedicated individuals and groups; operators of ambulance services, private associations, physicians, hospital professionals, and government personnel involved in Federal Health and Highway Safety Programs.

As a continuing result, significant progress has been made to ensure improved life-saving care for the public. The non-medical aspects of emergency medical care are beginning to receive more attention as the overall standards of the profession are raised. Principally, patient-handling tasks (e.g., lifting and moving patients) of the two-man ambulance team are being examined and proper methods documented.

243

Chapter 1

Introduction

A. Objectives and Scope of Patient-Handling

The objectives of patient-handling procedures are to prepare, position and transfer a sick or injured patient on and off appropriate carrying devices in order to transport the patient safely and expeditiously by ambulance usually to or from a medical facility.

An Emergency Medical Technician (EMT) must be able to analyze a situation, evaluate a patient's condition under the most stressful circumstances and know how to administer the necessary emergency medical care procedures that can mean life or death to the patient. He must also be able to lift and transfer the patient properly, position, cover and secure him to a stretcher or other carrying device, move the loaded stretcher, load and unload the patient into and out of an ambulance, care for the patient enroute and deliver him safely to his destination. In addition, an EMT must meet and interact effectively with many people including the patient, concerned friends and relatives of the patient, onlookers (especially at the scene of an emergency), police officers, physicians and hospital personnel, and ambulance partners. He may also be involved in various administrative or information gathering activities, not the least of which is the collection of pertinent information on the patient and his condition.

Generally, the many tasks of the EMT can be characterized as falling into one of three categories: 1) emergency medical care techniques, 2) patient-handling, and 3) administrative tasks. Although the distinction between emergency medical care and patient-handling is not always clear, the manual defines patient-handling as encompassing the non-medical emergency care tasks of the EMT, exclusive of any administrative functions. More specifically, the patient-handling activities can be described as six fundamental tasks, with some of the tasks not entailing direct physical handling of the patient but preparation to do so.

they usually occur during an ambulance run. First, the preparation of bedding and accessories for use with carrying equipment and the maintenance of the mechanical order of equipment is a secondary patient-handling task (i.e., it does not involve direct handling of the patient). Second, the EMT must select and carry all of the equipment (i.e., emergency medical care and patient-handling equipment) which he will need. The speed and effectiveness with which these tasks are done obviously help determine how quickly the EMT's can begin emergency medical care and patient-handling for the patient.

The third fundamental task in this discussion is the initial patient-handling task of the sequence involving direct physical contact with the patient. This task is the transfer of the patient from his bed, floor or ground location to a suitable carrying device for transport by ambulance. The transfer is actually composed of a number of sub-tasks which can be generally described as positioning equipment, positioning patient, covering patient, lifting and carrying patient to stretcher, and placing the patient on the carrying device. The fourth task can then be regarded as the preparation of the patient on a stretcher. Again, preparation involves several sub-tasks; namely, positioning the patient on a stretcher, covering and securing him (all accomplished prior to moving the patient-loaded stretcher). Fifth is the patient-handling task of lifting and carrying (or otherwise moving) the patient-loaded stretcher. The sixth, and final, patient-handling task considered fundamental in the manual are the activities of loading and unloading the ambulance. Loading and unloading an ambulance are essentially the same process, one being the reverse of the other. The above fundamental tasks of patient-handling and the usual sequence of their occurrence define the skeletal scope and organization of the manual.

B. Objectives, Scope and Organization of the Manual

The manual is intended as both an instructional text and a general reference document for EMT's. It is devoted exclusively to the tasks associated with lifting and moving the sick or injured person. Its scope is limited further to the range of situations ordinarily encountered by the Emergency Medical Technician in ambulance service.

The manual is a collection of narrative text and procedural descriptions defining the basic patient-handling tasks and presenting some proper methods for accomplishing each task. Reading the entire manual through will give the most instructional benefit, but is not necessary when the reader is interested in learning a particular method for a patient-handling task. The procedural description of a method, accompanied by illustrative diagrams and photographs, is believed to impart a complete understanding of the mechanics of each operation. Transitional and introductory text will enhance this understanding and, especially, aid in one's choice of method.

The procedures and approaches suggested in this manual were produced by consolidating the expressed practice of experienced ambulance service operators from over a dozen geographically distant locations in the United States. However, the particular methods and procedures described do not necessarily apply to all situations or all locales; they do reflect generally accepted principles of lifting and moving patients, and the methods can be used within the common range of ambulance service situations.

The manual consists of seven chapters and two appendices. All six fundamental tasks of patient-handling (outlined in the previous section) are examined and discussed in, more or less, the sequence of their occurrence on an ambulance run. Procedures and other technical material are presented principally in Chapters 3 through 6. These chapters cover equipment selection and preparation, transfer of a patient to a stretcher, preparation and moving a stretcher patient, and loading and unloading a ground ambulance. Additional technical material and/or modifications of basic techniques are presented in Chapter 7 for ambulance cases which are described as "special problems for patient-handling."

In addition to the introductory and background information in this chapter (Chapter 1), Chapter 2 describes principal types of patient-handling equipment, its usage and limitations. The appendices contain procedures on some peripheral patient-handling tasks, and list some suggestions for personal grooming and behavior for EMT's.

C. The Basics of Lifting and Moving

The Emergency Medical Technician in conducting the patient-handling procedures outlined in subsequent chapters must perform several basic tasks including lifting, lowering, pulling, holding and transporting individuals and equipment. If any of these tasks is conducted improperly, discomfort and injury could result to the patient, and possibly to the EMT. Even without these effects the EMT could expend unnecessary energy. It is the purpose of this section to describe procedures which, if utilized, will reduce the possibility of injury and assure the efficient lifting and moving of all patients.

The arms and legs are two major lever systems of the body. They are linked together by the spine. The bones forming these lever systems are hinged at the joints so they can move and perform work. The forces which operate these levers are applied through muscles which contract to produce movement.

Most bones in the body are connected by joints which permit movement. Of the various types of joints between bones, two are pertinent to this discussion. The first is the synovial joint that connects the bones of the limbs, and the second, the cartilaginous joint, found between the vertebrae in the spine. The bones of most joints are held together by muscles and inelastic ligaments. The elbow and knee are simple hinge joints which permit movement in one plane. The wrist and ankle move in two planes at right angles to each other due to joint surfaces which are almost flat. The joints of the hip and shoulder are characterized by a ball and socket arrangement which provides a wide range of movement. The ball of the hip joint is almost completely enclosed in a deep socket which results in great mechanical strength but limits somewhat its movement range. The shoulder socket is much shallower and wider range of movement is possible but at reduced strength. Damage may occur in a joint if force is applied suddenly in a direction in which the joint does not normally move or if the joint is misused over a period of time. The sudden application of force may result in a sprain (the stretching or laceration of the ligaments), a dislocation, or the release of fluid in the joint, expanding the joint cavity, and resulting in pain and reduced movement. If stretching occurs, the ligaments are less likely to withstand subsequent strains and dislocations may occur more easily.

The second type of joint to be considered is the cartilaginous joint between vertebrae. In each of these joints, there is a disc of fibrous cartilage with a central elastic area, which serves as an excellent shock absorber. Individual vertebrae are joined by a series of elastic ligaments which assist in maintaining the normal curvature of the spine. The body can bend forward easily but not far backward. In addition to bending, the spine also allows rotation which varies from approximately 90 degrees to about 30 degrees in the area of the neck to about 30 degrees in lower areas. It should be noted that although the total amount of movement whether bending or rotating permitted by the spine is substantial, the movement occurring between individual vertebrae is quite small.

The muscles that bend the body forward are mainly in the walls of the abdomen and are not able to exert a great deal of force. Some of the complex muscles that straighten the body act on the bony protuberances of the vertebrae and form a number of small levers. These muscles and small levers produce less powerful movements than the limbs. Therefore, the EMT's should in general avoid lifting or moving patients when they are themselves in postures which make it necessary for them to bend and then straighten their backs. Discomfort or injury may result if undue strain is placed on the back when lifting a patient or if frequent bending and straightening of the back takes place. Even a moderately bad posture over a period of time will result in muscular fatigue and an aching back.

The muscles related to lifting and moving are composed of bundles of long, thin cylindrical fibers. In order for these muscle fibers to contract, energy must be released through chemical reactions triggered by nerve impulses. In addition to this energy, unwanted and sometimes poisonous by-products are produced which must be removed. This is done by the action of oxygen stored in the red muscle fibers themselves or in the blood. If the supply of oxygen from these sources is inadequate, the by-products of the energy production will build up and cause the sensation of pain or muscular fatigue. This may result even if the force exerted is quite small provided the muscle is contracted for a long period of time. Pain will build up and will subside only when the muscle is relaxed and blood allowed to flow through it again. Consequently, any significant amount of force should not be sustained over a long period and all muscular activity should be intermittent.

Several types of injuries and discomfort may result if patient-handling tasks are performed improperly. EMT's are liable to experience muscle strain, sprained ligaments, dislocations, cramps, fatigue, or even permanent impairment if lifting and moving are not done in a manner which properly utilizes the body's natural system of levers. In order to protect an EMT and help him move patients safely, certain principles should be followed in conducting the patient-handling tasks to be described in this manual:

- Keep in mind your physical capabilities and limitations and do not try to handle too heavy a load. When in doubt, seek help.

- Do not attempt to lower a patient if you feel you could not lift him.

- Keep yourself balanced when carrying out all tasks.

- Maintain a firm footing.

- Maintain a constant and firm grip.

Chapter 2

Patient-Handling Equipment

A. Introduction

A variety of equipment is available to assist the EMT in performing the patient-handling tasks. The first section of this chapter identifies categories of carrying equipment and describes the types of equipment available in each category. It is recognized that not all ambulance services have identical carrying equipment nor necessarily equipment from each of the categories discussed. They are included in order to provide the EMT with an understanding of the range of equipment available, their common characteristics, specific equipment options available and functional (i.e., with respect to the tasks of patient-handling), advantages and limitation of various equipment types.

The section on carrying devices is followed by discussion of both ambulance vehicles and patient-handling supplies. The discussion of vehicles centers about design features that affect patient-handling regardless of the specific vehicle used for transporting the patient.

The discussions in this chapter are limited to equipment and design features common to ground ambulances. It is recognized that various types of fixed-wing aircraft and helicopters are being used increasingly for patient transport and have proved invaluable in instances where excessive time would be involved in the transfer of emergency patients by ground vehicles. Carrying equipment and vehicle design features for air transportation, however, are frequently specifically designed for the given aircraft in use and are not considered general enough for discussion in this chapter. EMT's who transport patients by air will need to become thoroughly familiar with the specific carrying devices utilized for the aircraft with which they deal as well as the specific aircraft design features, such as litter frames, fastening devices, side loading doors, etc., which will affect the conduct of patient-handling tasks.

- Lift and lower by bending the legs and not the back—keep the back as straight as possible at all times, bend knees and lift with one foot ahead of the other.
- When holding or transporting, keep the back straight and rely on shoulder and leg muscles; tighten muscles of the abdomen and buttocks.
- When performing a task that requires pulling, keep the back straight and pull using the arms and shoulders.
- Carry out all tasks slowly, smoothly and in unison with your partner.
- Move body gradually, avoid twisting and jerking when conducting the various patient-handling tasks.
- When handling a patient, try to keep the arms as close as possible to the body in order to maintain balance.
- Do not keep muscles contracted for a long period of time.
- Rest frequently and whenever possible.
- Remember to slide or roll heavy objects, rather than lift, whenever possible.

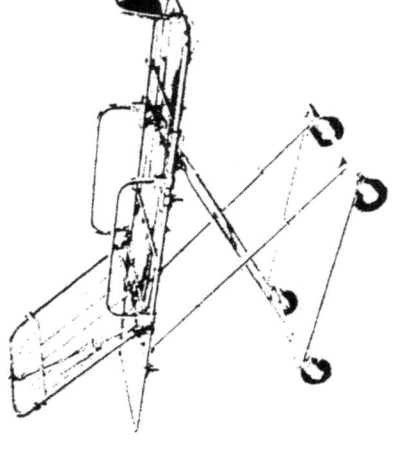

Photo No. 1. Multi-level wheeled stretcher (in elevated position).

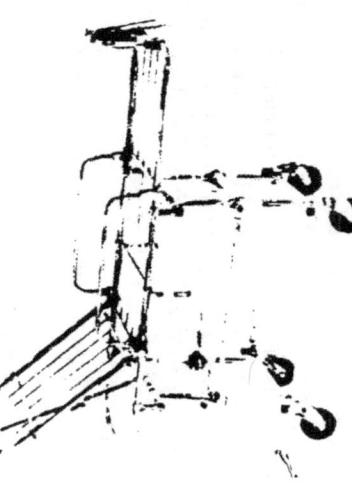

Photo No. 2. Two-level wheeled stretcher (in high position).

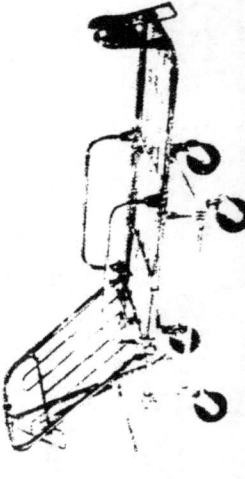

Photo No. 3. Single-level wheeled stretcher.

Equipment for Carrying Patient

This section provides brief descriptions of carrying devices commonly used by ambulance personnel. For each type of stretcher, descriptions are provided of its physical characteristics, equipment options available, its general use and its functional advantages and limitations.

The carrying devices described include those categories recently recommended by the NAS-NRC for inclusion on ambulances. These are: 1) wheeled stretchers, 2) folding or adjustable stretchers, and 3) devices designed to carry patients over stairways or through other narrow areas. For purposes of discussion, they will be referred to as wheeled stretchers, portable stretchers and stair chairs, respectively. It is recognized that the last two categories represent combination units in some equipment.

In addition to the preceding devices, ambulances carry or have available equipment for lifting and moving individuals with special medical problems. These include the short and long backboards recommended for immobilizing patients with suspected spine injuries. Scoop type stretchers are available for moving patients, under certain circumstances, with suspected spine or other injuries where it is desired to immobilize the patient on a carrying device without the necessity for first lifting and moving him.

The last carrying device discussed consists of a portable incubator for transfer of infants. Although space may not be provided for storage of such equipment directly on the vehicle, this carrying device is normally available to ambulance personnel on an as-needed basis and is frequently stored at the local emergency medical facility.

In summary, discussions of equipment will cover the following categories:

- Wheeled stretchers
- Portable stretchers
- Stair chairs
- Backboards
- Scoop type stretchers
- Incubators

1. Wheeled Stretchers

The wheeled stretcher is the standard ambulance cot. It is typically made of aluminum and has a multi-position backrest that permits the patient to rest in a variety of positions ranging from near-upright to fully supine. It may be single-level, two-level or multi-level. Special options available with the wheeled stretcher include, among others, a contour feature which permits the patient to rest in a knees-up position and a feature which tilts the stretcher surface at a 16° angle to accommodate patients in the shock position or in need of special airway care. Most are equipped with cot pull handles that permit the EMT to pull the stretcher without bending.

Typical physical characteristics of the wheeled stretcher are (all measures are approximate and represent those of the basic unit):

- Length: 75–76 inches
- Width: 22–23 inches
- Height: Single-level: 8 to 13 inches
  Two- and
  Multi-level: 8 to 13 inches minimum
  31 to 32 inches maximum
- Weight: 30–50 pounds

Of the wheeled stretchers, the single-level cot is lightest in weight and therefore easiest to carry. However, it lacks the special patient-transfer advantages provided by the two-level and multi-level stretchers. The latter require less bending on the part of the EMT in transferring the patient to and from the stretcher and permit easy transfer of the patient to a hospital bed, cot or examining table.

Because of its rigid structure and weight, the wheeled stretcher is designed primarily to be rolled rather than lifted. Wheeled stretchers may be difficult to maneuver through narrow hallways or on stairways (although models are available that convert into stair chairs).

2. Portable Stretchers

The portable stretcher serves primarily as an easily lifted device for those situations where a wheeled stretcher cannot be used; for example, where wheels do not roll smoothly or in multi-storied buildings where elevators are lacking. In addition, it serves as an auxiliary carrying device when two patients are to be transported in a single ambulance.

Portable stretchers range widely in design. They are typically constructed of nylon or canvas and have aluminum or wood frames. They include the standard pole and U-frame stretchers. Some models have special break-away features that permit the stretcher to be removed from beneath the patient without physically lifting the patient. Most models are designed with foldaway legs and wheels. Some have multi-position backrests and some convert into stair chairs. All have a slim-line feature and most fold either lengthwise or widthwise for easy storage. Some of the wheeled portable models are available with cot pull handles.

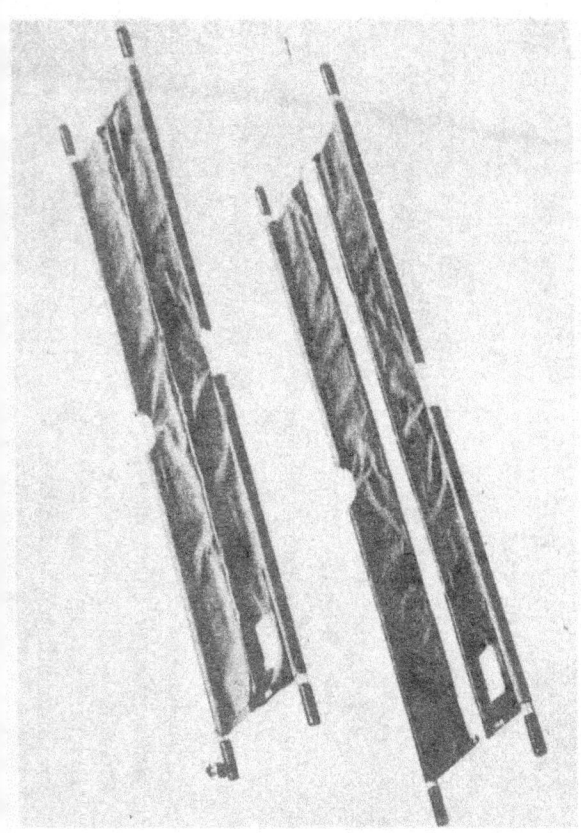

Photo No. 4. Break-away pole stretcher.

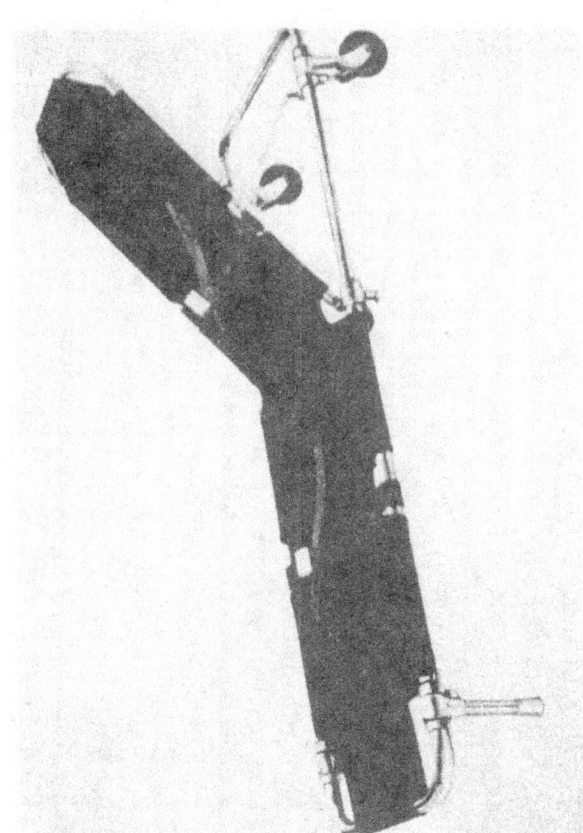

Photo No. 5. Portable stretcher with fold-away legs and wheels.

Typical physical characteristics of the portable stretcher are (all measures are approximate and represent those of the basic unit):

- Length: 72–82 inches
- Width: 17–20 inches
- Weight: 15 pounds (although they range from 8 to 25 pounds depending on the design of the basic unit)

The advantages of the portable stretcher are its easy maneuverability, light weight and compactness. Since they are single-level units, they have the disadvantage of the single-level wheeled stretcher of requiring considerable bending on the part of the EMT in transferring the patient to and from the stretcher. Since stretchers must keep the patient above the ambulance floor level, portable models without legs or wheels must be placed on the ambulance cot or bench when the patient is transported to the emergency medical facility. In addition, those without wheels lack the capability of being rolled into the vehicle and thus may require more lifting on the part of the EMT.

3. Stair Chairs

The stair chair is designed for patient-handling over stairways and through narrow halls or other confined areas. It is constructed typically of nylon with an aluminum frame. As stated previously, it may be a separate ambulance unit or it may be a feature combined with one of the other types of stretchers, most typically with the portable stretcher. It is normally light in weight and folds into a compact unit for easy storage. Some are designed with wheels for easier maneuverability.

Typical physical characteristics of the stair chair are (all measures are approximate and represent those of the basic unit):

- Height: 30–40 inches
- Width: 17–19 inches
- Weight: 8–20 pounds

4. Backboards

Backboards are designed primarily for immobilizing individuals with suspected spine injuries. Two sizes are available: one short and one long. The long board is used for immobilizing the prone or supine patient; the short board serves as an intermediate device for immobilizing patients in the seated position or other position

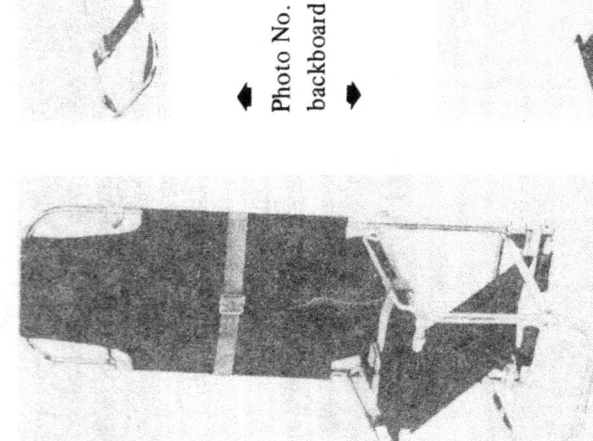

Photo No. 6. Combination stretcher chair.

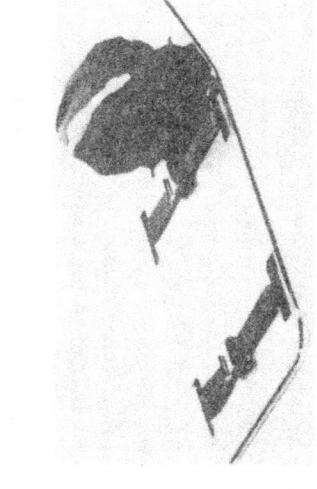

Photo No. 7, 8. Long backboard and short backboard.

Photo No. 9. Scoop type stretcher.

instant suction in case aspiration is needed, 2) nebulizer with a heating unit to ensure adequate moisture of the inspired gases, 3) A.C. thermostatic control of temperature, 4) resuscitator equipped with various sizes of face masks, 5) oxygen ratio controller to meet the needs of infants, and 6) oxygen analyzer that continuously monitors the oxygen concentration in the infant's environment.

Some incubators are equipped with portable stands. However, when inside the vehicle, the incubator is typically secured on the wheeled stretcher or so designed that it makes direct use of the wheeled stretcher or fastening devices used for securing the wheeled stretcher.

C. Ambulance Vehicles

Vehicles currently used to transport both emergency and non-emergency patients include: the standard ambulance, limousine, various sizes of heavy duty trucks, station wagons, fixed-wing aircraft, and helicopters. The type of vehicle selected by a given service depends on such factors as whether the vehicle is used for activities in addition to emergency ambulance services (such as non-emergency patient transfer, police cruising, funeral services, light or heavy duty rescue), terrain features of the area in which the vehicle operates, personal preferences of the purveyor of the service and economic considerations. The NAS-NRC states, "Although ambulances may be used for elective transport of non-ambulatory patients, e.g., hospital to home or nursing home, or for outpatient visits, a vehicle used for this purpose that is not designed, equipped or staffed to respond to emergency calls should not be termed an ambulance."*

Many articles have been devoted to comparisons of the various types of vehicles, and detailed performance and design criteria for emergency ambulances have been specified by the NAS-NRC.* It is not intended here to review these discussions nor to discuss the various factors that affect the safety of the vehicle and medical care provided to the patient. Rather, it is intended to limit discussion of vehicle design to those features directly relevant to patient-handling tasks, in particular, to loading and unloading the stretcher and securing it in the vehicle. Such vehicle design features include:

- Design of access and egress doors
- Height of the vehicle floor from ground level

(such as the floor well of a car) which would prohibit direct movement of the patient to the long board. The short board also provides a firm surface for administering external cardiac compression.

Backboards are typically constructed of aluminum or marine plywood. Wooden surfaces are well sanded, shellacked or varnished, and waxed to permit easy sliding of the patient onto the board. Both boards are equipped with two nine-foot straps for securing the patient to the board. For better immobilization of the patient, accessories include neckrolls, head and chin straps, foot rest and other body straps. Some long boards are designed to fold width-wise for easy transportability and storage. Both aluminum and wooden models permit X-rays to be taken of the patient without removing him from the board.

Typical physical characteristics of backboards are:

	Long Board	Short Board
Length:	72 inches	32–36 inches
Width:	18 inches	18 inches
Weight:	18 pounds	9 pounds

5. Scoop Type Stretchers

Scoop type stretchers are used for immobilizing patients with suspected spine or other injuries where it is desirable to immobilize the patient without physically moving him. Such stretchers typically are made of aluminum and utilize a scissor- or telescope-type action to enclose the patient. The patient is secured to the stretcher by means of straps. Such stretchers permit transfer of the immobilized patient to the examining table, X-ray table or hospital bed without disturbing him.

Typical physical characteristics of scoop type stretchers are:

- Length: adjustable from 63 inches to 84 inches
- Weight: 18 pounds

6. Incubators

The portable incubator provides a means for transporting the newborn, particularly the premature, in a controlled environment. As such, it typically contains means for manual or automatic temperature control. For other required patient care, such as oxygen, suction and resuscitation, the unit may be self-contained or designed to make use of standard equipment located on the vehicle.

Self-contained units are typically battery-operated to permit patient care outside the vehicle. Some of these more advanced mobile incubators offer an impressive range of features. For example,

---

*U.S. Department of Transportation, National Highway Safety Bureau. *Ambulance Design Criteria.*

- Size of the interior compartment
- Presence or absence of a fixed ambulance bench
- Type of fastening device for the cot
- Stretcher storage space

The effect of each of these design features on patient-handling is discussed below.

1. Design of Access and Egress Doors

Most ambulance doors are so designed and located to permit rear loading of the patient. For wheeled cots, therefore, the cot need only be lifted to the level of the vehicle floor and rolled into the vehicle. Once the lifting task is accomplished, the EMT's need only guide the cot smoothly into position in the vehicle interior.

Most rear doors open outwards to ease this task. A locking device should be incorporated as an important safety feature in the design of all outward opening doors and always used to ensure that the door(s) will not close accidentally. Where the door opens downward (a device found primarily on station wagons), tailgate plates can be used to cover the space between the tailgate and floor in order to eliminate bumping or jostling of the patient or the necessity for one EMT to enter the vehicle to ease the loading or unloading process.

2. Height of Vehicle from Ground Level

Height of the vehicle floor from ground level affects the distance the stretcher must be lifted before it can be rolled into or placed in the vehicle. For most standard ambulances, this height is approximately 24 inches from the ground and the lifting required of the EMT's is therefore minimal. However, depending on the vehicle and the necessity to adapt to local terrain features that dictate high road clearances, this height might vary.

It might be noted that the average male is able to lift a stretcher-type device to about 30 inches from ground level with his arms straight. When vehicle floor levels are higher than this figure, the EMT will need to bend his elbows to raise the stretcher into the vehicle.

3. Size of Interior Compartment

The size of the interior compartment affects the amount of bending required of the EMT once inside the vehicle while he is performing such tasks as fastening a portable stretcher in place or transferring a non-rolling stretcher into the vehicle or onto the ambulance bench. Although dimensions recommended by the NAS-NRC have been directed toward assuring adequate space for two litters and for providing life-saving emergency care to at least one of the victims, including external cardiac compression and administration of I.V.'s as required, the dimensions as specified also serve the function of providing extra space for the EMT's in their loading and unloading task. Vehicles that comply with the recommended values will permit the EMT to perform the stretcher handling tasks with less bodily strain. The values recommended by NAS-NRC are:

- Minimal length: 116 inches
- Optimal width: 71 inches
- Minimum height: 54 inches
- Optimal height: 60 inches

4. Presence or Absence of a Fixed Ambulance Bench

The presence of a fixed bench in a vehicle affects the loading task when there is more than one patient to be carried. The litter for one of the patients will need to be loaded into the vehicle and transferred to the bench prior to loading the second litter. Thus, with a fixed bench, additional patient-handling will be required when transporting more than one patient. Of course, without a fixed bench, as stated previously, both stretchers will need to have legs or wheels in order that the patient will be transported above floor level. The NAS-NRC recommends that litters *not* be suspended by wall brackets or from the ceiling.

5. Type of Fastening Device for Cot

Each cot, of course, must be securely fastened to the vehicle with crash-stable fasteners to assure that the cot does not move when the vehicle is in transit. These may be of the wall-mounted or floor-mounted type or a combination of the two. In addition, wheel and post cups are available to hold wheels and cot legs firmly in place.

Fastening devices are designed to require minimal effort on the part of EMT's. Wall- and floor-mounted devices for the wheeled stretcher permit the stretcher to be rolled into the vehicle and attached to the device both by maneuvering the stretcher into position and by adjustment of the fastener handle. Both of these tasks can be accomplished from the rear of the vehicle.

Wheel cups also provide a simple fastening device since the stretcher need only be rolled into the cups. For post cups, of course,

In addition to flat blankets, special zip-up versions are available that permit the patient to be completely enclosed in a warm fabric.

2. Foul Weather Accessories

Foul weather accessories are normally constructed of waterproof fabrics and designed to protect the patient and the bedding from inclement weather. These range from flat sheet-type supplies to full pouches which enclose the patient and the cot mattress. The latter have full length zipper openings, a hooded face opening and tabs which hold the pouch edges securely beneath the mattress.

3. Restraining Devices

Restraining devices are utilized to contain the unruly patient as well as to assure that all patients are held securely to the ambulance cot for their safety and comfort. They include wrist and ankle restraints, shoulder and waist restraints, and restraints that may be positioned at various other parts of the body. Some restraints are available in combination with others. They are typically straps made of two-inch wide nylon and utilize either self-adhesive closures or quick release buckles, or they may be constructed of softer fabrics which can be tied around patient and stretcher frame.

6. Stretcher Storage Space

The design of stretcher storage spaces affects accessibility of equipment for patient-handling. Therefore, equipment is normally stored so as to require minimum effort and time on the part of the EMT in gaining access to the device and readying it for use.

The wheeled stretcher is stored in the ambulance in a ready status, that is, it is normally made up in bed form and locked in its fastening device directly in the patient compartment. Portable stretchers and chair stairs are stored by various means depending on the design of the equipment and the storage capability of the vehicle. Techniques include strapping of devices to the interior compartment walls and, for fold-up equipment, storage in special compartments such as floor wells. Floor wells are typically located at the center rear of the vehicle to permit ready access by the EMT from outside the vehicle. Simple devices such as pole stretchers may be stored in flat form directly on the wheeled vehicle. Thus, when both devices are needed (for example, when the patient is in a building without elevator facilities), they may be removed from the vehicle simultaneously.

Portable incubators are frequently not stored directly on the vehicle. They most typically are held at a central source, such as the local hospital, and made available to ambulance crews on the as-needed basis.

D. Ambulance Stretcher Supplies

A range of supplies is available for use with the stretcher to assure the comfort and safety of the patient. These are discussed below in the categories of bedding, foul weather accessories and restraining devices.

1. Bedding

Ambulance stretcher bedding includes the standard items of linens, blankets and pillows, sized to fit the cot mattress. Sheets are available in both contour and flat form. In addition, special transfer sheets are available to minimize patient-handling; such sheets are typically constructed of nylon and have side handles for easy moving of the patient from ambulance to cot to hospital examining table or bed. With poles inserted, transfer sheets serve as a pole stretcher.

253

Chapter 3

Equipment Selection and Preparation

A. Selecting Appropriate Equipment

Emergency Medical Technicians in an ambulance crew must acquire the ability to diagnose the patient-handling *needs* of their patients, in addition to acquiring the skills to conduct patient-handling techniques properly. Most of the manual is devoted to describing the conduct of patient-handling techniques and, to a lesser extent, explaining the advantages, limitations, and typical circumstances surrounding the use of each technique.

It is recognized that the EMT will learn what equipment and method he should use to handle a particular situation principally through on-the-job experience and, also, in medical care training programs. This chapter does *not* provide equipment and method selection information in any greater detail than that which accompanies the description of techniques. Instead, this section consolidates such information and, in summary form, it is intended to guide the reader to the selection of proper equipment and method to meet a given set of common situations.

The modern, well-designed ambulance has storage space adequate to carry all of the patient-handling equipment (i.e., various patient carrying devices, for the most part) that might be required on the majority of the ambulance calls. For example, at least one patient-ready wheeled cot should be secured to the floor of the patient compartment; a portable stretcher, preferably convertible to a stair chair, can be kept ready by either storing it in the compartment wheel well or attaching it to holders on the wall of the compartment; and a backboard and/or scoop type stretcher should be stored in or attached to an accessible place in the patient compartment.

For a small percentage of the ambulance runs, the EMT's will find special additional equipment helpful to accomplish the patient-handling tasks. Such items as incubators, wheel chairs, and accessory attachments for life-support equipment can provide valuable assistance to the EMT's. Information obtained during the call for an

See footnotes on following page.

Summary of Equipment and Transfer Methods Appropriate to Selected Patient Conditions

Transfer Approach/ Patient Situation	Appropriate Equipment and Transfer Methods				
Bed-Level Patient Condition	Wheeled Stretcher	(Flat) Portable Stretcher	Stair Chair	Scoop Type Stretcher	Backboard
No Critical Medical Condition	1. Direct Carry 2. Draw Sheet 3. Slide Transfer	1. Direct Carry 2. Draw Sheet 3. Patient Roll (with stretcher on bed)	1. Extremity Transfer 2. Direct Carry	X	X
Injured Extremity	1. Slide Transfer 2. Draw Sheet (if bottom sheet exists)	1. Slide Transfer (with stretcher on bed) 2. Draw Sheet (if bottom sheet exists)	Z	X	X
Serious Fracture	1. Slide Transfer (if fracture is immobilized)	1. Slide Transfer (if fracture is immobilized and stretcher on bed)	Z	X	X
Unconscious	1. Direct Carry 2. Slide Transfer	1. Direct Carry	Z	X	X
Hard-To-Control	1. Direct Carry 2. Slide Transfer	1. Direct Carry	1. Extremity Transfer 2. Direct Carry	X	X

ambulance can allow time to prepare quickly for the special needs of the patient. For example, a portable incubator may be summoned for the transfer of a newborn, premature, sick or injured infant. In addition, specialized devices for carrying life-support equipment (e.g., oxygen, I.V. apparatus) can be made ready for attachment to the stretcher that will be used.

Subsequent chapters will show that there are a number of different tasks involved in the patient-handling role including, primarily, preparing and positioning patient carrying devices, transferring the patient to the stetcher, carrying the patient-loaded stretcher, and loading/unloading the ambulance. The key task is the transfer task. A transfer requires more direct contact with the patient than any other patient-handling task. Methods and procedures for this task are the most variable, depending upon patient condition and the equipment (carrying device) selected. To aid in the selection of transfer equipment and method, a table is provided which indicates generally preferred choices for various common patient conditions and situations. Procedures for the basic methods (and for variations within method) identified in the table are described in either Chapter 4 or 7.

B. Preparing Stretcher for Patient

To the extent possible, all patient carrying devices should be maintained in a clean, mechanically reliable state and prepared with bedding and other stretcher supplies at all times. Achieving this objective requires relatively few skills and little effort by the EMT's, even when dealing with the relatively complex wheeled ambulance cot. This section describes, in detail, procedures for placing the proper type and amount of bedding on the wheeled stretcher. In addition, general recommendations for covering and preparing other types of patient carrying devices are given in this section.

Many of the flat, horizontal ambulance stretchers can and should be prepared, with some modifications, as is described later for the wheeled stretcher. The primary difference in procedures for preparing the wheeled cot versus the other bed-like devices is *when* each should be prepared and not so much how they should be prepared. Lightweight portable stretchers, although typically flat, are desirable as supplemental carrying devices because they can be folded and readily stored out of the way until they are needed. The folding of these stretchers and the location of storage compartments (e.g., wheel wells, compartment floors, fastened to walls, etc.) render early preparation of linens inadvisable. Whereas, the wheeled cot can and should be stored in a ready state, made up with all necessary linens,

255

most other carrying devices should not. All portable stretchers, including scoop type stretchers and stair chairs, should be kept dry, clean and in good mechanical working order. Linens and covers for use with these carrying devices should be stored in proximity to the stretchers.

Backboards and scoop type stretchers should be used without linens while they are being used to immobilize the patient's spine. Once the patient has been immobilized to these devices, however, conventional covers may be placed over the patient (though no sheet or mattress should be between patient and stretcher).

Nylon portable stretchers should be prepared with a bottom sheet, folded lengthwise, shortly before the patient is to be transferred to the device. Once the patient is on the device he can be covered in the conventional manner. Linen typically is not placed directly on the stair chair, unless a pouch for the patient is to be used. In this case, the opened pouch may be draped across the chair prior to lifting the patient onto the device. The remainder of this section is devoted to detailed procedures for preparing, or making up, the wheeled stretcher with fresh linens.

PROCEDURES FOR PREPARING THE WHEELED STRETCHER

NOTE: The following procedures are suggested to be accomplished well in advance of a call for ambulance service, i.e., as soon as possible upon completion of a call for service. The procedures below start with a stretcher which had been used to transport a patient.

1. REMOVE unsoiled BLANKET(S) and PLACE ON CLEAN SURFACE
   - Blanket is usually a re-usable item; if cleaning is required, fold blanket and set aside

2. REMOVE PILLOW CASE and PLACE PILLOW ON CLEAN SURFACE
   - Pillow is usually a re-usable item

3. REMOVE all SOILED (used) LINEN from stretcher
   - Avoid additional soiling of linen

   Isolate soiled linen to prevent contamination.

Summary of Equipment and Transfer Methods Appropriate to Selected Patient Conditions—Continued

Transfer Approach/ Patient Situation	Appropriate Equipment and Transfer Methods				
Floor-/Ground-Level Patient Condition	Wheeled Stretcher	(Flat) Portable Stretcher	Stair Chair	Scoop Type Stretcher	Backboard
No Critical Medical Condition	1. Direct Carry 2. Extremity Transfer	1. Direct Carry 2. Slide Transfer	1. Extremity Transfer 2. Direct Carry	X	X
Injured Extremity	1. Direct Carry (if fracture is immobilized)	1. Direct Carry (if fracture is immobilized) 2. Slide Transfer	Z	1. Method unique to equipment	X
Serious Fracture	1. Direct Carry	1. Slide Transfer (if fracture is immobilized)	Z	1. Method unique to equipment	1. Special Slide Transfer
Unconscious	1. Direct Carry	1. Direct Carry 2. Slide Transfer	Z	X	X
Hard-To-Control	1. Direct Carry	1. Direct Carry	1. Extremity Transfer 2. Direct Carry	X	X

X = improbable transfer situation/equipment combination.
Z = equipment not recommended for patient condition (i.e., use of equipment may be detrimental to patient condition).

Place soiled linen in designated receptacle (if temporarily stored in ambulance compartment, remember to remove when at headquarters)

RAISE STRETCHER to highest LEVEL possible
- Will ease conduct of procedures

Relevant to multi-level or two-level wheeled stretchers.

4. LOWER HEADREST and CONTOUR FEATURE OF STRETCHER, if applicable
   - Stretcher should be in flat position

Relevant to wheeled stretchers having these options.

5. LOWER SIDE RAILS and DROP SAFETY STRAP

6. TURN MATTRESS OVER
   - Use proper cleaning agents on soiled mattress

Rotation of mattress adds to its life.

7. PLACE BOTTOM SHEET CENTERED on mattress and OPEN FULLY
   - One EMT at each end of stretcher
   - If contour sheet, slip over each corner of stretcher
   - If tunnel sheet, slip on from foot end and tuck excess under head end of mattress

If bed-sized sheet is used, fold lengthwise first.

8. TUCK SHEET under EACH END of mattress and SQUARE CORNERS

9. TUCK SHEET under SIDES of mattress
   PLACE disposable PAD in CENTER of mattress

10. PLACE SLIP-COVERED PILLOW at head end of MATTRESS
    - Can be placed lengthwise (as shown in photo no. 10 until

If desired.

11. FOLD TOP SHEET and PLACE ON MATTRESS
    - Open top sheet
    - Fold lengthwise first
    - Then fold sheet in half
    - Place folded top sheet at foot end of mattress

See text following.

As an option to Step 11, the ambulance top sheet may be handled as described below for blankets. In this alternate method, the top sheet would be opened across the mattress (as in Step 12) and the blanket(s) would be matched to the sheet before they are folded (as in Step 13). Alternatively, the blanket(s) may be folded and placed on the mattress as described in Step 11.

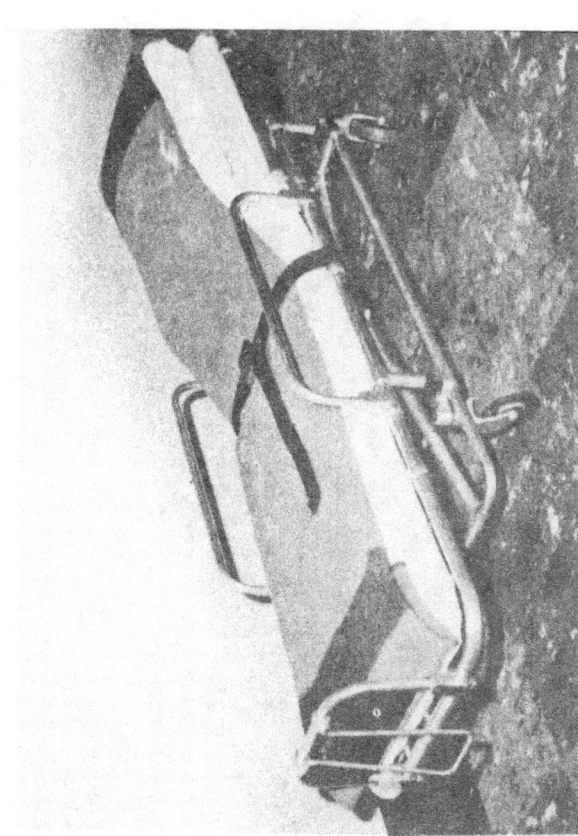

Photo No. 10. Wheeled stretcher with bedding prepared.

257

12. Fully OPEN BLANKET OVER STRETCHER
    - One EMT stands at each end of stretcher

    If second blanket desired, OPEN AND MATCH with first blanket

    Use same size blanket, if possible.

13. FOLD BLANKET(S) LENGTHWISE to match width of stretcher
    - Preferably, fold left side first and then right side of blanket(s)

    Helps to protect linen from soil, in addition to storing accessibly.

14. TUCK foot end of folded BLANKET UNDER foot end of mattress

15. TUCK head end of folded BLANKET UNDER upper end of MATTRESS

16. BUCKLE SAFETY STRAP(S)
    - Tuck excess strap over and under belt toward foot end of stretcher

17. RAISE SIDES AND FOOT REST of stretcher

    See photo no. 10.

18. LIFT HEAD REST of stretcher up ONE NOTCH

    To help prevent pillow from sliding off stretcher in transit.

The procedures above describe one method of preparing the stretcher to receive the patient. If any variations in method are preferred, bear in mind several objectives in this phase of patient-handling. First, all linens, blankets, pouches, etc., which are likely to be needed on the next ambulance call should be stored in a neat fashion with the carrying device (i.e., *on the wheeled stretcher*). Second, whatever preparation can be accomplished before the actual call should be done as soon as possible (e.g., cleaning and flipping over the stretcher mattress, placing the bottom sheet, etc.). Third, all linen and covers should be folded or tucked such that they will be contained within the stretcher frame. This will help to ensure cleanliness of the linen and keep a neat appearance of the stretcher. Remember, hanging folds of material can easily brush against soil or possibly get caught on objects.

Further discussion of the preparation of patient-handling equipment may be referred to in Appendix A. The appendix complements this section by providing procedures for adjusting the head elevation of stretchers and adjusting the mattress level of the multi-level wheeled ambulance cot.

C. Unloading and Carrying Equipment from Ambulance to Patient

This section refers specifically to handling techniques for patient carrying equipment only. However, medical and various accessory equipment is often needed for care of the patient and frequently must be carried with the stretcher to the scene. When the EMT's anticipate the need for such equipment (e.g., resuscitators, oxygen, etc.), they should be first secured to the stretcher (i.e., the stretcher can be a device for carrying equipment, too) and carried in such a way, or they can be transported by a third person. If accessory equipment is secured well by safety straps or other ties, the handling of all necessary equipment can be accomplished by two EMT's often in one trip to the scene. The key steps in this process are as follows:

1. Evaluate Situation

Use your own observation and all information at hand to determine the carrying devices and other equipment you may require to reach the patient, care for him at the scene and carry the patient back to the ambulance. Most frequently, the minimum amount of equipment that will be taken from the ambulance will be the wheeled cot and one portable stretcher; often the wheeled cot is carried only part of the way, while the portable stretcher is taken directly to the patient. When the wheeled cot can be delivered to the scene, it is the minimum amount of equipment the EMT will require in ordinary ambulance work.

Observation at the scene should include determining the best method of access to the patient. The characteristics of this route should be taken into consideration when deciding upon what and how much equipment should be carried the rest of the way to the patient. Alternatively, the availability of particular types of equipment should be considered in determining the best method of access.

2. Plan Exit Route

While on the way to the patient, look for features of the environment which will help in determining the best method of later carrying the patient to the ambulance. In particular, while carrying the

Chapter 4

Transfer Of Patient To Stretcher

A. Introduction to the Transfer Task

The transfer task is perhaps the most critical patient-handling task the EMT must learn to conduct properly. In its usual form, the task is essentially the lifting, carrying and placing of the patient onto a stretcher without aggravating his condition.* This chapter will discuss and describe various acceptable ways of accomplishing this task with a two-man ambulance crew.

There are several reasons why proper conduct of the transfer task is so important. First, the patient can be found in any of a number of environmental situations, physical positions and medical conditions. The methods of patient transfer are not all equally correct all of the time. The selection of an appropriate method must be made by the EMT's; thus, knowledge of the various transfer methods is critical. Second, a patient transfer may involve considerable direct contact with the patient. This is potentially hazardous to the patient, especially to the patient suffering from a fracture. There is also a greater risk of infection from bacteria carried by the EMT's as contact increases. Third, most patient transfers require that the entire weight of the patient be borne by just the two EMT's. It is therefore important that the EMT's know the correct way to carry that weight to ensure they will neither drop the patient nor injure themselves.

A number of methods have been devised to transfer a patient safely and efficiently to a stretcher. Many variations within methods have also evolved to deal with each set of circumstances arising from unique combinations of patient and environmental conditions. However, this variety of method can be reduced generally to three fundamental approaches to patient transfers. One approach is for the

---

*With some break-away devices, e.g., scoop type stretcher, the transfer task does *not* require lifting and carrying; the stretcher is carried and fastened around the patient.

---

unloaded stretcher, look for areas through which you will be unable to pass once the patient is on the stretcher and, where possible, remove obstacles from the route or select another route.

3. Avoid Taking Wheeled Cot Up or Down Stairs

The wheeled ambulance stretcher is relatively heavy and difficult to maneuver especially over stairs. If at all possible, take a stair chair or other light weight stretcher when access or egress routes involve traveling over stairs. The wheeled ambulance cot may be left on the ground floor or in another sheltered area for later receiving the patient-loaded portable stretcher.

Carrying any stretcher over stairs should be done by the End Carry method (Chapter 5, Section B) with each EMT facing the other. Head elevation should be lowered as much as possible to create a better weight distribution and the head end of the stretcher should be carried up stairs first and be brought down last. The head end EMT should carry the stretcher as low as possible with his arms extended while the foot end EMT should hold the stretcher at waist or chest level, particularly when the patient is on the stretcher. It is extremely dangerous to carry the stretcher in an extended arm position over one's head.

4. Roll Wheeled Stretcher Whenever Possible

This will save EMT's much strain. Guidelines are given in Appendix A; use your own judgment at the scene.

259

EMT's to lift and carry the patient in their arms to the stretcher. This approach is often referred to as the Direct Carry method, sometimes the Arm-Lift-Chest Carry, and is the most popular transfer method used by ambulance personnel. It is recommended whenever the patient can be handled directly. The second approach is the use of a sheet, or similar length of material, as an intermediate "stretcher." The sheet can be placed under the patient, held taut by the EMT's and used to draw the patient onto the stretcher. This approach is commonly known as the Draw Sheet method and is preferred when the patient cannot be handled directly, particularly if the patient is bed-ridden. The third fundamental approach is to bring the stretcher to the patient, rather than transfer the patient to the stretcher. This can be done with some types of stretchers using a Patient Roll or quite uniquely as with the scoop type stretcher. The scoop type stretcher is opened, placed on either side of the patient, and then fastened around the patient as he is found. This is a relatively new device for transferring the patient with a suspected spine injury. In the case of a Patient Roll, the patient is moved to a position of rest on one side and a portable stretcher, or backboard, is positioned parallel to the patient, then he is lowered to the device (this method requires at least four men if the patient has a spine injury).

The most generally applicable methods of the first two approaches will be described in detail in this chapter. The descriptions are essentially procedural, supplemented by illustrations and text, and are organized to fit the major types of patient transfer tasks. In general, the procedures which define the several transfer methods differ primarily in the sub-tasks of positioning equipment and lifting the patient. Procedures suggested for positioning patient, carrying patient to stretcher and placing/positioning patient on stretcher are relatively similar for various transfer methods and carrying devices.

Patient transfer tasks can be broadly categorized as either bed-level or floor-/ground-level transfers. The appropriateness of a particular method and its specific application depend on the location in which the patient is found, relative to the EMT's. Thus, one would want to know first if the patient is to be transferred from a bed, or surface of similar height, or from a ground or floor location in order to select an appropriate method and conduct it in an acceptable manner. The presentation of the procedural descriptions takes this consideration into account. Once the transfer method is chosen, however, the specific application of the method depends upon the carrying device selected. Indeed, some methods would not be used at all with some stretchers.

This chapter does not attempt to present all procedural modifications appropriate to all transfer situations. What is given is a set of methods appropriate to most transfer tasks and to the types of carrying devices most often on an ambulance. Transfer of the bed-level patient is considered the most fundamental transfer task; it tends to be a relatively uncomplicated task and detailed procedures for two basic transfer methods are given in Section B. Modifications of the bed-level patient transfer methods are described for floor-/ground-level patients in Section C, in addition to methods specific to this situation. In addition, special patient conditions and other complications, as they affect the transfer and other tasks, are discussed in Chapter 7.

B. Transfer of Bed-Level Patient

In a great majority of the ambulance calls the EMT's will find their patient on a bed, either of an institutional type or the ordinary home variety. The reason for this is that many ambulance calls are the so-called routine transfer type requiring that the patient be transported either to or from an institution or a home. If the patient is to be transported from an institution it is likely that a relatively favorable environmental situation will be found in terms of gaining access to the patient, working space, and transporting the stretcher patient to the ambulance. Under these circumstances it is generally desirable to take the wheeled ambulance stretcher directly to the patient, minimizing the number of times the patient must be moved from his position. If the wheeled stretcher cannot be brought to the patient, a transfer to a temporary stretcher may be required, usually followed by a transfer to the wheeled stretcher for the patient's journey in the ambulance.

There are three basic methods of patient transfer (introduced in Section A) and each is quite appropriately used with the bed-level patient. Each of these methods (i.e., Direct Carry, Draw Sheet, Patient Roll) is discussed, and the first two, described in procedural detail in this section (the Patient Roll method is discussed in Chapter 7 for the patient with a spine injury). The Direct Carry method is most widely practiced and most often appropriate to the bed-level patient transfer task. The EMT's have direct control over the patient in their arms and can deposit him safely and easily in almost any type of carrying device. If the patient cannot be handled directly, the Draw Sheet method is quite satisfactory, particularly when the patient can be transferred directly to a bed-level stretcher (using a multi-level wheeled stretcher alone or as a base for another type of stretcher, e.g., a portable pole stretcher). Occasionally, the

EMT must ensure that the bed-level patient remains anatomically straight throughout the transfer to a stretcher. In this situation, the EMT's can use a Patient Roll approach by rolling the patient on one of his sides and then rolled back onto a backboard or similar device (additional help would be required for the spine injured patient). Once the patient is secured to a board in this fashion, the transfer can proceed in much the same way as the Direct Carry method for bed-level patients.

This section now focuses on the detailed procedures to be observed in the proper conduct of the Direct Carry and Draw Sheet methods of bed-level patient transfers. Each procedure which is essential to proper performance of the transfer is numbered (non-numbered steps are recommended when the described equipment or capability is at hand). The exact sequence of procedures presented is not necessarily critical to proper performance of the transfer, but is suggested as one logical, efficient progression of steps. Upper case letters are used to highlight the essence of the procedure to facilitate a quick review of the entire method. A more detailed description is indented below each procedural step. The right-hand column is reserved for supplemental notes of qualification, reference or general interest. *Underscoring* in the right-hand column is for emphasis and is used sparingly for best effect in cautioning the EMT against accidental injury to the patient and/or himself. Lastly, transitional notes (bounded by solid lines) are occasionally inserted within the procedural description; such notes, although appropriately part of the text, are believed to be more useful where they appear.

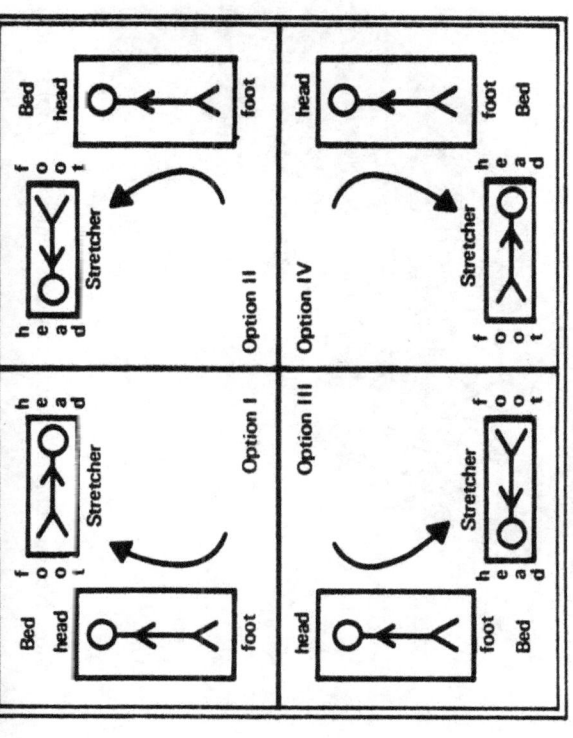

Diagram No. 11. Stretcher/bed configuration options.

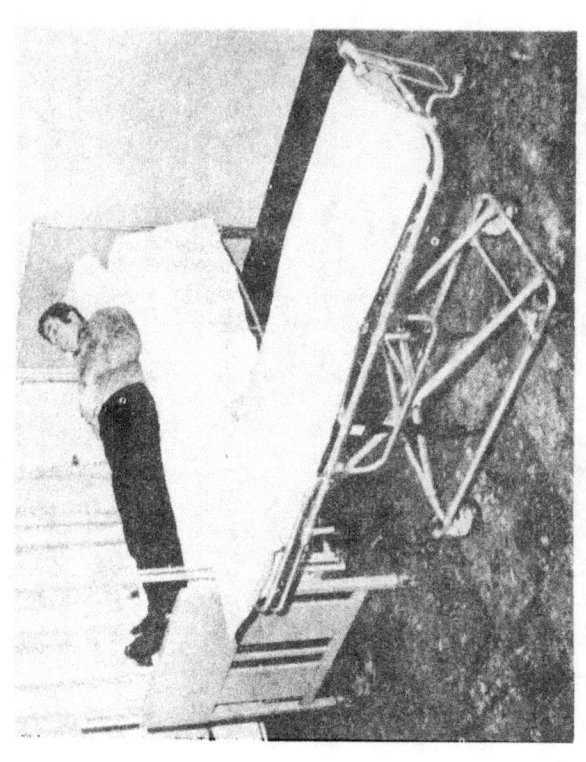

Photo No. 12. Patient and equipment positioned and prepared for transfer by Direct Carry method.

1. Transfer by Direct Carry Method

This method of transfer is also known by the more descriptive phrase of Arm-Lift-Chest Carry. The EMT's are required to lift and hold the patient in their arms, while keeping the patient as straight as possible (patient is almost resting on his side in the bent elbows of the EMT's), and carrying the patient from the bed to the stretcher. Ideally, the patient is then deposited onto a stretcher of bed-level height to eliminate additional strain on the EMT's which would exist in lowering the patient to a low-level stretcher.

The following procedures describe the proper conduct of a direct carry patient transfer from a bed, or similar surface, to a flat, bed-like carrying device. These procedures are generally appropriate (except as qualified) to any of the standard flat ambulance stretchers, in particular: 1) wheeled stretchers, including those of adjustable height or contour; and 2) all varieties of the full-length portable stretcher. As a general rule, the Direct Carry method should

261

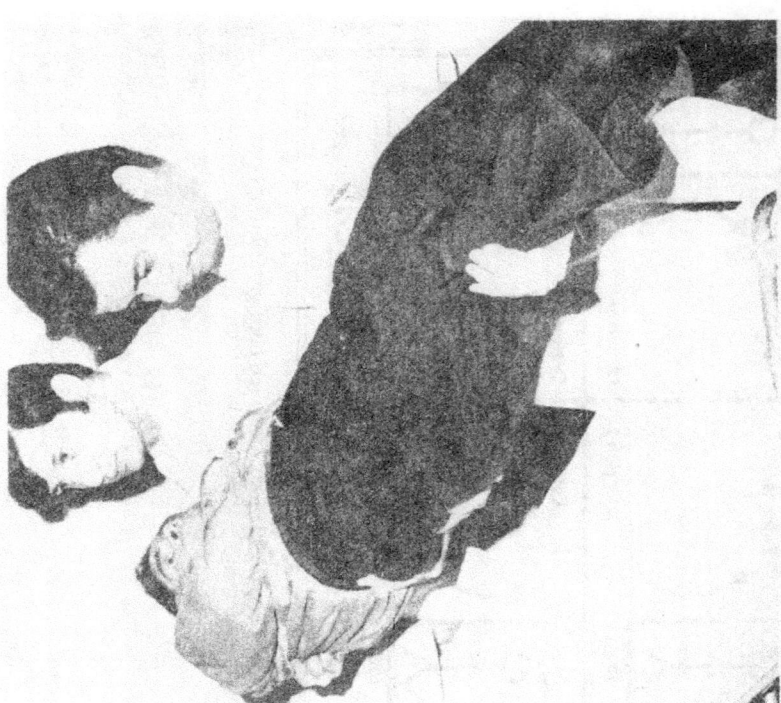

Photo No. 15. EMT's transferring patient by Direct Carry method.

Photo No. 16. EMT's ready to lower patient to low-level stretcher.

Photo No. 13. EMT's positioning arms for Direct Carry transfer (see Steps 11-15).

Photo No. 14. Close-up of EMT's arm positions.

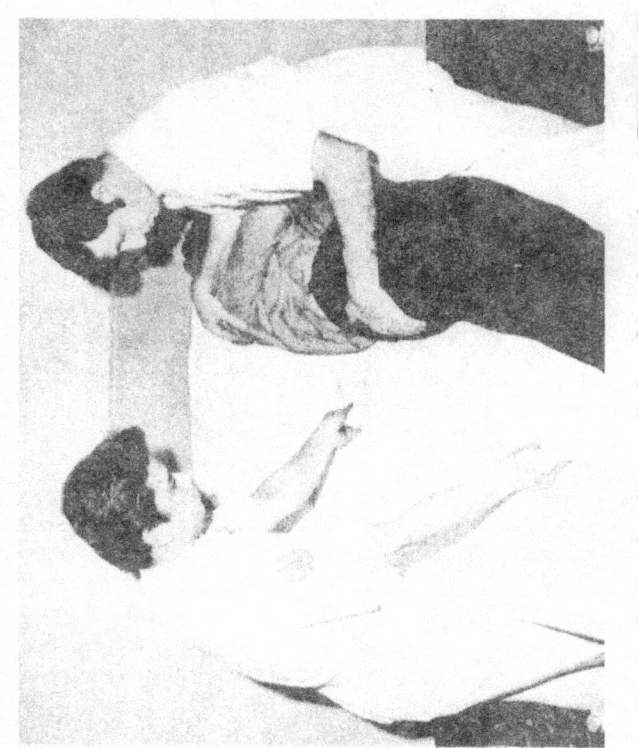

Photo No. 19. Patient has been rolled to his other side and EMT is pulling draw sheet through.

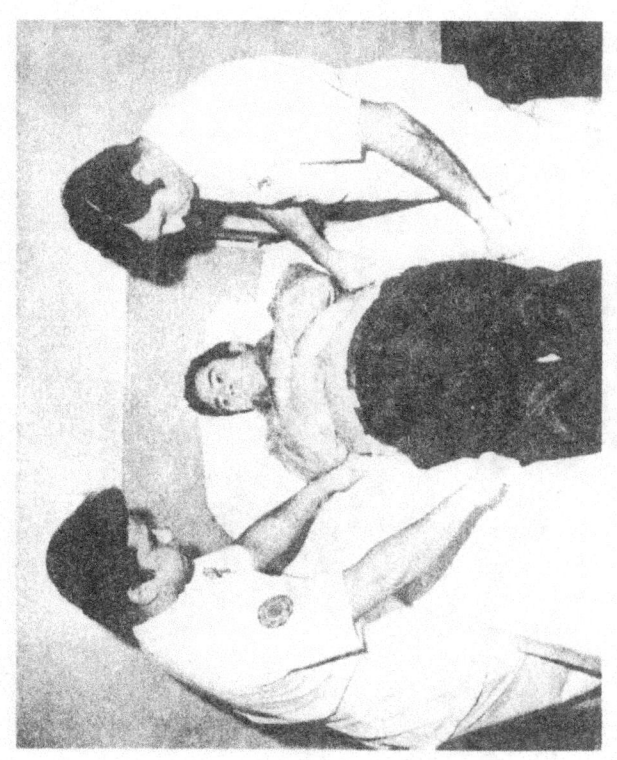

Photo No. 20. EMT's roll in both sides of draw sheet.

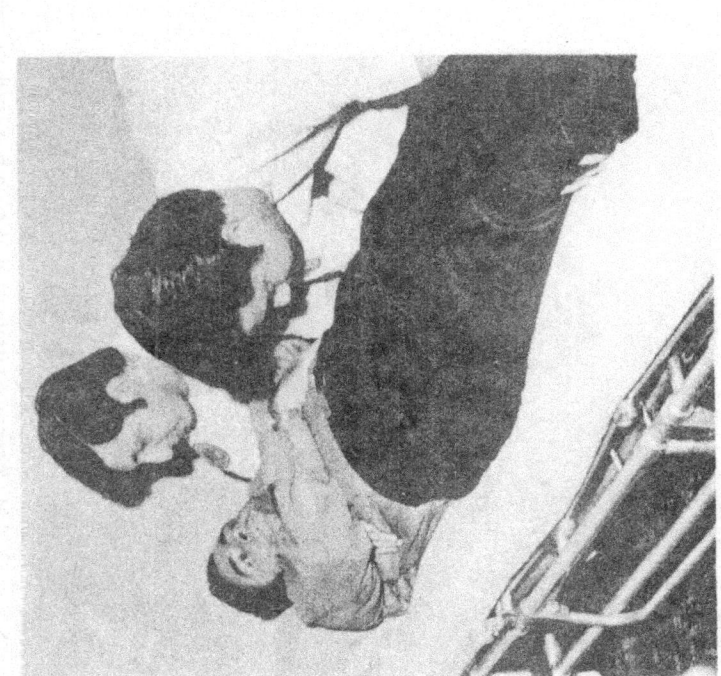

Photo No. 17. EMT's placing patient on low-level stretcher.

Photo No. 18. EMT tucking draw sheet under patient's back.

263

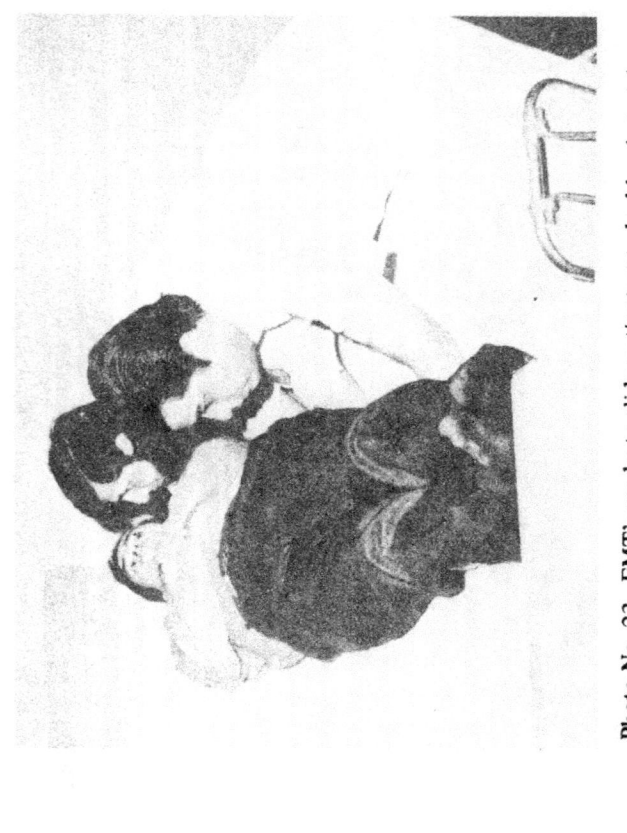

Photo No. 23. EMT's ready to slide patient onto bed-level stretcher.

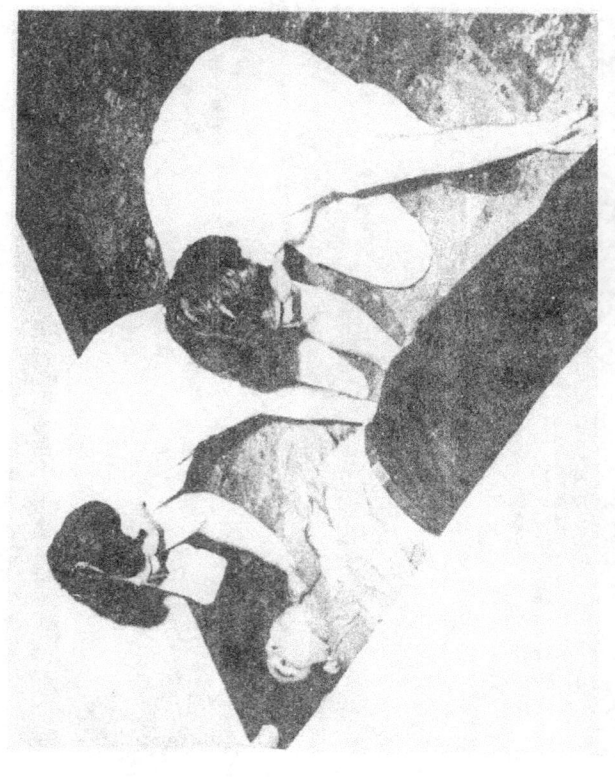

Photo No. 24. EMT's and stretcher positioned for Direct Carry transfer of floor-level patient.

Photo No. 21. EMT's have "hammock hold" on draw sheet to lower patient to low-level stretcher (see Steps a-e).

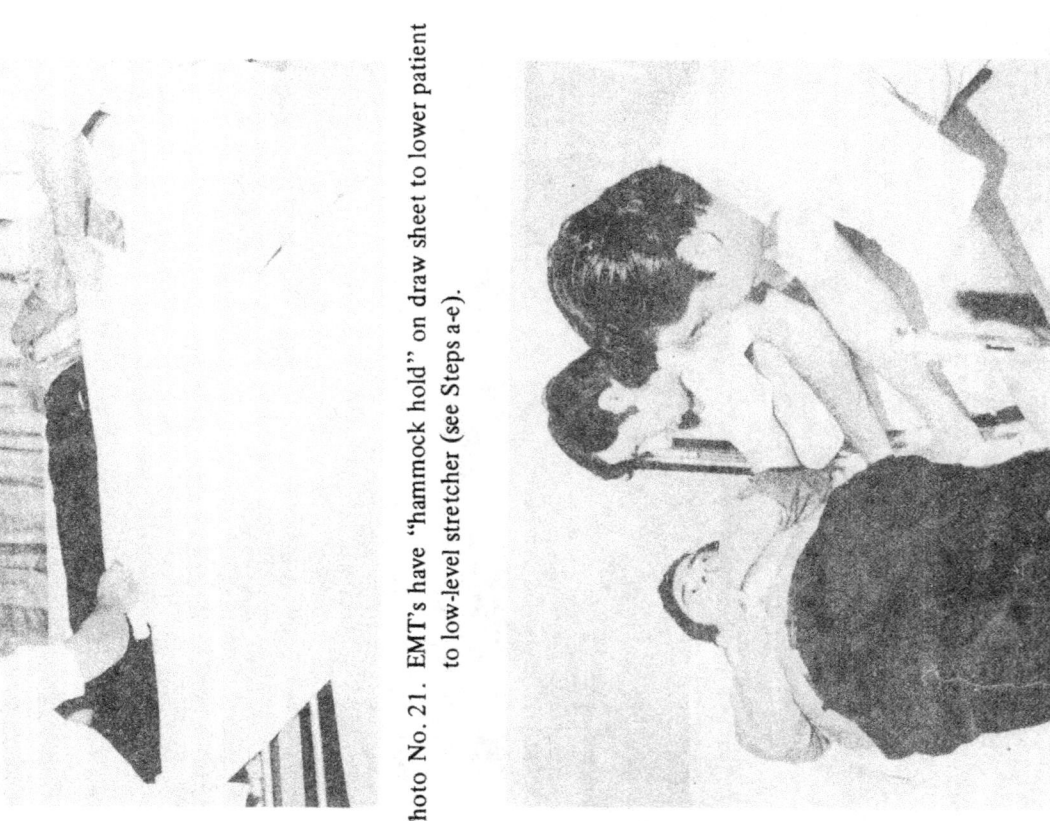

Photo No. 22. EMT's ready to draw patient onto bed-level stretcher.

Photo No. 25. EMT's assume alternative position on both knees.

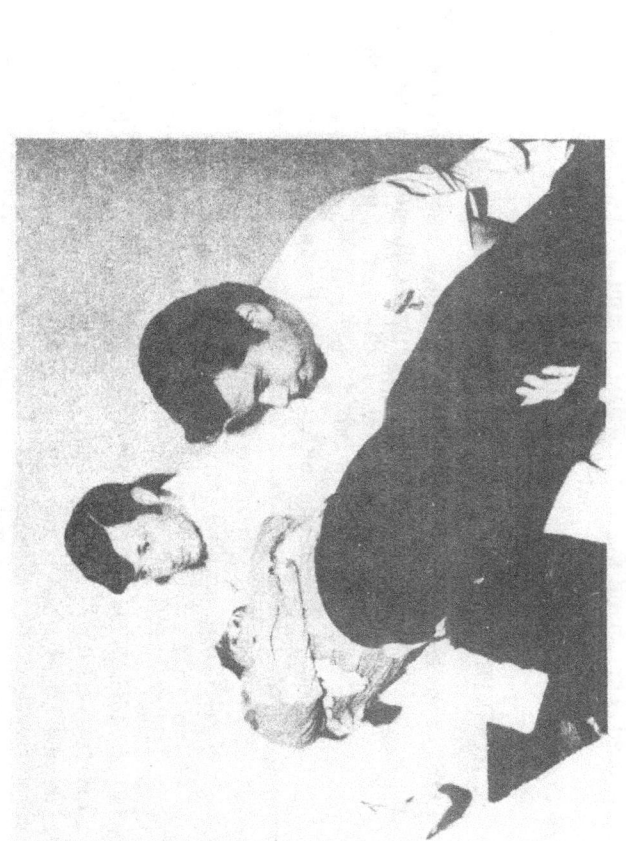

Photo No. 27. EMT's ready to drop to one knee and place patient on low-level stretcher.

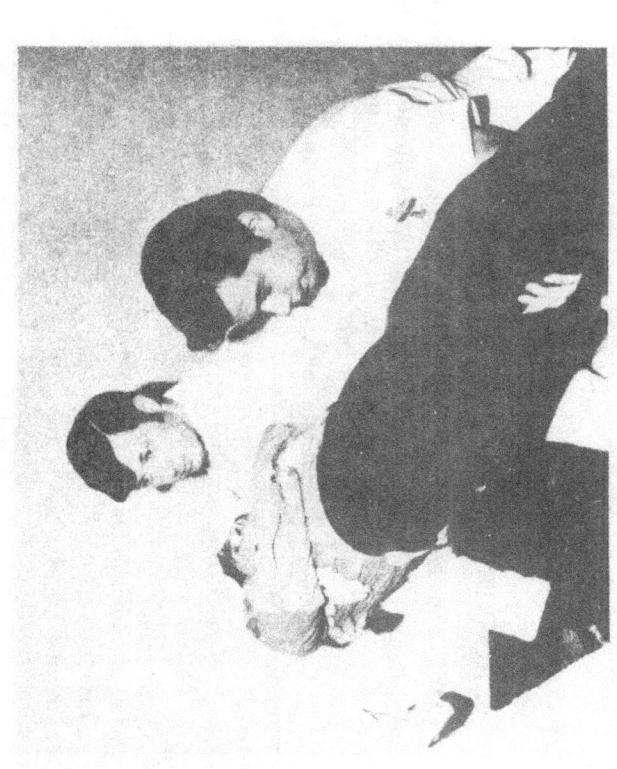

Photo No. 26. Direct Carry lift of floor-level patient.

Photo No. 28. EMT's ready to "draw" or slide patient onto floor-level portable stretcher.

not be used when handling a burn patient has, or is suspected to have, a spinal injury; in most other instances the Direct Carry method should be preferred.

PROCEDURES FOR DIRECT CARRY METHOD

1. **POSITION STRETCHER PERPENDICULAR TO BED**

   Angle configuration minimizes direct carrying distance of patient which reduces risk of strain on EMT's and injury to patient (see Diagram 12).

   - Choose side of bed nearest route of exit and form 90° angle between it and either end of stretcher
   - Roll head of stretcher to foot of bed, or, alternatively, foot of stretcher to head of bed

   If possible, **ADJUST ELEVATION of STRETCHER to BED-LEVEL HEIGHT**

   Relevant to multi-level wheeled stretchers only. *Know adjustment method for own make of stretcher.* (See Appendix A for general procedures.)

   - Method of mechanical adjustment specific to particular make of multi-level wheeled stretcher

2. **REMOVE SAFETY STRAPS** from stretcher mattress

   Be sure safety straps cannot entangle feet.

   - Unfasten and place aside all safety straps and restraining devices

3. **LOWER RAIL** on loading-side of stretcher

   Patient to be loaded onto stretcher within area formed by angle of stretcher and bed.

4. **IMMOBILIZE STRETCHER**

   Beware of "top heavy" characteristic of elevated multi-level stretcher.

   - In particular, lock wheels of stretcher (ensure that other types of stretchers will not shift or skid)

5. **IMMOBILIZE PATIENT'S BED**

   Most relevant to institutional type of beds which typically have wheels.

6. **REMOVE and SET ASIDE BLANKETS and TOP SHEET** from stretcher

   Usually placed along the head end of stretcher. Head piece recommended for cold weather protection and wrap-around sheet especially useful when using portable stretcher or chair mattress.

   - Fold top sheet length wise to prepare it for placement over patient at later time
   - Place blankets and top sheet on a clean, accessible surface

   PLACE PILLOW in appropriate position on **STRETCHER HEAD-PIECE** and/or opened **WRAP-AROUND SHEET** may be placed on stretcher

   > At the conclusion of Step 6 above, the EMT's have properly positioned, prepared and secured the equipment they will use in the patient transfer. Bedding and restraining devices have also been made accessible for later use. The diagram on the page opposite Step 1 illustrates the various options in the angle formation of bed and stretcher which are appropriate to this method. The photograph (no. 12) shows the stretcher placement chosen for this procedural description along with the result of completion of the procedures thus far (note patient is uncovered for photo illustrations but should always be covered in practice).

7. **COVER PATIENT** with **STRETCHER TOP SHEET**

   Be sure to keep patient covered at all times.

   - Place over existing bedding, if present

8. **REMOVE BEDDING UNDER TOP SHEET**

   - One EMT pulls bedding from under top sheet to bottom of bed while other EMT holds top sheet to keep it from slipping off patient

9. POSITION PATIENT in usually preferred manner
   - Supine with arms folded across chest; legs straight and close together

   If patient is conscious, explain what is to be done and have him position himself, if he is able. *Know medical conditions which preclude this patient position.*

10. BOTH STAND in area BETWEEN BED and STRETCHER and FACE PATIENT from same direction

---

The procedures which follow are specific to EMT's that are facing a supine patient's left side. Remember that arm placement must be reversed if the other side of the bed is selected.

---

11. ONE EMT SLIDES RIGHT ARM UNDER PATIENT'S NECK, and with right hand, CUPS PATIENT'S RIGHT SHOULDER
    - Patient's head cradled in driver's right elbow

    "Head-end" EMT See photo no. 13.

12. OTHER EMT SLIDES LEFT HAND UNDER EDGE OF PATIENT'S LEFT HIP and LIFTS slightly

    "Foot end" EMT

13. Head end EMT then SLIDES LEFT ARM UNDER PATIENT'S BACK (in the region of the 4th and 5th lumbar vertabrae) WHILE ATTENDANT SLIDES RIGHT ARM UNDER PATIENT'S HIPS (to the sacrum area)
    - EMT's arms inserted to their elbows under patient

    At completion of this step, driver's left arm and attendant's right arm should be parallel and almost touching.

    Foot end EMT REMOVES LEFT HAND from patient's hip

14. and SLIDES LEFT ARM UNDER PATIENT'S KNEES

15. Foot end EMT then SLIDES LEFT ARM to rest under MIDCALF AREA OF PATIENT'S LEGS

    EMT arms' position under the patient are shown in photo no. 14.

16. SLIDE PATIENT TO EDGE OF BED toward EMT

    Patient should be anatomically straight at all times.

17. BOTH BEND OVER TOWARD PATIENT

EMT's are now in the correct position to begin to lift the patient. (see photo number 13). At this point, the EMT's should be concentrating on maintaining the patient's position, controlling the patient's weight and conducting the lift with good body mechanics.

---

18. BEND KNEES TO STOOPED POSITION and CURL PATIENT TOWARD CHEST
    - Patient should be cradled now in flexed arms and resting against chests of EMT's

    Maintain a rigid, vertical back to reduce risk of back strain

19. RETURN SIMULTANEOUSLY TO A FULL STANDING POSITION
    - Use pre-arranged signal to coordinate move

    Support patient's weight on legs, not back. See photo no. 15.

20. BOTH TAKE ONE STEP BACK away from bed

    Be sure to have secure hold on patient and confidence that patient's weight can be borne.

21. EMT nearest stretcher STEPS BACKWARD while OTHER EMT STEPS FORWARD UNTIL PATIENT IS PARALLEL TO STRETCHER

22. WALK TO STRETCHER in unison — *Walk slowly and carefully.*

The procedures described in Steps 23 to 26 are specific to the low-level stretcher including light weight portable stretchers, chair mattresses and low-level wheeled stretchers placed on the floor or ground. Remember that these devices may often be placed securely on a bed-level surface, as on a multi-level wheeled stretcher, and the depositing-patient process can be simplified (as indicated in the alternate procedures below which can directly follow Step 22).

Procedures for Bed-Level Stretcher

a. BOTH PLACE RIGHT FOOT ON LOWER BAR OF STRETCHER — This ensures that the multi-level wheeled stretcher is immobilized and that the EMT's will not jar the stretcher while lowering patient.

b. FLEX KNEES and GENTLY LOWER PATIENT to center of mattress — *Maintain rigid, vertical back and support patient on legs, not back.*

Continue to Step 27.

23. STOP ONE STEP FROM STRETCHER — See photo no. 16.

24. BOTH PLACE LEFT FOOT FORWARD and ONE STEP FORWARD and BEND RIGHT KNEE TO FLOOR

 • Right knee should rest beside left foot
 • Knee and foot should be about 1 to 3 inches from base of stretcher

25. SWING LEFT KNEE TO PO-

26. BOTH ROLL FORWARD and PLACE PATIENT ON STRETCHER — *Be sure patient is placed in center of mattress. See photo no. 17.*

Rather than kneel, as in Step 24, the EMT's may prefer to assume a crouched position, maintaining rigid, vertical backs, and then use a forward roll to place the patient on the stretcher.

27. SLIDE the three ARMS FROM UNDER PATIENT's BACK and LEGS

28. Head end EMT USES LEFT HAND TO GENTLY RAISE PATIENT'S HEAD and SLIDES RIGHT ARM FROM UNDER PATIENT'S NECK — *Do this before removing arm from under patient's neck and head.*

Upon the completion of Step 28 above, the patient usually should be resting on his back (supine position) in the center of the stretcher mattress. The EMT's have successfully transferred the patient from a bed to a wheeled, portable or other level, flat carrying device by using a popular version of the Direct Carry method. This method would be used in almost all ambulance transfer work, unless the patient's condition precludes direct handling, and the EMT's would then proceed to positioning, covering, securing and moving the stretcher patient (procedures discussed in Chapter 5). An alternative to the Direct Carry method is occasionally used for bed-level transfers, especially on routine ambulance calls, and is actually the preferred method for some patients, e.g., burn cases. This method is known as the Draw Sheet transfer.

2. Transfer by Draw Sheet Method (and Slide Transfers)

The Draw Sheet method is used almost exclusively for transfer of bed-level patient to any of the standard, flat ambulance stretchers, but is best used with a wheeled stretcher adjustable to bed-level height. With this method, the EMT's rarely touch the patient directly and the sheet used to draw the patient onto the stretcher becomes an "intermediate stretcher." In other words, the sheet temporarily supports much of the patient's weight during the actual

If the patient's condition allows slightly more direct contact than the Draw Sheet method requires, the basic procedures can be used without a sheet, or similar length of material, and is called a Slide Transfer. This adaptation of the basic Draw Sheet method is explained in the detailed procedures given below. Although detailed procedures have been written with the wheeled stretcher of bed-level height in mind, low-level stretchers (e.g., single level wheeled or portable stretchers) can be used. The procedural description below recommends certain modifications of the basic method which should be observed when using a low-level stretcher. Format of detailed procedures and text are presented as in the description of the Direct Carry method.

PROCEDURES FOR DRAW SHEET (AND SLIDE TRANSFER) METHOD

*(Omit Step for Slide Transfer)

1. **COVER PATIENT** with **STRETCHER TOP SHEET**
   - Place over any existing bedding

2. **REMOVE BEDDING UNDER TOP SHEET**   *Be sure to keep patient covered at all times.*
   - Retain for later use

*3. **LOOSEN BOTTOM SHEET** under patient to prepare as draw sheet   (If there is no bottom sheet, see text below.)

In some cases the EMT's must insert their own draw sheet under the patient (i.e., when there is no bottom sheet on the bed, or when the one there is unsatisfactory). This can be accomplished as follows:

Procedures for Inserting Draw Sheet

a. **FAN-FOLD SHEET** lengthwise

b. **EMT's ROLL PATIENT AWAY to POSITION** on his **SIDE**   One EMT should be on each side of bed.
   - One EMT will then be facing patient's back

c. **TUCK LONG FOLD of SHEET BETWEEN PATIENT and BED**   See photo no. 18.

d. **ROLL PATIENT BACK** to rest on **OTHER SIDE**   Guide patient's roll and help keep him supported when on his side.
   - Use patient's uppermost arm to begin roll back
   - Reach over patient's body to grasp arm formerly under patient's body to help complete roll to his other side

e. EMT now facing patient's back **PULLS DRAW SHEET THROUGH**   See photo no. 19.

f. **ROLL PATIENT ON HIS BACK**
   Continue to Step 4.

4. **STRAIGHTEN SHEET AND ROLL IN BOTH SIDES TOWARD** patient

5. **LOWER RAILS** of stretcher and **REMOVE SAFETY STRAPS**   See photo no. 20.

   If using a wheeled stretcher with contour feature, ensure that **STRETCHER IS FLAT**

6. **ELEVATE ADJUSTABLE STRETCHER TO BED-LEVEL HEIGHT**
   - Ensure that it is locked in this position

   Know mechanical procedures for own make of stretcher.

7. Roll **STRETCHER PARALLEL** to and **TOUCHING LONG SIDE OF BED**

   These procedures are written specifically for stretcher placed along supine patient's left side.

8. IMMOBILIZE STRETCHER and BED

   If other side of bed selected, reverse arm placements.

   Know wheel locking mechanism.

9. PULL SHEET to MOVE PATIENT to side of bed nearest stretcher
   - If slide transfer rather than draw sheet method is to be used, pull bottom sheet, under patient, to move him over

10. POSITION PATIENT in usually preferred manner
    - Supine with arms folded across chest; legs straight and close together

The procedure for Draw Sheet transfer described in Steps 11 through 13 is specific to the use of the bed-level stretcher. If a low-level stretcher is used (usually a single level wheeled stretcher), the procedure is slightly modified as indicated below. Steps a through c would directly follow Step 10 and would then continue to Step 14.

Procedures for Low-Level Stretchers

a. BOTH STAND on side of bed NEAR STRETCHER and REACH ACROSS ENDS of STRETCHER to patient
   - EMT (usually driver) stands along short side of head end of stretcher
   - Other EMT (usually attendant) stands at short side of foot end of stretcher

b. Head end EMT GRASPS DRAW SHEET ON EITHER SIDE OF PATIENT'S HEAD
   - Grasps top corners of draw sheet

c. Foot end EMT GRASPS DRAW SHEET ON EITHER SIDE OF PATIENT'S FEET
   - Grasps bottom corners of draw sheet

For good grip on draw sheet, bunch up each corner. See photo no. 21.

11. BOTH STAND on side of bed NEAR STRETCHER and REACH ACROSS STRETCHER to patient
    - EMT (usually driver) stands along short side of head end of stretcher
    - Other EMT (usually attendant) stands at center of long side of stretcher

    FOR SLIDE TRANSFER, without draw sheet, refer now to text following Step 14

*12. Head end EMT LEANS OVER STRETCHER, SLIDES one ARM UNDER PATIENT'S HEAD and SHOULDERS and GRASPS DRAW SHEET with free hand

*13. Foot end EMT SLIDES one ARM UNDER PATIENT'S KNEES AND GRASPS DRAW SHEET with free hand
    - Lean against stretcher to ensure its stability

For good grip on draw sheet, bunch-up sheet to form a "handle." See photo no. 22.

MODIFICATION FOR SLIDE TRANSFER

(Procedures to substitute for Steps 11 through 13 of Draw Sheet method)

Continuation from Step 10 (of Draw Sheet Method)

11. Head end EMT SLIDES RIGHT ARM UNDER PATIENT'S NECK and with right hand, CUPS PATIENT'S RIGHT SHOULDER while placing OTHER HAND UNDER PATIENT'S LEFT SHOULDER
    - Patient's head is cradled in EMT's right elbow
    - EMT's left arm is in position to support patient during draw move

12. OTHER EMT reaches over to patient and ONE HAND UNDER BUTTOCKS TOWARD SMALL OF BACK and OTHER HAND UNDER BUTTOCKS NEAR THIGHS

    See photo no. 23.

13. (For bed-level stretcher) SLIDE PATIENT onto stretcher with an UPWARD DRAW motion

    (For low-level stretcher) SLIDE PATIENT to EDGE of bed and LOWER to stretcher

14. Simultaneously, DRAW PATIENT ONTO STRETCHER
    - This "slide" and "carry" should be a single, continuous motion

    Lean against stretcher to prevent it from moving.

The patient should now be resting supine, covered and in the center of the stretcher. The basic draw move, which is the essence of the Draw Sheet transfer method, can be accomplished in a similar fashion without the use of a sheet. Proper placement of the EMT's arms can give sufficient support to the patient to allow EMT's to "draw" patient onto either a bed-level or low-level stretcher. This process is called a Slide Transfer. It can be accomplished by following the steps outlined in the Draw Sheet method through Step 10 and substituting the following procedures for the previously described Steps 11 through 13.

It should be obvious from the discussion of the procedures for the simple Draw Sheet transfer and the modified procedures for the simple Slide Transfer, that the two "methods" are actually versions of the same set of moves and equipment/patient positions. The notable difference in the procedures is the use of a sheet for the "draw" move in the case of a Draw Sheet transfer and the same move with the patient supported by only the arms and hands of the EMT's, in a Slide Transfer. If a draw sheet must be inserted under the patient for the transfer (e.g., there is no bottom sheet under patient), a simple Slide Transfer can be accomplished more quickly. However, the Slide Transfer does require more direct handling of the patient than would be necessary with the aid of a draw sheet.

3. Transfer by Other Methods

Transfer of the bed-level patient is simplified, relative to the transfer of a patient from floor or ground, by several advantageous situational characteristics. First, the patient is to be moved from a comfortable surface and can be positioned generally in comfort on the mattress. Second, the EMT's are able to work on the patient in a comfortable standing position and the lifts that are required begin with the patient already at waist level. Third, clean work surfaces are probably accessible to the EMT's because such transfers are conducted indoors and, frequently, in a hospital.

Thus, the bed-level patient environment will usually not interfere with the conduct of either a Direct Carry transfer or a Draw Sheet transfer. Both these transfer methods are performed best with a bed-level (multi-level wheeled) stretcher but can be used when portable stretcher or straight chair mattress only can be brought to the patient. Sometimes, though, special transfer methods must be employed. If the patient cannot be moved on a flat, horizontal type of stretcher, a stair chair may be required, calling for special procedures. It is possible that the patient on a bed would be moved best by using a backboard, e.g., in a heart case requiring cardio-pulmonary resuscitation. These more specialized techniques are discussed for the floor-/ground-level patient in detail in Chapter 7 and could be applied, if necessary, to the bed-level patient.

There is one other transfer method for the bed-level patient which deserves special mention here. It is a particularly safe and easy transfer of a bed-ridden patient, but appropriate to only certain portable stretchers. For example, a light weight chair mattress (locked in flat position) or a portable canvas stretcher (minus its poles) can be placed directly on the bed, along side the patient who has been moved to one side of the bed. Then, both EMT's stand on the side of the bed nearest the stretcher and use a lift and pull motion, as in the Slide Transfer, to draw the patient onto the stretcher. The patient-loaded stretcher would then be loaded onto a standard flat wheeled stretcher, if and as soon as possible.

Another version of the above mentioned approach is to use the canvas section of a portable stretcher as a "draw sheet." In this instance, the EMT's would follow the basic instructions for insertion of the draw sheet with the exception of folding the sheet before insertion (this is not necessary with the narrow canvas stretcher). Removal of the patient from the bed is easier with this method than with the usual draw sheet. Often the canvas stretcher will have convenient hand holds for the EMT's, or the poles may be re-inserted, and the patient may be carried to the ambulance in this fashion (though it is usually preferable to place the patient *and* stretcher on a wheeled stretcher first).

C. Transfer of Floor-/Ground-Level Patient

The ambulance that responds to an emergency call will find the patient most often lying on the floor or, outdoors, on the ground. Although a relatively small percentage of the calls for ambulance service arise from a true medical emergency, when an emergency does occur the EMT must be especially skilled in the more difficult transfer of the floor-/ground-level patient. Such a transfer is likely to require handling compensations for more dire medical conditions and more efficient use of the strength of each EMT (more *lifting* required).

The basic transfer approaches discussed previously are also appropriate to the floor-/ground-level patient but procedures must be modified somewhat and the frequency with which a particular approach applies is different than for the bed-level patient. In general, the exception to this statement is limited to the basic inappropriateness of the Draw Sheet method. The use of the draw sheet would require too much rolling of the patient on a hard, often cold, surface and it would be difficult to achieve desirable support for the patient lifted from a floor or ground location. Thus, the method relies on soft maneuverable surface) for its usefulness. The related Slide Transfer method, however, is occasionally used with a flat portable stretcher (analogous to the method described in Section B. 3.) for the floor-ground-level patient.

There will be a choice typically among three methods of transferring the floor-/ground-level patient to a carrying device. In many cases, a version of a Direct Carry of the patient to a standard flat stretcher, or to a stair chair, will be selected. The procedures, as appropriate to the floor-/ground-level patient, will be discussed in detail in this section. A second, very useful method is called the Extremity Transfer; it is described in detail in Section H of Chapter 7. This is, perhaps, the easiest method for lifting and carrying a patient from the floor or ground, but it should not be used for the seriously injured or fracture patient. The third most common method will be the use of the hinged scoop type stretcher (or perhaps a background) to transfer the patient later to an ambulance wheeled stretcher. These procedures are considered in Chapter 7 as one of the special transfer tasks, because they are almost always used when it is suspected that the patient is suffering from a spine injury or a patient requires cardio-pulmonary resuscitation.

1. Transfer by Direct Carry Method

If, upon examination, the floor-/ground-level patient is found to be free of injury to an extremity or danger of a spine fracture, he will generally be lifted and rolled to the chests of the EMT's and transferred to a stretcher by Direct Carry. The arm placement of the EMT's, the positioning of the patient and the execution of the Direct Carry are all similar to its use in transferring a bed-level patient. The principal difference when the patient is on the floor or ground is the placement of the stretcher which should be alongside the patient (parallel to) rather than perpendicular and the position of the EMT's to enable them to conduct the more strenuous lift without undue strain.

The following procedures describe the proper conduct of a direct carry patient transfer from a floor or ground location to a flat, low-level carrying device. The procedures and options presented are generally appropriate (except as qualified) to any of the standard flat ambulance stretchers, in particular: 1) all wheeled stretchers, in low-level carry position; and 2) all varieties of the full-length portable stretcher. The format for the procedures below is identical to that described in the section of the bed-level patient. The procedures though some steps are repetitions of the version for bed-level patients, and for simplicity, it is assumed the EMT's are facing a supine patient's right side (in the procedures for bed-level patients, the EMT's are facing a supine patient's left side; these steps reflect reversed arm placement though the photographs do not).

MODIFIED PROCEDURES FOR DIRECT CARRY METHOD

1. REMOVE and SET ASIDE BLANKETS and TOP SHEET from stretcher
   - Most relevant to wheeled stretchers.

   PLACE PILLOW in appropriate position on STRETCHER

   HEAD-PIECE and/or opened WRAP-AROUND SHEET may be placed on stretcher
   - Head-piece recommended for cold weather protection and wrap-around sheet especially useful when using portable stretcher or chair mattress.

   COVER PATIENT with STRETCHER TOP SHEET
   - Other covers may be advisable for warmth or protection.

2. REMOVE SAFETY STRAPS from stretcher mattress
   - Unfasten and place aside all safety straps and restraining devices
   - *Be sure safety straps cannot entangle feet.*

3. LOWER RAIL on loading-side of stretcher
   - Relevant to wheeled stretcher only.

4. POSITION STRETCHER ALONGSIDE PATIENT
   - Parallel and as close as possible to patient
   - If EMT's are facing patient's right side, the stretcher should be along patient's left side

5. IMMOBILIZE STRETCHER
   - In particular, lock wheels of stretcher (ensure that other types of stretchers will not shift or skid)
   - *Know locking mechanism for own make of stretcher.*

6. POSITION PATIENT IN USUALLY PREFERRED MANNER
   - Supine with arms folded across chest; legs straight and close together
   - If patient conscious, explain what is to be done and have him position himself, if he is able.
   - *Know medical conditions which preclude this patient position.*

7. BOTH EMT'S drop to ONE KNEE side-by-side NEAREST and facing PATIENT
   - Head end EMT drops right knee, other EMT, left knee
   - Alternatively, EMT's may completely kneel, if they prefer. See photo nos. 24 and 25.

   At this point and as illustrated by photograph no. 24, the stretcher and patient have been positioned, prepared and the EMT's have assumed an acceptable stance for the actual transfer of the patient.
   ---

8. Head end EMT SLIDES LEFT ARM UNDER PATIENT'S NECK and with left hand, CUPS PATIENT'S LEFT SHOULDER
   - Patient's head cradled in elbow
   - Direct Carry procedures here assume EMT's to be facing supine patient's right side.

9. OTHER EMT SLIDES RIGHT HAND UNDER EDGE of PATIENT'S RIGHT HIP and LIFTS slightly

10. Head end EMT then SLIDES RIGHT ARM UNDER PATIENT'S BACK (in the region of the 4th and 5th lumbar vertebrae) WHILE OTHER EMT SLIDES LEFT ARM UNDER PATIENT'S HIPS
    - EMT's arms inserted to their elbows under patient

273

11. Foot end EMT REMOVES RIGHT HAND from PATIENT'S HIP and SLIDES RIGHT ARM UNDER PATIENT'S KNEES

    - Upon completion of step, EMT's arms should be parallel and almost touching

12. Same EMT then SLIDES RIGHT ARM TO REST under MID-CALF AREA OF PATIENT'S LEGS

    EMT's should be bent over toward patient (natural occurrence with performance of Steps 8 to 12) and should keep backs rigid and as vertical as possible.

13. Simultaneously, BOTH EMT's LIFT and ROLL PATIENT AGAINST their chests

    - Use pre-arranged signal to coordinate move

    Be sure to keep patient anatomically straight. See photo no. 26.

14. RETURN SIMULTANEOUSLY TO A FULL STANDING POSITION

    - Use pre-arranged signal to coordinate move

    Support patient's weight on legs, not back.

15. WALK TO STRETCHER in unison

    - One or two steps forward

    Walk slowly and carefully. See photo no. 27.

16. BOTH EMT's DROP TO ONE KNEE, as before

    - Use pre-arranged signal to coordinate move

    This step may be omitted if a high-level stretcher is used.

17. ROLL FORWARD and GENTLY LOWER PATIENT to stretcher

18. SLIDE the three ARMS FROM UNDER PATIENT'S BACK and LEGS

    Do this before removing arm from under patient's neck and head.

If it had not been possible to place the stretcher parallel to the patient, the above procedures could have been modified by using the perpendicular positioning (i.e., perpendicular to patient) that was described in the Direct Carry Method for the bed-level patient and adding Step 21 of that description to easily re-orient EMT's to the stretcher.

2. Transfer by Other Methods

If there is just a suspicion that the floor- or ground-level patient has a spine injury, e.g., if he had fallen, the EMT's should not hesitate to wait for additional help and use a scoop type stretcher or utilize specialized procedures (see Chapter 7). The other special transfer tasks examined in Chapter 7 also apply to the exclusion of the basic aforementioned approaches.

In addition to the Direct Carry method for floor-/ground-level patient, several other methods may be used if the right circumstances prevail. One method is a variation of the Slide Transfer (discussed in Section B) that can be used when the EMT's have at their disposal a portable stretcher which sits no more than 2 or 3 inches off the floor. In this instance, the EMT's kneel alongside the stretcher, rather than the patient, and slide or draw the patient toward themselves onto the stretcher, in one continuous motion (see photo no. 28). This method would not be desirable with a very heavy patient and a two-man ambulance crew. It could prove very useful, however, if the EMT's have access to only one side of the patient (e.g., patient lying parallel to and against wall, or other obstruction).

Another transfer option is available which utilizes the parallel positioning of the patient and stretcher described in the Modified Direct Carry and a third person. Rather than the EMT's lifting and *carrying* the patient from the floor or ground to the stretcher, a bystander may be able to slide the stretcher under the patient while the EMT's have the patient in their arms. The EMT's then merely lower the patient to the center of the stretcher.

Finally, the use of a canvas stretcher as a "draw sheet," as was described in Part 3 of the bed-level patient transfer section, can be also employed for the floor-/ground-level patient. Obviously, it is not as desirable for the patient to be rolled on the floor or ground as on a bed, which should be taken into account before deciding upon this method.

Chapter 5

Moving Stretcher Patients

A. Preparation of Patient on Stretcher

Positioning, covering and securing the patient on a stretcher are patient-handling tasks which logically follow the transfer of the patient to a stretcher. For purposes of this chapter, it is assumed the patient had been rendered emergency care and was transferred by some acceptable method to one of the standard ambulance carrying devices. All of the basic transfer methods described in Chapter 4 resulted in placing the patient in the center of the stretcher on his back, with his arms folded across his chest and his legs together. The patient must now be prepared, including positioning, covering and securing, before the EMT's should attempt to lift and transport the loaded stretcher to the ambulance.

This section treats each task in the preparation for moving patient as a separate unit for discussion and procedural description. The first section below will describe conventional positioning of the typical (i.e, conscious, non-critical) patient on a stretcher. Similar discussions for covering and securing the patient complete the sequence of tasks which define proper preparation of the patient for moving.

Procedures for proper positioning, covering and securing of the patient vary depending upon several factors: 1) the patient's medical condition; 2) the environments (i.e., interior and exterior) to which the patient will be exposed; and 3) the type of carrying device which will be used to move the patient. The patient's medical condition has, by far, the most significant effect on the conduct of these tasks because it must be taken into account before the EMT's decide how they will position, cover and secure the patient on the stretcher they had selected already (the patient's condition entered into this latter decision as well). The environmental factors, especially weather conditions at the time, will largely affect the way in which the patient is to be covered. Finally, the type of stretcher on which the patient is resting may limit the number of positions the patient can assume and will have an additional minor effect on procedures for covering and securing.

275

Since considering all of these factors at the same time will lead to complicated procedural descriptions and is likely to disguise the basic processes, the following subsections describe only the typical positioning, covering and securing of the stretcher patient. Though some variations and options are presented in the procedural descriptions in this chapter, for the most part, exceptions are due to special, and often critical, medical problems which are dealt with separately in Chapter 7. It is assumed in this Chapter that the patient is conscious, suffering no immediate life-threatening emergency and is to be positioned, covered and secured on a standard, horizontal ambulance stretcher.

The format for procedures in this chapter is identical to that used previously. That is, the essential steps in the performance of the task are numbered, supplemented by non-numbered, optional steps; uppercase-lettered words highlight the basic procedure; indented, bulleted remarks describe the basic procedure in more detail; the right-hand column presents notes of qualification, reference or general interest; and underscoring is intended to add emphasis. A reminder—the text occasionally interrupts the procedural description and is indicated by a solid-line boundary.

1. Positioning Patient on Stretcher

Under most circumstances, the patient's opinion of his own comfort can be used as an acceptable guide to correct positioning of the patient on the stretcher. Making the patient as comfortable as possible is always the key objective in meeting this task and the patient can often help in meeting this objective (patients with critical medical conditions, as discussed in Chapter 7, must be positioned usually without their aid). The following procedures describe the normally comfortable positioning of the non-critical patient on a flat, bed-like carrying device. These procedures are generally appropriate (except as qualified) to any of the standard flat ambulance stretchers, in particular all wheeled stretchers and all varieties of the full-length portable stretcher. In general, these procedures for positioning should not be used for an unconscious or vomiting patient, a patient in shock or having breathing difficulty, and are not directly appropriate to the use of the stair chair.

BASIC (USUAL) PROCEDURES FOR POSITIONING PATIENT

1. Place PATIENT ON BACK (su- PILLOW and ARMS ACROSS CHEST

   This step is usually the transfer of patient to stretcher (previously discussed in Chapter 4).

   - Merely check for these characteristics if step previously accomplished in the transfer process
   - Patient's arms may be resting at his sides or across his stomach, if preferred

2. ADJUST, if necessary, PATIENT'S HEAD, TORSO and LEGS to form STRAIGHT LINE down CENTER of stretcher

   If manipulating necessary, *do so gently.*

   Position PATIENT'S FEET flat AGAINST FOOTREST, if possible

   Most relevant for wheeled stretchers.

The above steps are the few basic requirements for correctly positioning the usual stretcher patient. At this point, the patient should be easily and comfortably positioned. Several easily accomplished additional steps are recommended below for enhancing patient comfort (usually employed at the discretion of the patient).

FLEX and SUPPORT KNEES slightly
- Can be accomplished with extra pillow or rolled blanket on any device or,
- Adjust contour feature on wheeled stretcher, if available

ELEVATE BACKREST of stretcher, if possible

Possible with wheeled stretchers and certain portable stretchers.

- Backrest should be only slightly elevated during wheeling or carrying of stretcher (unless breathing difficulty necessitates upright

- Once stretcher is stationary (e.g., secured in the ambulance), elevate backrest to 30°–45° for patient comfort

2. Covering Patient on Stretcher

Proper covering of the patient helps to maintain an acceptable body temperature, avoids exposure of the patient to drafts and keeps the patient covered at all times to ensure his privacy. These forms of patient protection are the principal objectives of the covering task; secondarily, the EMT's should also avoid excessive soiling of ambulance blankets and linen, if possible. The actual measures taken by the EMT's should be in keeping with environmental conditions (i.e., principally the weather), but the range of these conditions can be dealt with typically by one set of covering practice. The greatest percentage of patients will be adequately covered when the EMT's adhere to a set of basic procedures which are detailed below. The extremes of environment, adverse (e.g., foul weather) or very favorable (e.g., comfortable summer day) weather conditions can be met usually by either adding to or subtracting covers from the basic procedures. The EMT's should use their discretion to adjust these basic procedures to suit better prevailing patient and environmental conditions. The following procedures describe the usual way to cover a patient on any of the flat, horizontal carrying devices and include special recommendations for handling extreme environmental conditions.

PROCEDURES FOR COVERING PATIENT

1. Ensure that ALL BUT HEAD of patient COVERED by ambulance TOP SHEET — Use top sheet that had been placed on patient prior to transfer.
   - Check to see that sheet at bottom of stretcher is enough to completely cover feet

   One EMT STAND at HEAD and other EMT at FOOT of stretcher
   - Both facing patient

2. FANFOLD or DOUBLE EXCESS SHEET at head of patient UNDER CHIN — Do not allow sheet to cover patient's face.

3. PLACE HEAD-PIECE (often a towel) UNDER patient's HEAD ON PILLOW — *Protect patient's head from drafts.*

4. FOLD TOWEL AROUND patient's HEAD — In severe cold, cover more of face with towel. See photo no. 29.
   - Pull towel up from back of head to partially cover patient's forehead
   - Draw top corners of towel diagonally to patient's chest bone
   - Towel should drape each side of patient's head

5. TUCK HEAD-PIECE UNDER patient's SHOULDERS and UNDER CUFF of TOP SHEET

6. COVER PATIENT with 1 or 2 BLANKETS — Use none or 1 blanket in the summer or similar good weather. Place blanket according to procedures for making up stretcher (see Chapter 3).
   - Use fully opened blankets
   - Leave some excess blanket under chin of patient

7. CUFF BLANKETS at neck of patient

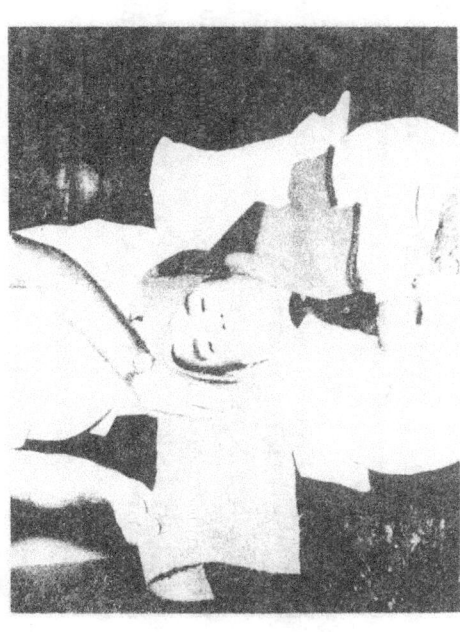

Photo No. 29. EMT folding head-piece (see Steps 3-5).

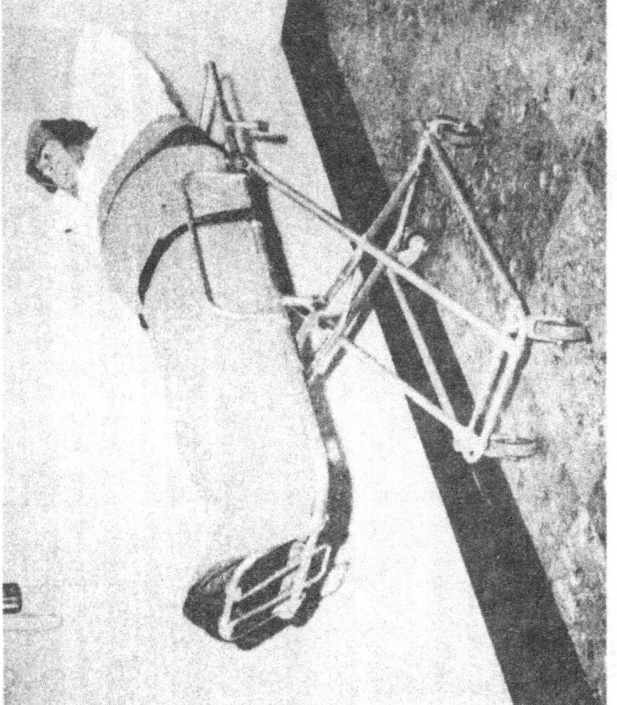

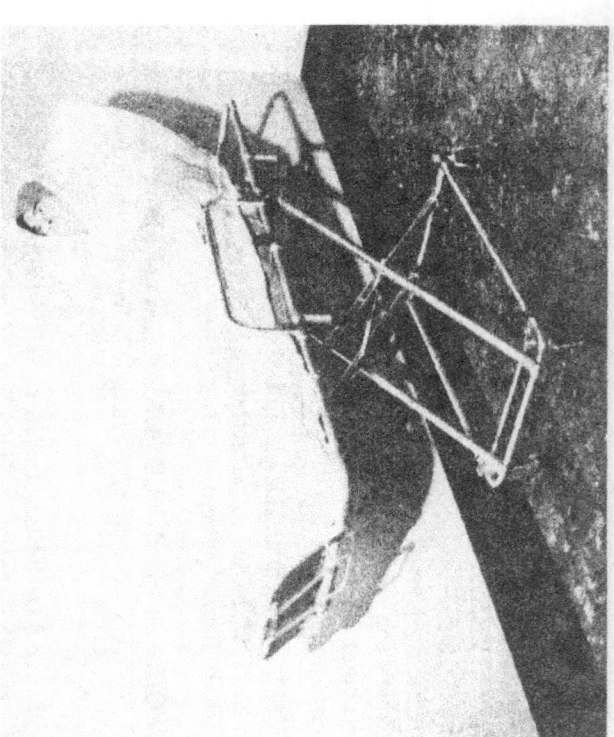

Photo No. 30. Patient covered for cold weather.

8. CUFF SHEET OVER BLANKETS at neck of patient

Provides neat finish to bedding and protects blanket.

9. TUCK BLANKETS and SHEET TOGETHER UNDER MATTRESS at foot of stretcher

Keep bedding off foot or leg injury by supporting bedding with foot rest and aluminum guide.

10. TUCK BLANKETS and SHEET UNDER SIDES OF MATTRESS
    - One EMT at each side of mattress

Avoid jarring stretcher; each EMT places one foot on lower bar of stretcher.

11. TUCK TOP OF BLANKET CUFF UNDER patient's SHOULDERS

In severe cold, draw blanket up around patient's face. See photo no. 30.

If necessary, APPLY FOUL WEATHER PROTECTION

Ideally use a plastic cover made for the purpose; if necessary, use other waterproof cover. See photo no. 31.

a. Open and partially un-zipper foul weather pouch

b. Place pouch over patient with un-zippered section toward head

c. Fit pouch over foot of stretcher and tuck around mattress sides only (leave frame of stretcher uncovered to allow grip for carrying)

d. Fit head section of pouch over head of stretcher with patient's head visible through un-zippered portion

e. Tuck top section of pouch over pillow and around edges of mattress

f. Zip top section closed over patient's face *only* while patient is exposed to the inclement weather

Minimize time that patient's face is not visible.

g. Re-open top section of pouch immediately after loading

These additional restraining measures are described in Chapter 7 entitled Special Problems for Patient-Handling.

B. Lifting and Moving the Loaded Stretcher

The patient should be comfortably positioned, covered and safely secured on the stretcher (described in Section A, Chapter 5) before the EMT's attempt to lift or move the stretcher. The EMT's may select one of two basic methods for lifting and moving the stretcher. The methods differ mainly in the positions of the EMT's relative to the stretcher and in the manner of carrying the stretcher. They are aptly termed, End Carry and Side Carry methods. In the former method, the EMT's face the patient from each end of the stretcher (i.e, foot end and head end); in the latter method, the EMT's face each other from opposite sides (long sides) of the stretcher. Either method can be used quite effectively with the wheeled stretcher and, in fact, both are typically used sometime during the course of lifting, carrying (or wheeling) and loading (into an ambulance). Alternatively, portable stretchers, and most other standard devices, are generally handled only by the End Carry method unless they are placed upon a wheeled stretcher and moved accordingly.

The End Carry method, which will be described in detail later, is the most common method of transporting a loaded stretcher to an ambulance by means of a flat, horizontal stretcher, they will most often use the End Carry method to do so. This method offers the advantages of good weight distribution, allowing the EMT's to walk with the stretcher in a near-natural manner and relatively easy maneuvering of the stretcher's position. The basic procedures of this method are defined below with different specifics, as required, for the portable and the wheeled stretchers. It is assumed for the procedural description that the method is being used for either the portable or the wheeled stretcher but, in actual practice, a portable stretcher will be placed upon a wheeled stretcher if, and as soon as, possible. As soon as this happens, of course, the End Carry method proceeds as if the wheeled stretcher is the only carrying device involved. (Remember that any method of lifting a loaded stretcher is strenuous; roll the stretcher when equipment and terrain permit.)

Photo No. 32. Patient covered and secured on a portable stretcher.

3. Securing Patient on Stretcher

Under most normal circumstances, this task simply involves enclosing the patient within the carrying device to protect him for the ambulance trip and the carrying or wheeling of the stretcher by the EMT's. Enclosure of the patient is accomplished by 1) always fastening at least one safety strap (attached to both sides of the stretcher) across the patient, and 2) locking any, and all, side rails in upright position around patient (see photo no. 30). For extra protection of the patient, particularly when more physical restraint is necessary (e.g., some psychiatric patients), special wrist, ankle, head and/or waist restraints may be used to secure the patient to and within the stretcher.

When the patient is being carried on a wheeled stretcher, the side rails should be snapped into upright position after the patient has been completely covered and safety belt should be fastened across the patient's waist. Since a portable stretcher typically has no side rails, *two* safety straps should be placed across patient, one over the chest and other across the lower extremities (see photo no. 32), and fastened securely (e.g., as firmly as recommended for auto safety belt) to frame of stretcher. If more elaborate securing of the stretcher patient is desired, selection of some of the measures recommended for hard-to-control or psychiatric patients may be employed.

Photo No. 33. End Carry of stretcher at waist-level with palms-up grip.

PROCEDURES FOR MOVING STRETCHER BY END CARRY

ASSUMPTION: Patient is centered on a low-level standard flat ambulance stretcher and has been properly positioned, covered and secured in the carrying device. Two EMT's are prepared to carry the loaded stretcher to the ambulance.

1. ONE EMT STANDS, at EACH END of STRETCHER, FACING PATIENT
   - Usually, driver at head and attendant at foot of stretcher

   Both should already have agreed upon route to ambulance.

2. HEAD END EMT GRIPS SLIDE BAR of wheeled stretcher
   - Grip lower bar of stretcher with hands toward corners of the end

   Do not carry stretcher by hand pull guides.

3. FOOT END EMT GRIPS LOWER BAR of wheeled stretcher frame
   - Grip at contour on both sides of foot rest

   Gripping procedures for portable stretchers are specific to the particular type being used. However, all portable stretchers provide hand holds, poles or other means by which the EMT's can firmly grip the end sides (i.e., head and foot sides) of the stretcher.

4. BOTH BEND KNEES and CROUCH with BACK STRAIGHT

5. RETURN to a STANDING POSITION keeping ARMS FLEXED at the elbows.
   - Should be coordinated; both beginning at the same time and moving smoothly

   Carry stretcher at waist level with palms-up grip (see photo no. 33) or carry with arms extended and palms-down (see photo 34).

Chapter 6

Loading And Unloading Ambulance

A. Introduction to the Tasks

This Chapter describes procedures for loading and unloading a ground ambulance with a stretcher patient. Several assumptions are implied by the procedural descriptions which should be made explicit here. For the purposes of patient-handling, most ground ambulances appear to share enough design characteristics to allow a generalized set of realistic procedures to be written. For example, all standard ambulances, including trucks used mostly for rescue functions, 1) have one of their doors located at the rear of the vehicle, 2) have a directly accessible compartment which is large enough to accommodate at least one stretcher patient, 3) have a level floor in the patient compartment, 4) have floors close enough to the ground allowing the stretcher to be raised into the ambulance without requiring the EMT's to lift the load above their waists, and 5) have wheel cups, wall hooks or similar devices for securing the stretcher within the ambulance.

These characteristics reduce almost all ground ambulances to essentially the same type of vehicle as far as loading and unloading procedures are concerned. However, there are some air ambulances which may have enough of these design features to enable the EMT to use the procedures presented in this Chapter for such vehicles. In general, though, fixed wing aircraft and helicopter ambulances have very unique characteristics which make generalized procedures for them practically impossible. For such specialized vehicles, it is recommended that ambulance personnel become thoroughly familiar with techniques and procedures which are tailored to the characteristics of their particular air, or other, specialized ambulance.

Another assumption underlies the presentation of procedures in this chapter. Namely, that a stretcher patient will be on either a wheeled or a portable horizontal stretcher during the conduct of the loading and unloading tasks. The patient should be positioned

---

FOOT END EMT prepares to LEAD transport of stretcher to ambulance

Allow patient to see where he is going.

- Should initiate move, set pace of walk and move backwards while "pulling" stretcher

6. WALK at same pace to AMBULANCE

Use signal to coordinate move.

- Head end EMT walks forward and foot-end EMT walks backward
- Progress by means of a shortened, natural walk at a smooth, fairly slow pace
- Attempt to keep stretcher as level as possible

7. When near loading door of ambulance, SLOWLY seat STRETCHER TO GROUND

Remember to place stretcher to allow ease in loading patient head first.

- EMT's bend knees, keep back straight and produce semi-crouched position to put stretcher on ground

---

If the patient is being transported on a wheeled stretcher over smooth surfaces and regular terrain, the EMT's may prefer to wheel, rather than carry, the patient-loaded stretcher. This option should be used carefully and under the right terrain conditions. Sometimes, the transport situation is handled best by combining both options and carrying and wheeling the stretcher over various segments of the walk to the ambulance.

The other method for transporting the patient-loaded stretcher to the ambulance is called the Side Carry. This is essentially the same method as the End Carry except the EMT's work from the long sides of the stretcher rather than the ends. This method is employed best in loading and unloading the ambulance; it is described in detail in Chapter 6. The Side Carry is not ordinarily recommended for carrying the stretcher over any distance. The method is more vulnerable (than End Carry) to weight shifts and changes in balance, and requires the EMT's to use an oblique, rather than normal, stepping pattern.

directly on a wheeled stretcher or the device on which he is secured (with the exception of the stair chair) should be placed, with the patient, on top of the wheeled stretcher prior to loading the ambulance. If the patient has been carried to the ambulance in a stair chair he should be transferred from the device and positioned, covered and secured on the wheeled stretcher for the ambulance loading and subsequent journey. Perhaps the only time a patient will have to be loaded into the ambulance supported by only a portable stretcher will be on the rare occasion when more than one stretcher patient must be carried in the vehicle at the same time. This situation is dealt with most often (ambulances usually have only one wheeled stretcher) by securing one patient on the portable stretcher and the other patient on the wheeled stretcher. Loading the ambulance under these circumstances utilizes procedures both for portable and wheeled stretchers, described in this chapter, and should always begin with the loading of the patient on the portable stretcher into the ambulance.

This Chapter is organized into two technical sections which follow this brief introduction. One section focuses on the loading procedures for placing a stretcher patient into a ground ambulance. This section covers the tasks of lifting the stretcher, rolling or sliding it into the ambulance and securing the stretcher to the vehicle; different procedures are recommended for wheeled and portable stretchers. The second section, in a similar format, describes procedures for unloading a ground ambulance with a stretcher patient.

B. Loading the Ground Ambulance

The sub-tasks involved in loading the ambulance are 1) positioning the stretcher outside the ambulance, 2) lifting the stretcher to the patient compartment floor, 3) rolling or sliding the stretcher into the compartment, and 4) fastening the stretcher to the interior of the vehicle. Two sets of procedures are given below. One set describes the conduct of the loading task when working with a patient on a wheeled stretcher. This will be the context of the task encountered on a very high percentage of the ambulance calls. For those uncommon instances when the EMT's must load the ambulance with two patients, the second set of procedures is appropriate and describes proper loading of the non-wheeled portable stretcher.

PROCEDURES FOR LOADING AMBULANCE WITH WHEELED STRETCHER

NOTE: These procedures are recommended for the rear-loading ground ambulance when using the standard ambulance wheeled cot,

or stretchers to transport patient (or the patient may be on another device which is secured to the wheeled stretcher).

1. PLACE or roll head end of STRETCHER to within THREE FEET of ambulance REAR DOOR   Bend knees to lower stretcher to ground.
   - If possible, place stretcher perpendicular to rear door

   ENSURE STRETCHER IS LOCKED IN POSITION OF LOWEST HEIGHT FROM GROUND   *Know locking mechanism for own make of stretcher.*

2. OPEN REAR DOOR(S) of ambulance   Be sure door cannot swing into loading area accidentally.
   - Open door as wide as possible and lock in open position, if possible

3. USE SIDE CARRY METHOD TO LIFT STRETCHER to ambulance floor   Refer to text below for procedures of Side Carry method.
   - Follow Steps a through e

The Side Carry method, as opposed to End Carry, is the only method recommended for two men to lift and move a patient-loaded wheeled stretcher into a ground ambulance. The End Carry method, described in Chapter 5, is appropriate for lifting and moving the stretcher *to* the ambulance and for loading a light weight portable stretcher. The procedures for the Side Carry are given below.

Procedures for Side Carry

ASSUMPTION: Patient-loaded stretcher is positioned near rear door, loading door is open and wheeled stretcher is locked in lowest level.

a. ONE EMT STANDS at EACH LONG SIDE of STRETCHER facing each other
   - For later convenience, EMT who will be driving usually stands at side of

Photo No. 35. EMT's-loading ambulance using Side Carry method for wheeled stretcher.

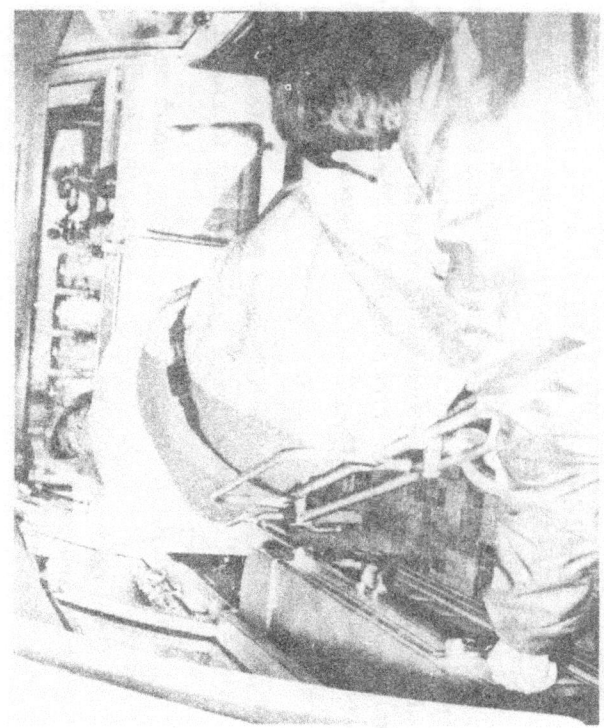

Photo No. 36. Securing wheeled stretcher with ambulance slide bar.

stretcher nearest driver's side of vehicle	
b. EMT's GRASP LOWER BAR of stretcher frame	*Bend knees* to assume lower position.
• Each hand toward nearest end of stretcher	
• Grasp bar with one palm up and one palm down	Produces strong grip and good control of weight shifts.
c. FLEX ARMS and LIFT STRETCHER BY RISING to a full standing position	
• Signal to coordinate lift	
• Rise slowly and simultaneously	
HOLD stretcher level UNLESS STRETCHER'S ELEVATED HEAD END will not pass freely through door opening (e.g., some station wagon ambulances)	*Use caution* to protect patient's head.
• If necessary, lift foot end of stretcher higher than head end	
• Place elevated end of stretcher in ambulance with scooping motion	
d. USE OBLIQUE STEPPING to ambulance door opening	
e. PLACE FRONT WHEELS of STRETCHER on COMPARTMENT FLOOR	See photo no. 35.

4. With stretcher on compartment floor, ROLL STRETCHER CAREFULLY into position for securing devices

Do not bump stretcher into anything.

There are many different devices for securing a stretcher to the interior of an ambulance vehicle. The most common fastening devices for wheeled stretchers are 1) four wheel cups in the floor into which the stretcher wheels are rolled and held secure, and 2) slide bars which secure one side (usually left side, looking from rear of vehicle) of the stretcher firmly to the wall of the vehicle. The procedures below assume a slide bar is being used for this function.

5. EMT's ROLL head end of STRETCHER FRAME into half-ring HOOK
   - Hook is at far end of slide bar (loading from rear of vehicle)

   See photo no. 36.

6. ONE EMT PUSHES spring-loaded HANDLE on opposite end of bar UNTIL half-ring HOOK at center of bar OPENS EMT ENSURES END OF STRETCHER IN POSITION FOR HOOK

   Open just enough to catch stretcher frame.

7. EMT then RELEASES BAR HANDLE and hook catches stretcher frame

   Be sure stretcher is secured.

8. ONE EMT ENTERS PATIENT COMPARTMENT

9. OTHER EMT CLOSES REAR DOOR(S) OF AMBULANCE from outside the vehicle

These procedures are basically the same for loading any carrying device into any ground ambulance. Nevertheless, the specific steps are different enough for the non-wheeled portable stretcher to warrant an additional procedural description (given below) for loading the ambulance. The reader is reminded that whenever possible, it is preferable to place the patient, prior to loading the ambulance, on the wheeled stretcher even if this means the device on which the patient has been carried must be placed and secured on the

PROCEDURES FOR LOADING AMBULANCE WITH PORTABLE STRETCHER

NOTE: These procedures are recommended when the patient is on a non-wheeled portable stretcher and must be transported in the ambulance on that device. Further, the procedures are for a rear-loading ground ambulance. If a wheeled stretcher patient will be transported in addition to the patient on the portable stretcher, load this patient first.

1. PLACE STRETCHER NEAR REAR DOOR of ambulance

   Bend knees to lower stretcher to ground.

2. OPEN REAR DOOR(S) of ambulance
   - Open doors as wide as possible and lock in open position, if possible

   Be sure doors cannot swing into loading area accidentally.

3. USE END CARRY METHOD TO LIFT and carry STRETCHER to ambulance

   Procedures for End Carry described in Chapter 5.

   Bystander may be elected to open ambulance doors. If this happens, EMT's would omit Steps 1 and 2, above, and would not have to place stretcher on ground at all; they would carry the portable stretcher directly from scene to ambulance floor.

4. PLACE HEAD END of stretcher on FLOOR of ambulance patient compartment

5. FOOT END EMT KEEPS STRETCHER LEVEL
   - Stretcher supported by floor of compartment and by one EMT

   See photo no. 37.

6. HEAD END EMT ENTERS PATIENT COMPARTMENT of

7. EMT in patient compartment CROUCHES TO GRASP HEAD END of stretcher
   - Bend knees to assume position

8. BOTH LIFT STRETCHER slightly and MOVE IT INTO PATIENT COMPARTMENT
   - Foot end EMT walks forward as head end EMT moves carefully backward

9. PLACE PORTABLE STRETCHER PARALLEL TO its eventual POSITION FOR TRANSPORT
   - Resting on the floor of the patient compartment, completely inside the ambulance

10. FOOT END EMT ENTERS PATIENT COMPARTMENT of ambulance

Keep stretcher level. See photo no. 38. Some portable stretchers may be slid into the compartment.

Upon completion of Step 10, both EMT's are within the patient compartment and must now properly place and secure the portable stretcher for the ambulance journey. Several options may be available to the EMT's depending upon the type of ambulance vehicle, the size and features of the patient compartment and the type of portable stretcher they are using. If the portable stretcher has wheels and/or leg posts, the ambulance should have corresponding cups, recessed in the compartment floor, to stabilize the stretcher and provide the opportunity for lashing it in position. The portable stretcher having no legs and wheels must be raised off the compartment floor, secured, ideally, on a squad bench or similar structure. Another method of carrying two patients in the same ambulance (one patient on an unsupported portable stretcher) is used by some ambulance services but it is explicitly disapproved by the National Academy of Sciences. The method is the suspension of the portable stretcher by wall- or ceiling-mounted brackets; it should not be used unless absolutely necessary.

Regardless of the method employed for a two-patient transport, crash-stable fasteners should be used to secure each stretcher and

Photo No. 37. Placing head-end of portable stretcher on compartment floor (see Steps 3-5).

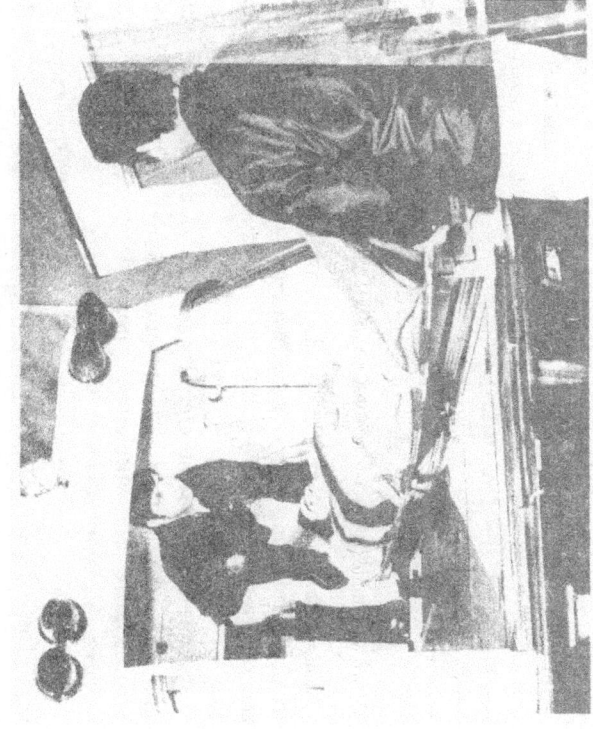

Photo No. 38. Loading ambulance with portable stretcher by End Carry method (see Steps 6-9).

restraining devices should ensure minimal longitudinal and transverse motion of the patient. Another general rule to follow in loading all ground ambulances is to place the stretcher with the patient's head toward the front of the ambulance. This affords the patient the greatest protection in the event of an accident and allows the EMT to administer to the patient more easily enroute.

C. Unloading the Ground Ambulance

The task of removing a stretcher patient from a ground ambulance involves releasing the devices which had fastened the stretcher to the compartment, rolling or otherwise moving the stretcher to the rear of the compartment, and lifting and lowering the stretcher to the ground outside the ambulance. These are the basic steps in the process of unloading the ground ambulance. The details of unloading differ for wheeled and portable stretchers as did the details in procedures for *loading* the ambulance. The format of this section parallels the presentation of procedures appearing in Section B of this chapter. Procedures for the wheeled stretcher are given first, followed by a similar description of unloading the ambulance with a portable stretcher. When more than one patient is being transported in the ambulance, and one patient is on a portable stretcher, the wheeled stretcher patient should be unloaded first.

PROCEDURES FOR UNLOADING AMBULANCE WITH WHEELED STRETCHER

NOTE: These procedures are recommended for the rear-loading ground ambulance when using the standard ambulance wheeled cot, or stretcher, to transport patient (or the patient may be on another device which is secured to the wheeled stretcher).

1. **EMT** in patient compartment **OPENS REAR DOOR(S)** of ambulance and exits compartment
   - Open door as wide as possible and lock in open position, if possible

   Wait until ambulance has stopped completely.

   Be sure door cannot swing accidentally into unloading area.

2. **EMT PUSHES** spring-loaded **HANDLE** and **RELEASES HOOKS** from stretcher frame
   - If cot is in wheel cups both EMT's should roll stretcher

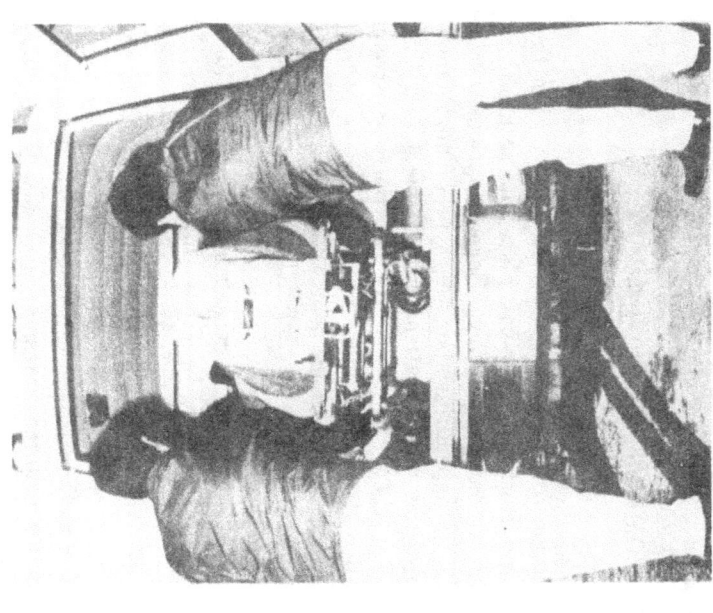

Photo No. 39. EMT's grasp stretcher frame with outside arms to unload ambulance by Side Carry (see Step 6).

3. **EMT'S POSITIONED** at EITHER **CORNER** of **FOOT END** of stretcher
   - Both should be standing on ground at the rear door opening

4. **EMT'S GRASP LOWER BAR** of stretcher frame with **INSIDE HAND EACH**
   - EMT on driver's side with right hand
   - EMT on other side with left hand

   See photo no. 39.

5. **BOTH EMT'S ROLL OUT STRETCHER** carefully UNTIL

   Do not allow rear wheels to drop when

stretcher FRONT WHEELS are resting on the floor toward the REAR of the compartment — rolling out stretcher.

6. When accessible, EACH EMT GRASP LOWER BAR of stretcher frame NEAR HEAD END of side with OUTSIDE HAND — As in photo no. 35. *Keep stretcher as level as possible.*

7. LIFT STRETCHER ABOVE ambulance FLOOR — Lift with arms.
   - Signal to coordinate lift

8. EMT'S SIDE STEP with STRETCHER until it is away from rear of ambulance — See Side Carry method in Section B.

9. When clear of ambulance, LOWER STRETCHER TO GROUND
   - Bend knees and flex arms to lower stretcher

The method of unloading the non-wheeled portable stretcher is somewhat different than described in the procedures for the wheeled stretcher. If the portable stretcher is secured to an ambulance squad bench, it is first unfastened (leaving the patient secured to the stretcher only), both EMT's face the rear of the ambulance and grasp the ends of the stretcher, as in the End Carry method, and lift the stretcher off the bench. The EMT's then move the stretcher patient to the center of the compartment floor and lower the stretcher to the floor, resulting in the foot end of the stretcher being close to the rear of the vehicle. The stretcher patient is then removed from the ambulance in the manner described below. The following procedures describe the unloading of a ground ambulance with a non-wheeled portable stretcher that had been secured to the interior of the patient compartment by means of roof and wall hooks. It is essentially the same method for the portable stretcher on an ambulance bench except Steps 2 to 4 do not apply.

PROCEDURES FOR UNLOADING AMBULANCE WITH PORTABLE STRETCHER

NOTE: These procedures are recommended when unloading a rear-loading ground ambulance with a patient on a non-wheeled portable stretcher which had been secured by wall and roof hooks.

1. DRIVER EMT ENTERS PATIENT COMPARTMENT by rear door and OPENS DOORS(S) WIDELY — Be sure door cannot swing closed during unloading.
   - Lock doors in opened position, if possible

2. ONE EMT STANDS TOWARD EACH END OF stretcher on LONG SIDE suspended by roof-mounted hanging hooks

3. BOTH EMT'S LIFT STRETCHER OFF ROOF HOOKS
   - Replace hooks in their roof holders while supporting side of stretcher with one hand each

4. USE END CARRY and BOTH EMT'S LIFT entire STRETCHER FROM WALL-MOUNTED HOOKS — Procedures for End Carry in Chapter 5.

5. LOWER STRETCHER TO FLOOR placing foot end of stretcher near rear of ambulance — Keep stretcher level.
   - Signal to coordinate move

6. Foot end EMT LEAVES COMPARTMENT and GRASPS foot end of STRETCHER

7. BOTH EMT'S SLIDE OR LIFT STRETCHER UNTIL ONLY HEAD END RESTS ON AMBULANCE FLOOR

8. OTHER EMT LEAVES COMPARTMENT and GRASPS head end of stretcher

9. STRETCHER MOVED AWAY FROM AMBULANCE by End Carry method

Chapter 7

Special Problems For Patient-Handling

A. Introduction to Chapter

There are several relatively common medical conditions, encountered in emergency ambulance work, that complicate the basic procedures observed in patient-handling. Among these conditions are injury to the spine, unconscious or vomitus patients, patients requiring life support equipment, psychiatric or hard-to-control patients, etc. These and other similar problems are examined in this chapter with respect to their effects on patient-handling tasks. Each special case is discussed as a separate unit in the chapter and applicable unique or modified procedures in the conduct of patient transfer, positioning, covering, securing, stretcher carry and ambulance loading/unloading are explained comprehensively.

Procedures appearing in the Chapter follow the previously used and described format. However, some of the sections which follow describe only modifications of the basic procedures.

In these instances, the modifications may be outlined in narrative form, in complete procedural form, or may be presented as a sub-set of procedures to substitute for a sub-set in the previously described basic procedures. If the latter description of a method is used, adequate reference to previously stated procedures should enable the reader to make proper substitutions.

B. Patient with Suspected Spine Injury

No patient condition demands more care in handling than the patient with a suspected injury of the spine. One of the main functions of the vertebrae column, or spine, is to protect the spinal cord contained within it. Once the spine is fractured or vertebra displaced, the spinal cord is in great danger at the points of injury. The danger to the spinal cord consists of possible pinching or sev-

1. Use of Backboards

The size of the short backboard does not make it a very useful carrying device. It was designed to aid in handling the spine injured patient particularly during extrication from an automobile accident. The long backboard, on the other hand, is a fine carrying device for the spine injured patient, once he has been secured properly.

The short backboard is used to immobilize a patient's spine before the patient is transferred to a longer, fully supporting device, such as a long backboard, wheeled or portable stretcher. A unique feature of the short backboard is its maneuverable size which is just sufficient to support the entire spine, but not the patient's legs. A spine injured patient should *not* be covered, positioned or moved from his seated or sitting-like position until he has first been secured to a short backboard.

The EMT's now have the relatively easy task of transferring patient and short backboard, as a unit, to a full-sized carrying device, usually to a long backboard. If the board is properly secured, the patient's spine will be immobilized and will remain that way even during extrication procedures and transfer to a long backboard or stretcher. The best way to accomplish the transfer of a patient secured to a short board is to place the patient in a sitting position on the floor or ground with the edge of one end of a long backboard at his back (the patient is facing away from the long board). Then the patient can be gently tipped backward on the lower half of the long backboard (this must not be attempted with a spine injured patient who has not been secured first to a short board). The EMT's now can slide patient and short board completely onto long backboard. The patient then may be secured to the long board in the normal manner. Once a short backboard is secured to the patient, it should not be removed until directed by a physician at the hospital (usually after examination and X-rays).

The long backboard is an excellent carrying device for all patients with serious fractures, especially of the back and neck but also for pelvic fractures and fractures of both legs. In addition to the method recommended for transferring a patient secured to a short backboard onto a long backboard there are two other distinct methods commonly used. One method is log-rolling, also called a Patient Roll, which usually requires a minimum of four people to conduct properly. The other method is an adaptation of the slide transfer

central nervous system. Very few victims of spine injury immediately suffer the severe consequences of an injured spinal cord. It is typically the result of improper or careless patient-handling, particularly at the time of the actual transfer of the patient to a carrying device.

This section discusses several basic techniques for properly handling the patient suspected to have a spine injury. In addition, the section presents detailed procedures recommended for the use of scoop type stretchers in these patient transfers. The recommended devices for handling the spine injured patient are the short and long backboards. A backboard of wood or aluminum is an excellent device for immobilizing the spine, once the patient is *on* the device and secured properly to it. The problem with these devices is that it is difficult for only two men to ensure the patient's spine will remain immobile during the transfer process. However, with adequate training the transfer can be accomplished safely. Instead, the basic principles to be followed and certain cautions to be observed are described; trained EMT's must in fact improvise specific hand grips and movements appropriate to the posture and position of the patient. A patient is likely to have a fracture of the spine, and should be handled accordingly, if he has suffered any kind of severe fall, a diving accident, whiplash in a head-on or rear-end collision, or a heavy weight hitting the patient's back. Both backboards and scoop type stretchers were designed for immobilizing a patient with a suspected fracture and thereby prevent spine movement during a transfer operation. In general, a patient should not be moved until his spine has been immobilized. A spine injury will occur most often in either the neck region (a cervical fracture), or in the lumbar area of the spine. Injuries of these types require primarily that the head, neck and trunk be kept immobile and generally in the alignment in which they are found; only secondarily must consideration be given to how the patient is moved from his initial position to an ambulance by some carrying device. This primary requirement for immobilization places emphasis on the splinting role for which backboards and scoop type stretchers were designed. Although techniques for immobilization of the spine (or any other type of fracture) are beyond the scope of this manual, repetition of a cautionary comment on the positioning and securing of a patient on these devices is appropriate before discussing their secondary function as carrying devices.

Extreme caution should be exercised when moving the spine injured patient. Two strong, experienced men working slowly and with coordination can slide a long backboard under a patient but, generally, it would be wiser to wait for additional help.

which utilizes little direct handling of the patient. This second method can be performed with only three men but again, more help is advisable.

Patients who have severe fractures are found often in unusual positions. Unless a neck fracture is suspected, the patient may be transferred and secured to the backboard as he is found, either supine or prone. To ensure proper immobilization of the head and neck, however, the patient with a suspected neck fracture must be secured in the supine position on the backboard.

In properly conducted transfers, the patient is usually centered on the backboard. If he is not, then carefully slide him to the center. One person should hold the backboard while others grasp the patient's clothing and gently, in unison, slide the patient to the desired position.

The proper placement of straps is of the utmost importance to secure and immobilize a spine injured patient on a long backboard. The patient must be not only secured to the board but, more importantly, the straps must completely immobilize the patient's spine. One strap should be fastened around or through the board and secured firmly just above patient's knees. This will prevent the patient's legs from lifting off the board. Another strap should be placed across the patient's hip region. This middle strap should pass over the patient's wrists and hold the patient's arms securely to his sides. The third body strap is fastened around the patient's chest, just below his shoulders. Most manufactured backboards have strap slots which should be used in securing the patient, providing the slots align properly with the patient's anatomy. In the event that strap slots do not exist in the board or do not align properly, all straps should be passed around the outside edge of the backboard. Body straps should not be passed through hand holds in the board.

In addition to these body straps, restraining straps are usually used to secure the patient's head and feet, particularly if the patient is going to be carried for any distance on the backboard. In any neck injury case, head immobilization must, of course, be ensured with proper strap placement and the uses of a cervical collar or other device. A neck roll under the patient's head secured with chin and forehead straps will keep the patient's head immobilized. Feet then can be secured to a foot rest with bandage or strap applied in a figure-eight pattern. With these procedures completed a patient will remain safely secured to the backboard while being carried up or down almost any slope or distance. The backboard may then be

for transportation to hospital. Lifting and carrying the long backboard should be conducted as was recommended for other ground-level carrying devices, particularly the portable stretchers. If possible, place the long board on a wheeled stretcher before loading it into the ambulance.

2. Use of Scoop Type Stretcher

The unique feature of the scoop type stretcher is that it enables the EMT's to fasten a firm stretcher around the spine injured patient rather than first having to transfer and then secure the patient to a carrying device. This device must not be treated as a short-cut or fool-proof method for handling the spine injured patient and is not a replacement for the two types of backboards. Although two people are frequently sufficient to use the device, the general rule of waiting for additional help applies with this device as well. When using a scoop type stretcher, the patient must be positioned as straight as possible before applying the device and, of course, in possible neck injury cases, the head must be adequately supported and immobilized at all times. These handling requirements again make more than two people desirable.

When a patient is supine and lying fairly straight, with his legs close together and arms placed across his stomach, two men can fasten a scoop type stretcher around the patient and scoop him into it, providing there is sufficient space on both sides of the patient to position the stretcher. Three men should be the minimum-size team if the patient may be suffering an injury to the neck. In this case, the third person positioned at the head of the patient should immobilize the neck region. Detailed procedures are given which describe the use of the scoop type stretcher in handling spine injuries when the patient is free of injury to the neck region. Under these circumstances, the procedures are written for a minimum of two people.

PROCEDURES FOR TRANSFER BY SCOOP TYPE STRETCHER

1. PLACE WHEELED STRETCHER NEAR BY preferably parallel to PATIENT
   - Leave enough space on either side of patient to allow placement of each side of scoop type stretcher

2. REMOVE BLANKETS, SHEETS and PILLOW from wheeled stretcher

   Preparation of the wheeled stretcher to receive the patient-loaded scoop type stretcher.

3. UNFASTEN SAFETY STRAPS from wheeled stretcher
   If necessary, ADJUST LENGTH OF SCOOP TYPE STRETCHER TO FIT HEIGHT OF PATIENT

4. PLACE ONE-HALF of SCOOP TYPE STRETCHER ON EITHER SIDE of PATIENT
   - If using hinged variety, place opened end toward patient's feet

5. ONE EMT SUPPORTS PATIENT'S HEAD and assists in positioning stretcher

   See photo no. 40.

Photo No. 41. EMT's guide scoop type stretcher to fasten around patient without moving him.

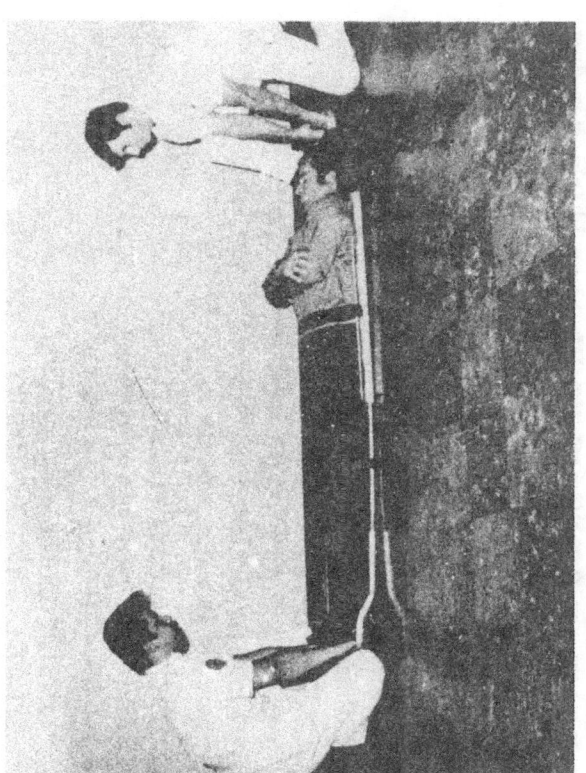

Photo No. 42. Patient secured to scoop type stretcher and EMT's ready to lift by End Carry.

6. DRAW IN SIDES OF EACH HALF OF STRETCHER toward patient

   - Carefully guide edges of stretcher sides underneath patient, one side at a time
   - Head end EMT aligns stretcher frame while other EMT closes in sides

   Avoid taking in debris, grass, etc. See photo no. 41.

7. SECURE LATCH AT OPEN END OF STRETCHER and check to see both ends are locked

   Know mechanism for own make of stretcher.

8. SECURE HEAD OF PATIENT to stretcher by means of chin and forehead straps

   As described.

9. FASTEN BODY STRAPS and SECURE FEET to stretcher

   - One strap across legs just above knees
   - Another strap across patient's hip region
   - Third strap across patient's chest, just below shoulders

10. COVER PATIENT with BLANKET

11. LIFT STRETCHER BY END CARRY METHOD and PLACE ON WHEELED STRETCHER
    - Method as described in Chapter 5

    Be sure stretcher has not caught something (while scooping) that will prevent lifting of stretcher. See photo no. 42.

C. Patient with Injured Extremity

This medical condition includes all types of severe wounds and fractures of the patient's arms or legs which render direct handling of the injured extremity painful (and often harmful) to the patient. Normally, the only changes in patient-handling procedures which are recommended for the patient with an injured extremity are typically ways to avoid direct contact with the extremity. These recommendations hinge usually on moving the patient as little as injured extremity. One additional important principle to follow when handling this type of case is to maintain adequate support of the injured extremity during handling and transport.

After splinting or bandaging of the fracture or wound, the EMT should determine if the injured extremity can be protected further by loosely securing it to the patient's trunk or uninjured extremity. If this is not advisable, one EMT should support the injured extremity during the transfer of the patient to a stretcher, or the patient may be in a position to do this himself. When lifting an injured extremity, especially as in positioning it, two hands should be used; one placed above and the other hand placed below the injured area. Also, the lower hand should be positioned under the injured extremity with palm facing up. The injured extremity then may be raised carefully and placed on a pillow, either directly on the stretcher or (in the case of an injured arm) placed on the patient. An arthritic or injured joint should be supported by the EMT's forearm during lifting of the patient, or just the extremity.

Whenever possible, the patient suffering from a fractured extremity should be transported on a portable stretcher or backboard (which then can be placed on a wheeled stretcher, if desired). Portable devices offer the distinct advantage to a fracture case of being placed directly on an X-ray table causing no disruption of the patient during examination.

D. Unconscious (or Vomiting) Patient

The unconscious patient is in a state of complete unawareness of what is going on around him and is unable to make any meaningful or purposeful movements. The EMT should be prepared for this state (i.e., position patient accordingly and do not rely on patient aid in handling) whenever the patient is suffering any of the common causes of unconsciousness: stroke, head injury, heat stroke, poisoning, alcoholism, epilepsy, or emotional stress.

The primary objective when handling the unconscious patient is to keep the airway free of obstruction. If the unconscious patient is positioned in the ordinary supine position on the stretcher, his tongue will drop back into his throat, most surely producing an obstruction in the airway. Also, vomiting may occur during or following unconsciousness; this is a great threat to an open airway. The EMT's will drastically reduce the risk of airway obstruction if the patient's head is positioned with a slight down-tilt while the patient is on his side or stomach. This positioning of the patient will tend to drain out any fluid in the air passages through the mouth or nose and can

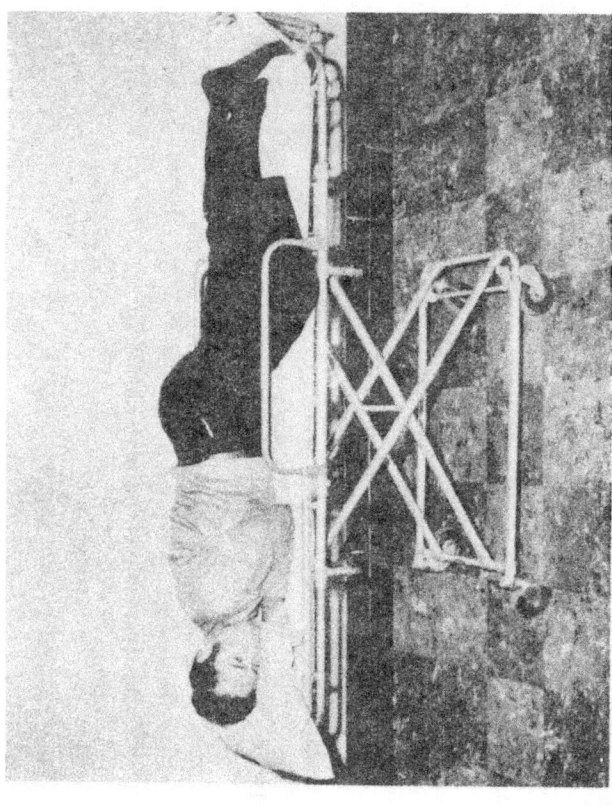

Photo No. 43. Unconscious or vomiting patient position.

Photo No. 44. Optional position for an unconscious or vomiting patient.

below describe the process by which the prone patient on a stretcher may be made to assume the unconscious (or vomiting) patient position.

PROCEDURES FOR POSITIONING UNCONSCIOUS (OR VOMITING) PATIENT

ASSUMPTION: Patient has been placed in prone position on a flat ambulance stretcher, with no pillow under his head.

1. ROLL PATIENT ONTO one (usually left) SIDE
   - Patient should be facing side of stretcher which will be accessible to attendant in ambulance

2. BEND UPPERMOST LEG and PLACE KNEE ON MATTRESS
   - Thigh should be at right angles to trunk and lower leg almost right angle with thigh

   Patient's knee and lower leg help support his weight.

3. PULL ARM under patient GENTLY BY ELBOW from patient's back
   - Arm should be positioned parallel to patient's back

4. BEND UPPER ARM of patient and PLACE PALM OF HAND on stretcher IN LINE WITH patient's FACE

   Patient's forearm and elbow help support his weight.

5. BEND HEAD AND NECK BACK slightly
   - So that patient's chin juts out

6. EASE PATIENT'S CHIN FORWARD SLIGHTLY

   Ensures tongue will not block air passages at back of throat. See photo no. 43 for correctly-positioned unconscious patient.

Ideally, the unconscious patient in this position will be tilted forward more by the angle at which the stretcher is carried, both as a

293

result of the EMT's and by the stretcher position in the ambulance. This means that a portable stretcher should be carried, as much as possible, with the head end of the stretcher lower than the foot end. This is not as easy when the patient is being carried on the conventional heavier wheeled stretcher. However, some of the wheeled ambulance cots are equipped with an optional feature that allows the EMT's to tilt the entire mattress frame to the desired incline.

Other patient-handling tasks are conducted for the unconscious or vomiting patient as was described in the typical procedures. The basic transfer methods are appropriate to the needs of the unconscious patient except they must be adapted slightly to handle the prone patient rather than supine patient. Procedures for covering and securing the patient are the same but use extra precaution to protect blankets and linens from soiling by the patient.

E. Handling the Psychiatric or Hard-to-Control Patient

In most cases, psychiatric patients will not be hard-to-control patients and should be handled by the EMT's as any other patient. Also, psychiatric patients frequently are sedated by a physician prior to the time they are to be handled by ambulance personnel (this is particularly true if the ambulance was called for a home-to-hospital or hospital-to-hospital routine transfer).

However rare, there are those instances when ambulance personnel are confronted with a violent or otherwise physically unmanageable person. The patient may be psychotic, intoxicated or a drug addict, to name the more common conditions of the hard-to-control patient. These are the special cases to which this section refers. Under such circumstances, the EMT's may have to use physical force and special restraining devices. These should be employed only with good discretion and always limited to measures which are absolutely necessary for the patient's protection and for the protection of others. Handling the hard-to-control patient requires more good judgment at the time by ambulance personnel than perhaps for any other type of patient. Handling procedures must be adapted to fit the needs of the situation.

The patient-handling tasks which are most affected by the hard-to-control patient are those of transferring the patient to the stretcher, including prior positioning and lifting of the patient, and securing the patient to the stretcher. Procedures are suggested below for these tasks and include somewhat drastic measures which may not be drastic enough for the rare encounter with the very violent patient. The EMT's may elect only some of the steps and not others;

handling procedures do not render the patient manageable, some or all of the following measures may be appropriate to the hard-to-control patient.

TRANSFER PROCEDURES FOR HARD-TO-CONTROL PATIENT

1. PLACE WHEELED STRETCHER AT LOWEST POSITION possible
   - Stretcher is most stable in this position (to protect patient against tipping over stretcher).

2. POSITION PATIENT FACE DOWN on floor
   - Extreme measure prior to applying extremity restraints. See text below.

> If possible, avoid Step 2 and carry patient to stretcher. Position patient face down and apply wrist and ankle restraints to patient once on stretcher. Restraints should be secured to the frame of the stretcher.

3. APPLY WRIST and ANKLE RESTRAINTS while holding down patient
   - Fasten wrist restraints behind patient's back
   - Secure ankle restraints to each other
   - Enables EMT's to move patient more easily and is comfortable for patient.

4. LIFT PRONE PATIENT ONTO STRETCHER
   - Adapt usual lift procedures to ensure good grip on the hard-to-control patient at all times

5. PATIENT POSITIONED FACE DOWN ON STRETCHER

6. COVER PATIENT
   - In usual manner

7. SECURE PATIENT TO STRETCHER

- One strap across patient's back just below shoulders
- Abdominal strap fastened across small of patient's neck
- Third safety strap across patient's legs

Once the patient has been secured to and within the stretcher, he may be moved to the ambulance in the usual manner.

F. Transfers Involving Ancillary Equipment

In many emergency situations the patient's critical condition demands application of life support equipment that must continue to be administered even while ambulance personnel are lifting or otherwise moving the patient. In particular, the common forms of life support equipment are oxygen, heart-lung resuscitator and I.V. administration of liquids. The use of equipment such as these makes many of the patient-handling tasks more difficult for the EMT's but, for the most part, with the aid of a third person the obstacles are readily overcome. The effects of ancillary equipment in the conduct of patient-handling tasks are discussed in three sections; one devoted to each of the common types of equipment.

1. Patient Receiving Oxygen

The ideal procedure is to have a third person hold the oxygen cylinder while the EMT's transfer the patient to the stretcher. This enables the patient to receive the oxygen without interruption; otherwise, oxygen must be disconnected for the transfer task and resumed once the patient has been placed on the stretcher. If a third person is available to hold the oxygen during transfer, the EMT's must be careful to keep oxygen tubing free of entanglement.

After the patient is comfortably positioned on the stretcher (usually a wheeled stretcher is preferred), the oxygen cylinder may be placed on patient's legs, on stretcher beside patient (see photo no. 47), resting on stretcher frame of head rest under mattress (see photo no. 48) or placed on a special cot-mounted cylinder holder.

All other patient-handling tasks may be conducted as for any other patient. The patient should be supine in the stretcher, covered, secured and transported as with the typical patient. The patient

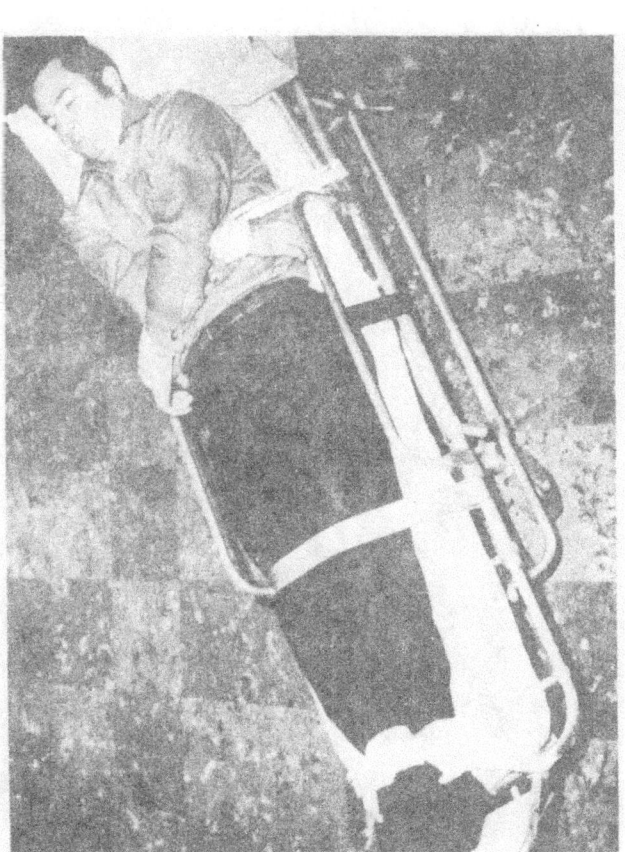

Photo No. 45. Hard-to-control patient secured with soft ties in supine position.

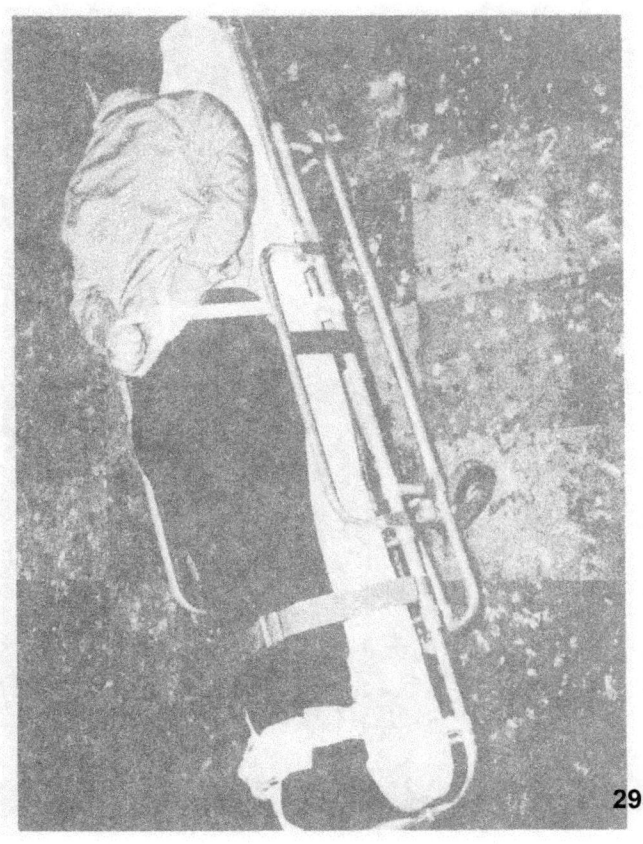

Photo No. 46. Hard-to-control patient secured with soft ties in prone position.

295

receiving oxygen will usually be most comfortable with the stretcher head rest elevated to 30° or 45° and, if the oxygen cylinder is to be placed between patient's legs, do so preferably after the patient has been covered. Use extra care to maintain the stretcher in a level position (so as not to disturb the oxygen cylinder) and proceed to transport the stretcher slowly and carefully.

2. Patient in Heart-Lung Resuscitation Unit

Oxygen-powered, mechanical heart-lung resuscitators (or cardio-pulmonary resuscitators) are becoming more common ambulance equipment. They hopefully will become effective devices in performing the critical life-saving techniques of external cardiac compression and respiratory ventilation. EMT's require special training by a physician in the proper use of this equipment. The equipment is typically entirely portable, weighs under thirty pounds and can be applied to the patient at the scene of the emergency.

While the patient is being manually maintained with cardio-pulmonary resuscitation, the base of the mechanical heart-lung resuscitator should be positioned under patient in the prescribed manner (know procedures for own type of heart-lung resuscitator). The resuscitation unit is then applied to the patient's chest and activation of the unit follows as soon as possible. A long backboard, or other firm surfaced carrying device, is positioned parallel to the patient. The EMT's may follow any of the usual transfer methods to place patient on the backboard. The heart-lung resuscitator as well as the patient should be firmly secured to the backboard. The patient in the heart-lung resuscitator on the backboard now may be lifted easily and carried to a wheeled stretcher. Also, once the patient has been secured properly to a backboard, one person can monitor the machine and maintain the airway during transport in the ambulance (a third person is required for these functions while the EMT's are carrying or rolling the stretcher). When covering patient, be sure to keep resuscitator unit exposed for monitoring by EMT's.

If the patient must be moved any distance before placing the backboard on the ambulance wheeled stretcher, care must be exercised to ensure the machine and patient are secured to the board. This is necessary to avoid any shifting of the patient which could result in displacement of the compressor from the correct point on the sternum; ineffective cardiac compression can cause serious consequences.

When carrying or wheeling the stretcher, it is ideal to have the

Photo No. 47. Oxygen cylinder fastened alongside patient.

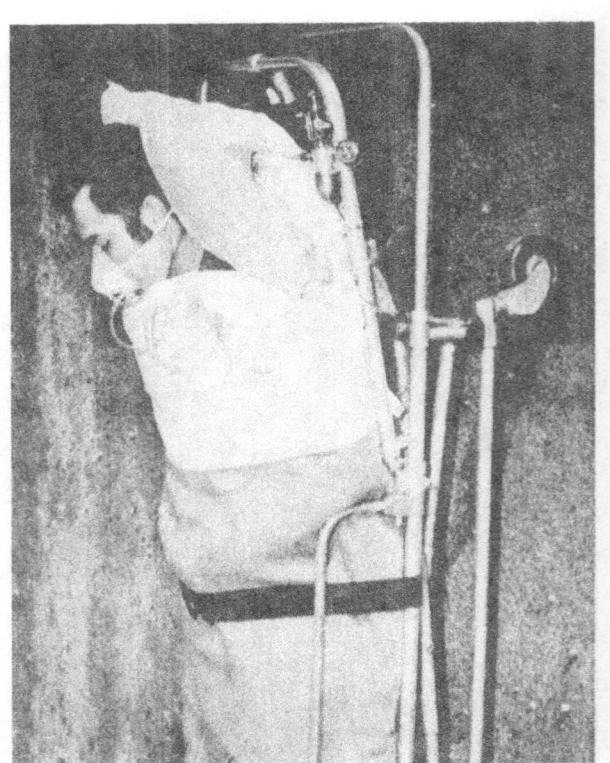

Photo No. 48. Smaller oxygen cylinder may be secured under stretcher

an adequate blood supply to the brain. Take care when attempting this over stairs, embankments or other terrain difficulties.

3. Patient Attached to I.V. Apparatus

When the patient requires administration of liquids by I.V. apparatus, the tasks of transferring the patient to the stretcher and of moving the loaded stretcher are complicated somewhat. In addition, minor modifications in positioning and covering the patient are usually observed.

Once the patient has been attached to the I.V. apparatus, the bottle must always be held well above patient's arm level. A third person is almost a necessity to transfer properly the patient attached to an I.V. The EMT's should position themselves on the patient's side away from the I.V. connection and lift the patient with one of the usual methods while a third person supports patient's I.V. arm and holds bottle up with other hand. Ideally, the patient is placed on a wheeled stretcher having a cot-mounted bottle holder and the two EMT's then can move the stretcher in the ordinary manner (see photo no. 49). If there is no cot-mounted holder, one EMT must carry the bottle during the entire transport. A glass bottle must be protected from breakage, or should be replaced by a non-breakable type.

The patient may be positioned on the stretcher in the usual manner but his I.V. arm should be placed on an extra pillow and left exposed for observation. Covering of the patient should include all practices except the patient's I.V. arm is above bedding. During all phases of handling, the EMT's must exercise caution to ensure I.V. tubing is free of all obstacles.

G. Handling the Infant Patient

Most non-premature infants will be transported in their mother's arms and the EMT's will not be required to handle the infant directly. Even when this method is not possible, handling of the infant by the EMT's is still a relatively simple task. Because of the infant's size, he can be lifted and carried easily from almost any position and then held in one's arms or placed in a carrying device. Normally, only one EMT should lift the infant patient at the same time. This should be done by placing the palm of one

Photo No. 50. Incubator attached to wheeled stretcher for transport.

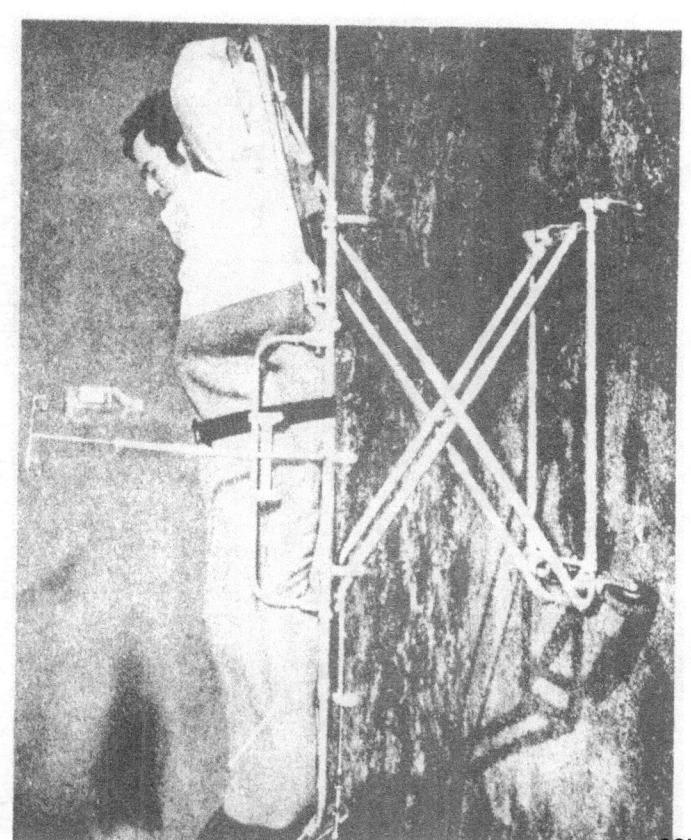

Photo No. 49. I.V. bottle cot holder in position.

hand under the infant's buttocks and supporting the small of the back and, with the other hand, cradling the head and neck while supporting the infant's shoulders.

If an incubator is available to ambulance personnel, the infant patient can be assured a carefully controlled environment. If possible, this type of carrying device should be used whenever a newborn and especially premature infant is to be transported. The infant is lifted as described earlier and placed in the center of the incubator which should contain a flat mattress without a pillow on it. Usually, the infant patient is placed on his stomach, with his face to one side, and is covered with a small sheet or receiving blanket that leaves the head exposed. If the patient is suffering any respiratory difficulty, he should be placed on his back with a folded sheet under his shoulders, to ensure a hyper-extended neck. The infant patient may be secured in the incubator by placing small pillows or rolled blankets on either side of patient. This precaution will keep the patient from rolling during the transfer but, again, one must be certain to keep pillows and covers away from infant's face. Once the cover on the incubator is fastened the incubator may be lifted by the EMT's (usually by End Carry) and carried to the ambulance or, preferably, first placed and secured on a wheeled stretcher, and then loaded into the ambulance. Although incubators frequently have their own stand, a wheeled stretcher is recommended generally as a better base for the unit during transfer and transport (carry the incubator base separately).

H. Patient-Handling in Confined Areas

Quite often, and especially when ambulance personnel are called to transport a patient from a home, the EMT's can find stairways, narrow corridors and/or other confined areas prohibit them from getting the ambulance wheeled stretcher near enough to the patient for a direct transfer to the cot. In these situations, many of the portable stretchers, including the stair chair or chair mattress, or long backboards will prove to be useful devices to carry the patient out or down to the wheeled stretcher for transport by ambulance. With any of these devices, the key to proper transfer in confined areas and over obstacles, such as stairways, is the task of securing the patient to the stretcher. The patient must be secured well enough to the device to enable the EMT's to conduct all necessary maneuvering around corners, down steep stairs, through narrow corridors, etc. A foot rest attached to the backboard or portable

greatly the stretcher's maneuverability. But, in many cases, the stair chair will be the preferred solution.

Because of its unorthodox design as a carrying device, the stair chair or the more versatile chair mattress (both may be folded flat, horizontal stretcher) require more specialized techniques than the previously discussed basic procedure for the proper conduct of patient-handling. Almost all of the tasks ordinarily conducted in lifting and moving the patient must be modified somewhat to suit the relatively unique stair chair. This section describes procedures for transfer, patient positioning, covering and securing and of transport of the stair chair. The device makes very efficient use of limited work space and can be easily maneuvered, but generally should *not* be used for unconscious or slightly comatose patients or when transferring patients with spine injuries or fractures of the lower extremities.

1. Patient Transfer to Stair Chair

There are two basic methods of lifting a patient onto a stair chair. One method is essentially the Direct Carry method (described in Chapter 4) with the exception that one EMT places his arm under the patient's thighs rather than under the mid-calf region of the

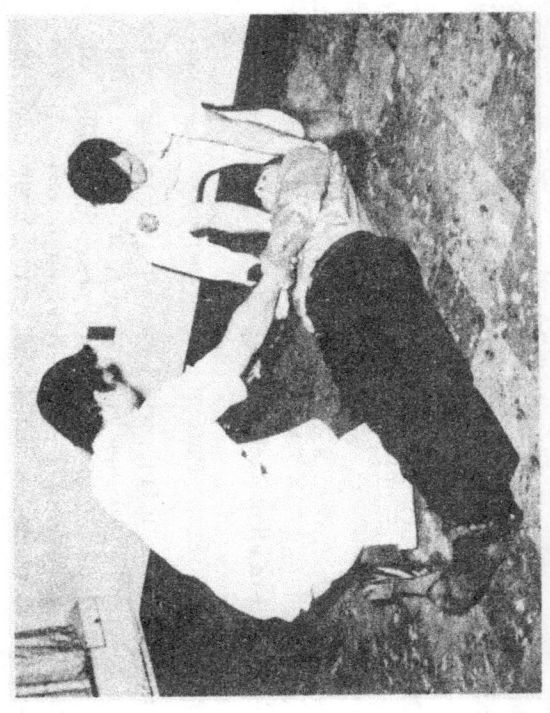

Photo No. 51. EMT's ready to raise patient to sitting position for Extremity

2. POSITION PATIENT SUPINE with LEGS STRAIGHT and FEET TOGETHER

3. ONE EMT STANDS ALONGSIDE PATIENT'S LEGS facing patient and other EMT — "Foot end" EMT.

4. OTHER EMT STANDS AT PATIENT'S HEAD facing patient and other EMT — "Head end" EMT.

5. Foot end EMT GRASPS PATIENT'S WRISTS
   - Preparation for raising patient to sitting position

6. Head end EMT PLACES HANDS UNDER PATIENT'S SHOULDERS
   - Grasps shoulders by placing hands in patient's arm pits
   - Preparation for raising patient to sitting position

   See photo no. 51.

7. Foot end EMT PULLS PATIENT TO SITTING POSITION AS head end EMT ASSISTS RAISE
   - Foot end EMT pulls *as* head end EMT lifts

8. Head end EMT DROPS TO ONE KNEE and SUPPORTS PATIENT'S BACK with knee and thigh

9. Head end EMT then EXTENDS HANDS palms down and GRASPS firmly PATIENT'S WRISTS
   - EMT's arms pass under patient's arm pits
   - Foot end EMT places patient's wrists in head end EMT's hands

   See photo no. 52.

Photo No. 52. Patient raised to sitting position for Extremity Transfer.

legs. This modification of the Direct Carry causes the lower part of the legs to drop down to a sitting position as the EMT's ease the patient into the stair chair. This modified Direct Carry is the best method to use when transferring the patient from bed-level height to a stair chair and may be used, if preferred, for the floor-/ground-level patient as well. However, there is a generally better method for the floor-/ground-level patient transfer to a stair chair, often called the Extremity Transfer.

This second method (i.e., Extremity Transfer) is inappropriate to the bed-level patient transfer but is not limited in its application to the stair chair alone. It is an excellent method for two men to lift a patient off the floor or ground to any standard carrying device. The major limitation of the Extremity Transfer method is that it must not be used if the patient has any fractures. Detailed procedures are presented below for employing this method to transfer a patient from a floor to a stair chair. Although the Extremity Transfer is not described elsewhere in the manual, modification of these procedures to suit flat, horizontal carrying devices should be obvious.

PROCEDURES FOR EXTREMITY TRANSFER TO STAIR CHAIR

NOTE: Do *not* use method if patient has any fractures.

1. PLACE STAIR CHAIR NEAR PATIENT

Photo No. 53. EMT's ready to lift patient by Extremity Transfer method.

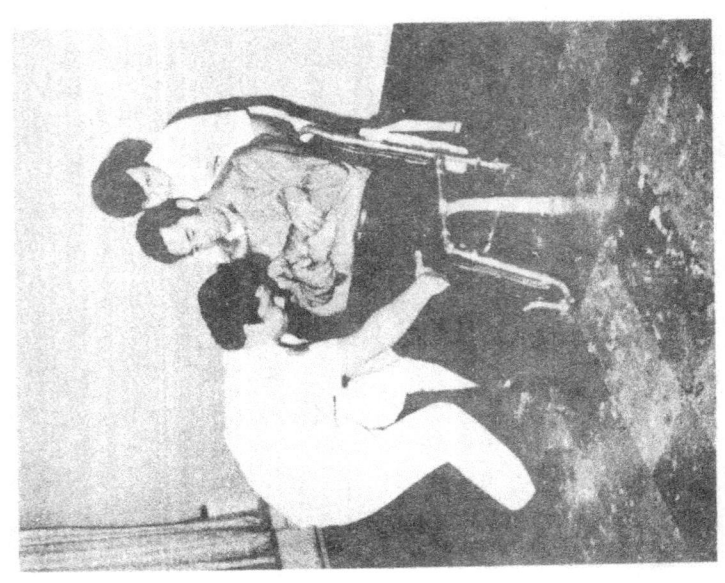

Photo No. 55. EMT's placing patient into stair chair.

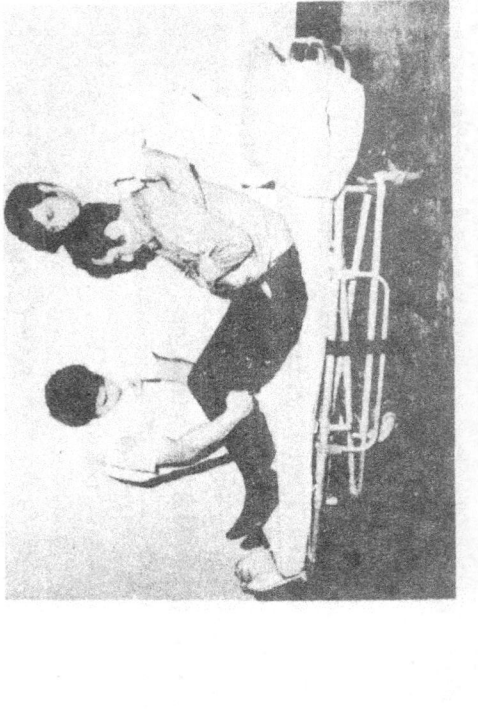

Photo No. 56. Extremity Transfer method may be used with other carrying devices, too.

10. Foot end EMT CURLS HANDS on either side UNDER PATIENT'S KNEES
 * Assumes position like that of baseball catcher

11. Head end EMT CROUCHES ON BOTH FEET

    Keep back vertical and rigid.

12. BOTH EMT'S STAND simultaneously
 * Use signal to coordinate move

13. CARRY PATIENT TO CHAIR (or other device) and GENTLY LOWER PATIENT

    See photo nos. 54, 55.

The patient who can be transferred by a stair chair is a non-fracture patient and as such can be lifted readily by a variety of methods. A two-man seat carry is another good method for placing a patient on a chair. The EMT's work on opposite sides of the patient and link their arms under the patient's back and thighs, lift and carry the patient in a sitting position. With most of the methods (except in the Extremity Transfer), the patient may find he is more comfortable with his arm or arms draped across the EMT's shoulders and this practice is perfectly permissible.

2. Positioning/Covering/Securing Patient on Stair Chair

The patient must be placed on the stair chair in a seated position, of course. He can most easily be covered in this position by means of a wrap-around sheet tucked around patient. A head cover towel may be added for extra warmth but is not as easy to keep on patient's head as it is for a patient on a flat stretcher. Pin the towel around patient's head and tuck it in well under the wrap-around sheet.

The most important task in preparing the patient for moving is to secure the patient well enough to keep him in the chair throughout the carry. This should be done with at least one belt around the patient's waist if the patient is merely going to be carried over level surfaces. If the EMT's will have to accomplish more difficult maneuvers safety belts should be fastened around patient and chair in the following manner: 1) across patient's thighs and around seat of chair; 2) around patient's chest and his arms and back rest of chair; and 3) around patient's lower legs and chair legs.

3. Carrying the Loaded Stair Chair

Once the patient is secured to the stair chair the EMT's will find the loaded unit fairly easy to carry and maneuver. However, the EMT's must remember to proceed to move with the stair chair carefully, slowly and keeping the chair as level as possible at all times. Some stair chairs are equipped with wheels which make moving the stretcher over level surfaces even easier. When the stair chair must be carried several procedures should be observed; these steps are given in Procedures for Chair Carry.

PROCEDURES FOR CHAIR CARRY

1. ONE EMT STANDS BEHIND CHAIR FACING PATIENT

    "Head end" EMT.

2. Head end EMT HOLDS TOP or sides of CHAIR BACKREST
 * Obtain a good grip, depending upon chair design, with hands spread wide

3. Head end EMT TILTS BACK CHAIR
 * Preparation for positioning other EMT at patient's feet

    Carefully. If chair has wheels be especially careful.

4. OTHER EMT with back to patient, GRASPS CORNERS UNDER SEAT or grips chair legs
 * Obtain a good grip, depending upon chair design, with hands spread wide
 * EMT should bend knees and crouch slightly to get into position

    "Foot end" EMT.

5. BOTH EMT'S LIFT CHAIR simultaneously
 * Use signal to coordinate move

The EMT's may now proceed to move the patient with both of them facing the same forward direction. They should carry the patient in the stair chair only until they reach the ambulance wheeled stretcher. The patient should be then transferred to the wheeled stretcher prior to loading the ambulance. The patient should generally be secured to a standard flat stretcher for the ambulance "journey."

Appendix A

Equipment Adjustment And Operating Procedures

A. Procedures for Adjusting Height of Multi-Level Stretcher

NOTE: The following also describe the method for adjusting the two-level stretcher; however, the two-level stretcher typically has a foot release bar rather than the hand release as noted below.

1. DETERMINE LEVEL desired for stretcher — Advise patient of your intentions.
2. One EMT STANDS at each END of stretcher FACING each other
3. Head end EMT GRIPS carrying or SLIDE BAR — Do not use headrest portion of frame as means of lifting.
4. Foot end EMT GRIPS CONTOUR portion of main FRAME, WITH ONE HAND on RELEASE BAR — Signal when grip is secure.
5. BOTH LIFT weight upward slightly
   - Signal to coordinate lift — *Do not jar patient.*
6. Foot end EMT SQUEEZES RELEASE BAR
   - Advise partner prior to squeezing release bar — *Do not release until signal has been given.*
7. Gently LOWER OR RAISE stretcher — Ensure it is locked before releasing grip.
8. LOCK STRETCHER in desired level
   - Listen for "click"

B. Procedures for Adjusting Head Elevation of Stretcher

NOTE: Patient is resting on a flat horizontal stretcher. Procedures below are written primarily with the wheeled stretcher in mind but the steps are applicable generally to all stretchers with adjustable headrests.

1. ADVISE PATIENT OF INTENTION to raise headrest elevation
   - Assure patient it will be raised slowly, safely and that he should relax

2. ONE EMT STANDS on EACH SIDE of stretcher at HEAD END

3. HOLD RELEASE HANDLE with one hand — Do *not* squeeze handle yet.

4. EACH EMT GRIPS FRAME OF headrest with one hand — Palms-up method best here.

5. LIFT HEADREST FRAME slightly — To reduce patient's weight on stretcher.

6. SQUEEZE RELEASE HANDLE gently — Be prepared for a *sudden increase in weight* on hands holding headrest frame.

7. RAISE or LOWER HEADREST to desired elevation
   - Maintain pressure on release handle while adjusting headrest

8. REMOVE GRIP ON RELEASE HANDLE when desired head elevation is desired — Do *not* remove hands from headrest frame yet.
   - Relaxation of grip on release handle engages the locking mechanism

9. LISTEN FOR "CLICK"
   - Headrest should be locked into position when this "click" sound is heard — While maintaining support of frame, apply slight pressure against headrest to check if it is properly locked.

10. RELEASE GRIP on headrest frame SLOWLY — Be sure headrest is locked before removing hands.

C. Procedures for Rolling Wheeled Stretcher

NOTE: These guidelines are most appropriate to the wheeled ambulance cot or stretcher, but the general principles described are applicable to all stretchers which can be rolled on wheels.

1. USUALLY ROLL WHEELED STRETCHERS when TERRAIN CONDITIONS PERMIT — Less strain on EMT's.
   - *Indoors* when corridors and door openings are wide enough; naturally, stretcher must be carried over stairs when there is no elevator
   - *Outdoors* when terrain is flat, smooth and firm

2. When rolling standard wheeled cot, USE COT PULL HANDLES TO WHEEL AND MANEUVER STRETCHER
   - An elongated U-shaped handle is attached to each end of the standard wheeled stretcher (i.e., it is permanently attached to the stretcher frame but swings out of the way for ease in carrying stretcher)

3. BOTH EMT'S AGREE ON EXIT ROUTE prior to wheeling stretcher — Less bending required of EMT's reduces back fatigue.

4. ROLL STRETCHER AT SAFE AND CONSTANT SPEED

5. TURN CORNERS SLOWLY AND SQUARELY — To avoid wasted movement and minimize motion to patient
   - A drifting turn can produce motion sickness in patient

303

6. LIFT STRETCHER OVER THRESHOLDS AND RUGS

   Rugs can abruptly stop stretcher. Rolling over thresholds can jar patient.

7. USE CAUTION WHEN MANEUVERING NEAR WALLS AND AROUND FURNITURE
   - "Nicks" can be costly

Appendix B

Suggestions For Peripheral Tasks

A. Introduction

Much of what could be discussed in this appendix has been covered in basic reference texts for ambulance service personnel. These include a number of general principles which should be followed by anyone working with the public and others that are generally recommended for effectively operating in an emergency situation. Qualities of courtesy, honesty, cooperativeness, responsibility, etc., are all, obviously, desirable characteristics for EMT's. Since these attributes are covered adequately elsewhere, the guidelines and principles outlined in this manual are items that are useful particularly when ambulance personnel are lifting or moving the patient. However, the tips, principles and procedures discussed here and not limited in their usefulness to patient-handling functions alone; they can better equip the individual for the entire EMT role. Finally, it should be borne in mind that the practices recommended in this section are only part of the total requirements for the "successful ambulance technician."

B. Suggestions for EMT Dress

1. WEAR SHOES PROVIDING GOOD SUPPORT and having NON-SLIP SOLES
   - Double-knot shoelaces (to ensure they will not become untied) or wear buckle or snap shoes or boots

2. DO NOT WEAR WATCHES, JEWELRY, ETC., which can harm patient or catch on objects while lifting or moving patient

3. IF NECKTIE is desired, WEAR BREAKAWAY KIND

www.ingramcontent.com/pod-product-compliance
Lightning Source LLC
Chambersburg PA
CBHW081758300426
44116CB00014B/2169